The Intelligent Unconscious in Modernist Literature and Science

This book reassesses the philosophical, psychological and, above all, the literary representations of the unconscious in the early twentieth century. This period is distinctive in the history of responses to the unconscious because it gave rise to a line of thought according to which the unconscious is an intelligent agent able to perform judgements and formulate its own thoughts. The roots of this theory stretch back to nineteenth-century British physiologists. Despite the production of a number of studies on modernist theories of the relation of the unconscious to conscious cognition, the degree to which the notion of the intelligent unconscious influenced modernist thinkers and writers remains understudied. This study seeks to look back at modernism from beyond the Freudian model. It is striking that although we tend not to explore the importance of this way of thinking about the unconscious and its relationship to consciousness during this period, modernist writers adopted it widely. The intelligent unconscious was particularly appealing to literary authors as it is intertwined with creativity and artistic novelty through its ability to move beyond discursive logic. The book concentrates primarily on the works of D.H. Lawrence, Virginia Woolf and T.S. Eliot, authors who engaged the notion of the intelligent unconscious, reworked it and offered it for the consumption of the general populace in varied ways and for different purposes, whether aesthetic, philosophical, societal or ideological.

Thalia Trigoni is a Postdoctoral Research Fellow at the Department of English Studies, University of Cyprus. She holds a PhD in English from the University of Cambridge and an MA in American Literature from King's College, University of London. She has published on D.H. Lawrence, William James, E.S. Dallas, Salvador Dali and Thomas De Quincey in Routledge, Palgrave MacMillan, Bloomsbury, Springer and De Gruyter.

Among the Victorians and Modernists
Edited by Dennis Denisoff

This series publishes monographs and essay collections on literature, art, and culture in the context of the diverse aesthetic, political, social, technological, and scientific innovations that arose among the Victorians and Modernists. Viable topics include, but are not limited to, artistic and cultural debates and movements; influential figures and communities; and agitations and developments regarding subjects such as animals, commodification, decadence, degeneracy, democracy, desire, ecology, gender, nationalism, the paranormal, performance, public art, sex, socialism, spiritualities, transnationalism, and the urban. Studies that address continuities between the Victorians and Modernists are welcome. Work on recent responses to the periods such as Neo-Victorian novels, graphic novels, and film will also be considered.

Contemporary Rewritings of Liminal Women
Echoes of the Past
Miriam Borham-Puyal

Desire and Time in Modern English Fiction: 1919–2017
Richard Dellamora

Catherine Crowe: Gender, Genre, and Radical Politics
Ruth Heholt

Peril and Protection in British Courtship Novels
A Study in Continuity and Change
Geri Giebel Chavis

The Intelligent Unconscious in Modernist Literature and Science
Thalia Trigoni

For more information about this series, please visit: https://www.routledge.com/Among-the-Victorians-and-Modernists/book-series/ASHSER4035

The Intelligent Unconscious in Modernist Literature and Science

Thalia Trigoni

Routledge
Taylor & Francis Group

NEW YORK AND LONDON

First published 2021
by Routledge
605 Third Avenue, New York, NY 10017

and by Routledge
2 Park Square, Milton Park, Abingdon, Oxon, OX14 4RN

First issued in paperback 2022

Routledge is an imprint of the Taylor & Francis Group, an informa business

Publisher's Note
The publisher has gone to great lengths to ensure the quality of this
reprint but points out that some imperfections in the original copies may
be apparent.

Library of Congress Cataloging-in-Publication Data
A catalog record for this title has been requested

ISBN: 978-0-367-55090-5 (pbk)
ISBN: 978-0-367-55089-9 (hbk)
ISBN: 978-1-003-09194-3 (ebk)

DOI: 10.4324/9781003091943

Typeset in Sabon
by codeMantra

Contents

Acknowledgments   vii
List of Abbreviations   ix

1   Introduction: The Intelligent Unconscious in the
    Modernist World   1

2   The Psychology of Unconscious Consciousness   18

3   D.H. Lawrence on the Intelligent Unconscious
    and the Allotropic State of Being   67

4   Virginia Woolf's Stream of (Un)Consciousness:
    The Ontology of Unconscious Androgyny   108

5   Feeling Unconscious Thoughts in T.S. Eliot   146

6   Conclusion: From Modernism to
    21st-century Cognitive Science   192

Index   209

Acknowledgments

This book began as a PhD thesis undertaken in the Faculty of English at the University of Cambridge, and so it is with gratitude that I would like to thank Kathleen Wheeler, my supervisor, for her scholarly example as well as for her continual guidance and support. I would also like to thank my dissertation examiners, Adrian Poole and Patricia Waugh, for their insightful reports. I feel fortunate to have had the privilege to receive their advice and I thank them unreservedly. I am also grateful to John Forrester, Ian Patterson, Deborah Bowman and Trudi Tate who read and offered incisive comments on earlier versions of this work, at crucial stages in its development. This book has benefited immensely from their exceptional intelligence and critical cast of mind. I also owe thanks to Andrew Zurcher for inspiring me, for more than a decade now, with the energy he brought in class and with his striking sharpness that was a pleasure to observe.

I could not have undertaken this research project without the financial assistance of the Cambridge European Trust and the Charter Studentship. This research was also awarded The Toby Jackman Prize at St. Edmund's College in Cambridge. The thesis was turned into a book with the support of the Research Fellowship I currently hold at the Department of English Studies, University of Cyprus. Special thanks must go to Antonis Balasopoulos for his steadfast support, ongoing encouragement and stimulating discussions at the final stages of this project.

The first academic to inspire me was Anna Despotopoulou. She was the reason I decided to pursue modernism in the first place. I thank her immensely for her encouragement and support. Her generosity and grace will always stay with me. I am also indebted to Eleni Berki, who opened my eyes to the world of academia. Further, I am deeply grateful to Michele Gemelos for her precious feedback, advice, our lively exchanges and friendship.

I am especially glad that this book will form part of the Routledge series "Among the Victorians and Modernists." It was a pleasure to work with Bryony Reece and Michelle Salyga at Routledge, who I thank for their editorial patience. Special thanks also go to the anonymous reviewers of the press whose expertise made the book immeasurably better.

Parts of Chapter 2 have previously appeared elsewhere: "Corporeal Cognition: Pragmatist Aesthetics in William James," in *Aesthetics and the Embodied Mind: Beyond Art Theory and the Cartesian Mind-Body Dichotomy*, ed. by Alfonsina Scarinzi. (New York; London: Springer, 2015), 55–70. Parts of Chapter 3 have appeared in: "Lawrence's Radical Dualism: The Bodily Unconscious," *English Studies* 95:3 (2014): 302–21; and "Lawrence's Allotropic Gladiatorial: Resisting the Mechanisation of the Human in Women in Love," in *D.H. Lawrence: Technology and Modernity*, ed. by Indrek Männiste (New York: Bloomsbury, 2019), 137–47.

I am fortunate to have been able to rely for support, comfort and encouragement on very dear friends. My gratitude goes to Hamid Zulnawas, Ali Ahmad, Luke Fletcher, Ulrich Linden, Arjun Ananthalingam, Arsalan Ghani, Eleftheria Fillipidi, Rena Tsafantaki and Andy Kotsifaki. My parents, Menios and Despoina, who have strived to make my life easier in every respect, and supported me in every way possible and step of my life, I cannot thank enough. My sister, Lydia Trigoni, has been present in my life in so many meaningful ways, even from afar, for that, I thank her dearly.

This work and every happiness that there is in life, I owe to my husband, my better half, my Pinio. He is the guiding force behind this project as he has been ungrudgingly living with it for years. He read through the manuscript throughout its development painstakingly, made crucial suggestions, opened my eyes to points and problems I couldn't see, lifted me when I fell and offered purpose. He has been more than I could ever hope for, or deserve, and I am fortunate and privileged to have him in my life. Without the guidance, security, emotional strength and self-abnegation that he showed, this book could not have been written. As a small gesture of appreciation for being my better self, this book I dedicate to him.

Abbreviations

In multi-volume works the volume number appears before the abbreviated form of the work cited.

PS   *Boris Sidis, The Psychology of Suggestion (New York: Appleton & Company, 1919 [1898])*

SPD   *Boris Sidis, Symptomatology, Psychognosis, and Diagnosis of Psychopathic Diseases (Boston: Richard G. Badger, 1914)*

PFU   *D.H. Lawrence, Psychoanalysis and the Unconscious and Fantasia of the Unconscious, ed. by Bruce Steele (Cambridge: Cambridge University Press, 2004)*

LD   *D. H. Lawrence, The Letters of D. H. Lawrence, ed. by James T. Boulton, 8 vols. (Cambridge: Cambridge University Press, 1979–2002)*

WL   *D.H. Lawrence, Women in Love, ed. by David Farmer, Lindeth Vasey, and John Worthen (Cambridge: Cambridge University Press, 1987)*

U   *Morton Prince, The Unconscious (New York: The Macmillan Company, [1914] 1921)*

FQ   *T.S. Eliot, "The Four Quartets," in The Complete Poems and Plays (London: Faber and Faber, 2004), 169–198*

SE   *T.S. Eliot, Selected Essays 1917–1932 (London: Faber, 1999)*

KE   *T.S. Eliot, Knowledge and Experience in the Philosophy of F.H. Bradley (London: Faber and Faber, 1964)*

UP   *T.S. Eliot, The Use of Poetry and the Use of Criticism: Studies in the Relation of Criticism to Poetry in England (London: Faber, 1933)*

E   *Virginia Woolf, The Essays of Virginia Woolf, 6 vols., vols. 1–4 ed. by Andrew McNeillie, vols. 5–6 ed. by Stuart N. Clarke (London: Hogarth Press, 1986–2011)*

W   *Virginia Woolf, The Waves, ed. by Gillian Beer (Oxford: Oxford University Press, 2008)*

O   *Virginia Woolf, Orlando: A Biography, ed. by Rachel Bowlby (Oxford: Oxford University Press, 2008)*

D   *Virginia Woolf, The Diary of Virginia Woolf, ed. by Anne*
       Oliver Bell, 5 vols. (London: Penguin, 1977–1984)
RO   *Virginia Woolf, A Room of One's Own; and, Three Guineas*
       (London: Chatto & Windus, 1984)
LV   *Virginia Woolf, The Letters of Virginia Woolf, ed. by Nigel*
       Nicholson, 6 vols (London: Hogarth, 1975–1982)
SPP   *William James, Some Problems of Philosophy: A Beginning of*
       an Introduction to Philosophy (New York: Longmans, Green,
       1911)
PP   *William, James, The Principles of Psychology (Cambridge:*
       Harvard University Press, 1983)

1 Introduction

The Intelligent Unconscious in the Modernist World

This book reassesses the philosophical, psychological and, above all, the literary representations of the unconscious in the early 20th century. This period is distinctive in the history of responses to the unconscious because it gave rise to a line of thought according to which the unconscious is an intelligent agent able to perform judgements and formulate its own thoughts. The roots of this theory stretch at least back to 19th-century British physiologists. Despite the production of a number of modern studies on modernist theories of the relation of the unconscious to conscious cognition, the degree to which the notion of the intelligent unconscious influenced modernist thinkers and writers remains understudied. The intelligent unconscious was particularly appealing to literary authors as it is intertwined with creativity and artistic novelty through its ability to move beyond discursive logic. In *The Unconscious Mind*, published in 1901, Alfred T. Schofield summarized some of the reasons behind the appeal of the intelligent unconscious:

> The value of the unconscious not only to consciousness but to the *man* himself is enormous. It guides him aright when otherwise he would go wrong, it inspires him, it warns him, it furnishes him with names, facts, and scenes from the stores of memory. It is really not only the guiding power of the body; accomplishing tasks so intricate, that no conscious mind, even if it had the power, has the capacity for; but it also guides behind the scenes the direction of his thoughts, his tastes.[1]

Modernist writers developed this strand of thought, and often present us with an understanding of the unconscious as an independent and intelligent entity that does not fit into the theoretical models we currently employ in order to unlock contemporary representations and articulations of unconscious processes. That said, this is no attempt to underestimate the pervasive influence of Freudian psychoanalysis in the modernist period but rather to bring to light another mode of understanding of the unconscious, which took different forms and names in the literature and the burgeoning sciences of psychology, neurology and physiology during what Alan Gauld has referred to as "the golden age of the subconscious, 1889–1914."[2] William Carpenter (1813–1885), for example, was the originator of the notion "unconscious cerebration," Herbert Spencer (1820–1903) was a major theorist of "unconscious memory," George Henry Lewes (1817–1878) theorized the distinction between "consciousness" and "consciousness of consciousness," Alfred Binet (1857–1911) propounded the existence of an "unconscious reasoning," Fredric William Henry Myers (1843–1901) was a major theorist of "subliminal consciousness," Pierre Janet (1859–1947) was the originator of the term "secondary consciousness," and Morton Prince (1854–1929) coined the concept "coconsciousness" and analysed the nature and processes of a "subconscious intelligence."

Accordingly, this book has two overarching aims. First, to uncover a hitherto understudied theory of the unconscious and unknown lines of reception. Second, to explore how literary writers adapted this theory in order to achieve their respective aesthetic, philosophical and/or ideological purposes. To satisfy these two aims, the book includes a substantial focus on the theoretical/historical context of the period, while each chapter discusses first the place of the literary writer under discussion within the theoretical/philosophical context before engaging with their literary work.

The "intelligent unconscious" is used to denote a mechanism able to execute complex reasoning processes, often more effectively than deliberate thought, while operating outside conscious awareness. These processes are rational in aim and physiological in origin. The intelligent unconscious does not simply reproduce mental contents, it further processes them on a complex level and influences one's conscious ideas and beliefs, and it even possesses the ability to perform independent decisions and actions. It therefore involves a similar mode of reasoning, complexity and rationality as the conscious mind. It only differs in terms of availability to conscious awareness. The term "intelligent unconscious," used in the title of this book and throughout its main body, is taken from the essay "Unconscious Intelligence" published in 1914 by William James Sidis, the child prodigy and son of the psychiatrist Boris Sidis, who was named after his godfather William James. Like Sidis, I use the term to encompass the ensemble of the unconscious mind's cognitive abilities which are indicative of the existence of a second consciousness or intelligence whose thinking powers not only resemble those of the personal consciousness but often exceed them. The use of an umbrella term, like "unconscious intelligence," is instructive because as we will see in the pages that follow, during the late 19th and early 20th centuries, this concept came under an entire rubric of multiple terms, including "reflex thought," "latent thought," "subconscious," "subliminal consciousness," "coconscious," "subwaking consciousness," "latent consciousness," "obscure perception," "the hidden soul," "reflex action of the brain," "unconscious psychical activity," "unconscious psychical processes" and "unconscious sensual and volitional processes."

Freud's topography of the unconscious partially overlaps with the psychology studied here. Freud's theory of the unconscious is approached through the lens of modernist writers, such as Lawrence, Woolf and Eliot. Partial and incomplete as their views of Freud's theory as they may be, it is instructive for our historical understanding to tap into the ways in which such literary authors understood Freud as well as into the ways in which they attempted to formulate alternative theories of the unconscious which they perceived to stand in opposition to the Freudian paradigm. As we will see in this book, these writers believed their theories to be more congenial with, for example, William James's (1842–1910), Pierre Janet's and F.W.H. Myers's rather than Freud's (1856–1939).

For Rilke, Freud was "to be sure, uncongenial and in places hair-raising."[3] For Pound "the Viennese sewage" had been going 40 years "and not produced ONE interesting work,"[4] while for Joyce psychoanalysis was "neither more nor less than blackmail."[5] As late as in 1973, Joyce's close friend, Maria Jolas, was asked at the Joyce Symposium in Dublin about Joyce's attitude towards Freud and Jung. She responded that "it was a remarkable sign of his intelligence that he didn't fall for psychoanalysis when it was so current. He started beyond it."[6] Joyce found an agreeable theory of human subjectivity in the work of Morton Prince, who formulated his theory as an alternative to the Freudian model. Prince's famous case of Miss Christine Beauchamp "proved a fascinating resource for Joyce, and it is densely woven into the textual fabric of *Finnegans Wake*."[7] Wyndham Lewis had also rejected the "dogma of the Unconscious" and levelled several major critiques against psychoanalysis across *The Art of Being Ruled*, *Time and Western Man* and *Paleface*,[8] while Thomas Mann characterized the relationship as an "official meeting between the two spheres" of literature and science, an "hour of formal encounter."[9] In a 1934 letter to Laurence Binyon, Ezra Pound wrote, "My use of 'idiotic' is loose [...] Have always been interested in intelligence, escaped the germy epoch of Freud and am so bored with *all* lacks of intelletto that I haven't used any discrimination when I have referred to 'em."[10] Pound, Lawrence and Lewis made direct addresses to their readers in their work which often took on a particularly aggressive tenor when the reader was perceived to be psychoanalytically inclined. In Lawrence's posthumously published novel *Mr Noon*, for example, the narrator admonishes:

> you sniffing mongrel bitch of a reader, you can't sniff out any specific why or any specific wherefore, with your carrion-smelling, psycho-analysing nose, because there *is* no why and wherefore. If fire meets water there's sure to be a dust. That's the why and the wherefore.[11]

There are even various examples of modernist writers who refused analysis because they felt it could be damaging to their inspiration. Like Woolf, Rilke's struggle with depression, exhaustion and hypersensitivity made him consider undergoing analysis, but he spontaneously reacted to the idea of "getting swept clean," which would lead to a "disinfected soul."[12] The view of psychoanalysis as damaging to creativity also led to another reaction in the form of caricatures of the psychoanalytic technique. Along with Lawrence's and Huxley's extensive parodies, Thomas Mann in *The Magic Mountain* caricatured psychoanalysis through the character of Dr Krokowski. Similarly, Italo Svevo's *The Confessions of Zeno* (1923)—a memoir—started as part of the psychoanalytic treatment to cure the protagonist's addiction to smoking but the novel only takes shape as it escapes the control of Dr S. and his Oedipal interpretations.

In the summer of 1922, Mina Loy was introduced to Sigmund Freud by Scofield Thayer, poet and editor of *The Dial*, who was at that time in therapy with the father of psychoanalysis. As Loy and her daughter Joella were staying in Vienna for several weeks, she was able to meet with Freud on a few occasions.[13] For Mina Loy, psychoanalysis was a typical product of the age of mechanical reproduction representing a mechanized form of mysticism, one trafficking in "readymade" absolutes.[14] She was suspicious of the pseudo-religious role that analysts had assumed in American and European culture. In "Conversion," Loy jokes that if Freud isn't on the Church payroll already, he certainly ought to be.[15] Rather than following closely the work of Freud, Loy and her friend, writer and patron Mabel Dodge Luhan, both immersed themselves in the work of Frederic Myers, one of the founders of the Society for Psychical Research (SPR). Loy's letters to Dodge suggest her sense of the limitations of the Freudian apparatus: "Freud who seems to have been a sort of wet nurse to sub-c[onscious] would not leave much room in it for evolving creative inspiration." To Loy, the Freudian subconscious sounded like "a dumping ground for cast off impressions" and she endorsed instead Dodge's new notion of a limitless, imaginative "superconsciousness."[16]

While the ambivalence of numerous authors towards Freud has been acknowledged,[17] there is still a need to trace the ideological and formal qualities of this strain of resistant discourse. The idea of the intelligent unconscious offers an alternative epistemology, a new paradigm for the understanding of human cognition. The intelligent unconscious, propounded by psycho-physiologists and psychical researchers, was said to be the source of some of our most sophisticated thinking and some of our most moral behaviour. This book shows how the emphasis on the cognitive unconscious offered exciting and comprehensive revisions of the understanding of thinking in the modernist period. As writers of the period were influenced by developments in the field of experimental psychology and physiology, they began to re-examine the nature of unconscious thinking—with its close ties to emotion, the imagination and the body. In the early 20th century, some of the most eminent literary authors incorporated into their works the notion of the intelligent unconscious, shaping their ontological view and literary output. This concept was studied and expanded by psychical researchers and psychologists alike. Literary authors, far from simply narrativizing problems of psychology, addressed aspects of the debates over the unconscious through innovations of style and technique. The consideration of this alternative route into modernism allows the mapping of interdisciplinary intersections and dialogues about the unconscious that complicate the Freudian paradigm. The overall aim of this book is to show what the period's science and philosophy have to tell us about the intelligent unconscious, how it can help us to understand the literary writing of the period and the ways in which writers adopted and incorporated it in their work.

The contribution of psychoanalytic studies to the unravelling of the history of the unconscious prior to the emergence of psychoanalysis is immensely significant, but this approach is often injected with the assumption that the unconscious, as theorized before Freud's time, is foreshadowed by Freud's ideas.[18] As Elke Völmicke characteristically argues, the hunt for "psychoanalytical seeds" distorts a historical analysis because it predefines the principles of the subject under discussion.[19] There is therefore a need to move beyond a teleological understanding of the unconscious and the authority of psychoanalysis.[20] In *The Mind of Modernism*, Mark Micale suggested that the development of various psychological schools between 1880 and 1940 was as momentous as the evolution of modernist art and literature. According to Micale, although the modernist era is typically associated with psychoanalysis, Freud's theories in the beginning of the 20th century were neither the most well-known nor the most influential of the psychological schools. Rather, "psychoanalysis was only one of many emerging models of mind that contributed to the constitution of the modern psychological self."[21] Henri Ellenberger's *The Discovery of the Unconscious* also argued that notions of the unconscious were diverse and pervasive in late 19th-century culture. For him, it no longer seems adequate to think of the late 19th-century unconscious as merely a fore-runner to the invention of psychoanalysis.[22] The early 20th-century concern with the role of the unconscious has its own complex set of determinants and meanings. These lead towards a variety of different issues, including memory, dreams, instinct, the nervous system, hysteria, criminology, creativity, mesmerism and metaphysics. As Matt Ffytche notes, when it comes to modernism, it is instructive to "proceed across psychoanalytic terrain, if only to develop alternative strategies, an independent version of depth psychology."[23]

Vanessa L. Ryan's *Thinking without Thinking in the Victorian Novel* explores several major Victorian writers in dialogue with the new psychology, demonstrating how these authors, in their plots and through their formal techniques, contemplated those occasions in which thought and action take place outside consciousness. She engages with theories of mind that proclaim productive unconscious processes, and she makes extensive use of the physiologist William B. Carpenter's theory of unconscious cerebration.[24] Markus Iseli's *Thomas De Quincey and the Cognitive Unconscious* examines De Quincey's notion of the unconscious in the light of modern cognitive science and 19th-century science. Iseli traces the close analogies of De Quincey's subconscious with the cognitive unconscious of modern science.[25] The present book complements these studies by showing that modernism is significant in our understanding of the historical and literary development of the notion of the intelligent unconscious because it is during this period that it gained momentum and recognition, which we stand to overlook.

Forms of the intelligent unconscious in the 19th- and early 20th-century thought have been identified and explored by critics within the context of spiritualism and the occult.[26] The theories of such figures as William James, Pierre Janet, William Carpenter, F.W.H. Myers, which entail an unconscious that exhibits volition and thinking processes independent of conscious activity, have been interpreted as lending support to and explaining a series of spiritual and occult phenomena. An equally if not more fertile field of enquiry to study 19th-century formulations of the intelligent unconscious and their legacy on modernist thought and literature is psychology, physiology and early neurology. This book is tasked to explore intelligent unconscious within this very context.

Pierre Janet's research work on hysteria marked the beginning of the field of experimental psychology of the subconscious. His first publication on Léonie in 1886 provided evidence of the existence of a secondary self, initiating what Alan Gauld referred to as the "golden age of the subconscious." At the same time, research on secondary selves was also conducted by Edmund Gurney and Alfred Binet. The French clinical research on the unconscious attracted the interest of researchers from England, the United States and Switzerland.[27] A close circle of prominent researchers was formed that included the psychologists Janet and Binet in France, the psychologist Theodore Flournoy in Switzerland, the psychical researchers F. Myers and Edmund Gurney in Britain and James, Boris Sidis and Morton Prince in America. The group has been called by Alan Gauld as the "Franco-American school" and by Eugene Taylor as the "French-Swiss-English-and-American psycho-therapeutic alliance."[28] It was through this group that the concept of the intelligent unconscious rose, mainly through two strands of research: psychology and spiritualism. The former was represented mainly by French experimental psychologists of the subconscious, including Janet, Binet and Théodule Ribot, as well as by American physicians who were influenced by the French clinical studies. Among these physicians were William

James, Boris Sidis and Morton Prince, referred to as the Boston group of psychotherapy. The latter took shape through the Society for Psychical Research established in Britain, founded by Frederic Myers, and its American branch of the SPR, which examined psychical phenomena. There was a clear cross-pollination between the two groups, but no figure was more actively involved with both than William James. The last major contributor of this group of researchers of the "golden age of the subconscious" was Morton Prince with his *The Unconscious*, published in 1914.

During the mid-19th century, physiological research into the nature of the nervous system and the brain was about to change the understanding of the role of the body and its relation to the mind, which was a highly contested topic. Science and in particular physiology provided a map of the nervous system and the brain that suggested an active and unconsciously operating mind. Questions addressed the functions of the nerves and the brain and the role of the body in mental action. These debates had implications for and a considerable impact on the conceptualization of unconscious processes. Physiology not only established the brain as the origin of mentation but also led to more sophisticated theories, according to which mentation is not exclusively conscious. Roger Smith, for example, stresses the "particular historical significance" of the first mechanical reflex concept with its categorization of "a unit of purposive behaviour in terms of existing physical structures instead of in terms of a directing mental agency."[29] Certain behaviours now had to be considered as automatic—acting independently of any influence of the will—but nevertheless purposive. It was Marshall Hall's (1790–1857) concept of reflex action, which enabled the conception of embodied unconscious mental action. Even though Hall never discusses the unconscious, "the issue could not but surface in any attempted integration of his model into Psychology."[30]

The first scientific basis for the corporeality of mentation was provided by Hall and it was swiftly developed by Thomas Laycock and William B. Carpenter. Laycock (1812–1876) asserted the idea that "[T]he human mind is none other than this unconscious principle of intelligence individualized, become cognisant thereby of its own workings in the cerebrum, and deriving its ideas from its own constructive or material changes in the organ of mind."[31] The conception of an embodied mind meant that conscious will was no more the sole originator of human action. According to Jonathan Miller, Carpenter and Laycock proposed "an altogether productive institution, actively generating the processes which are integral to memory, perception, and behavior."[32] Consciousness was no longer considered the sole source of mental cognition. Mesmerism was the starting point for psychophysiological investigations since these states of mind provided a fertile ground for research in unconscious mentation: "somnambulism, psychotic dissociation, and drug and hypnotic trances [...] all suggested that many 'complex' mental events happened automatically, without conscious control and sometimes without consciousness."[33] The "discovery of the unconscious" and its influence on behaviour, thought and memory was demonstrated through the mesmeric practice and later hypnosis, which caused "the doctrine of the unconscious mind [to] cease to be merely a philosophical abstraction."[34] Hypnosis played a crucial role in the development of the theory of the intelligent unconscious. Thus, according to Miller, "Human beings owe a surprisingly large proportion of their cognitive and behavioural capacities to the existence of an 'automatic self' of which they have no conscious knowledge and over which they have little voluntary control." Miller further laments that the "role of hypnosis in developing this distinctively enabling view of the Unconscious has been regrettably overshadowed by its contribution to the more widely recognized Freudian Unconscious."[35]

Laycock and Carpenter were highly intrigued by the mesmeric demonstrations they witnessed and extended that material for their own psychophysiological research on unconscious cognition. Through this understanding of unconscious processes, rooted in the nervous system, physiologists developed theories of perception, thought and behaviour. Laycock and Carpenter gave special emphasis on involuntary memory, the well-known experience of effortlessly recalling a forgotten name after strenuously trying to remember it. And Carpenter records in his books many examples of solving intractable problems just by sleeping on them.[36] Carpenter called it "unconscious cerebration," which can only be perceived through "the results of which [...] we are at last made conscious."[37] Laycock retained the phrase with which he claimed to have originated the idea, "reflex function of the brain" and observed that "On the one hand, [...] we have consciousness; on the other, unconscious yet intelligent action."[38]

Physiology in the 19th century made key contributions to the understanding of unconscious mental processes—including complex, reasoned ones—as a helpful and necessary part of the physical system. By the time of the publication of George Henry Lewes's (1817–1878) *Physiology and Common Life* (1859), nerves were perceived as so conscious of the world that it was necessary for Lewes to distinguish between "consciousness" and "consciousness of one's consciousness."[39] This distinction is representative of a tendency to conceive of the unconscious bodily process as intelligent, forming a consciousness distinct from the conscious one. The conception of the intelligent physiological unconscious undermined the Cartesian dualism by attributing consciousness to the body.[40] For Lewes, the ability of the neural system to perform judgements as a response to stimuli meant that it constituted a consciousness of its own.[41] This introduced the notion that the neural system is able to respond and grasp sensations not experienced by the conscious mind, and of whose workings it is oblivious. Lewes asserted that it was false to believe "that no sensation can be produced by an impression, unless that impression reach the Brain." Instead, "To have a sensation and to know that we have it, are two things."[42] In the spinal cord, for instance, "consciousness may, and often does, exist without knowledge" of this consciousness in the brain.[43] The sophistication of the body revealed to Lewes that "we may properly say that there can be unconscious thinking, and unconscious sensation."[44] Lewes was also the first author to write in English a detailed discussion of the "stream of consciousness," which presupposed that all mental operations are in fact the results of biological unconscious pulses forming a physiological consciousness. Proposing an argument similar to Carpenter's theory of "sensational consciousness," Lewes undermined the view of the brain as the sole centre of the nervous system. He argued that the somatic nerves have the same properties as the nerves that compose the brain forming a distinct consciousness.[45]

The late 19th century saw an unseating of the mind as an agent in control of the body and a shift towards the examination of the cognitive capacities of the body, marking a new understanding of the somatic and psychological experience.[46] This intellectual current became a major preoccupation for many writers of the period: Wundt asserted the importance of "unconscious logical processes"[47] and Lewes postulated the "existence of unconscious judgements, unconscious reasonings, and unconscious registrations of experience."[48] C.S. Peirce distinguished between two main operations of reasoning performed by the "instinctive mind": perceptual judgements which he considered to be the "very most important of all constituents of practical reasoning"[49] and abduction which "comes to us like a flash. It is an act of *insight*."[50] In his discussion of Eduard von Hartmann, Léon Dumont (1837–1877) asserted that the ability to perform voluntary movements without an idea of the specific processes required to execute them means that "this idea does not exist in consciousness." Therefore, it must exist "in an unconscious intelligence, of which my conscious intelligence is doubtless only a mode, a manifestation."[51] The idea that conscious intelligence is only a manifestation of unconscious intelligence was popular at the time. Irish poet and philosopher Joseph John Murphy (1827–1894) noted, "Intelligence, unconscious and conscious, formative and mental, is fundamentally the same."[52] Murphy's argument points at the development of the notion of the reasoning unconscious emerging from the physiological discourse, which was extended to the highest cognitive processes. Countering the scientific discourse surrounding the mechanical body, Murphy argued that "vitalized matter is endowed with intelligence—Intelligence tends to guide all vital actions in the direction that is best for the health of the organism."[53] And he argued for a continuity between unconscious and conscious intelligence: "I believe the unconscious intelligence that directs the formation of the bodily structures is the same intelligence that becomes conscious in the mind."[54] Like Lewes, Murphy distinguished between thought and the consciousness of thought, noting

> what I wish to insist on here is, that intelligence is not the same thing with the consciousness of intelligence [...] the consciousness of distinct thought is a distinct thing from the thought itself, and there may be thought without the consciousness of it.[55]

Murphy located the processes that unravel in the stream or train of consciousness in this unconscious consciousness, calling for a significant reassessment of the role of the unconscious in thinking. This crucial recognition marked, for Murphy, the starting point of research into the nature of consciousness: "it is only by admitting that trains of thought, or suggestion, may go on in unconsciousness, that we can account for the mental phenomenon."[56] In each human being, according to Murphy, there are two intelligences: "Intelligence is not always conscious, and even when conscious it is not always conscious of itself."[57] We will return to the role of the unconscious in thinking in Chapters 2 and 4, when the notion of the stream of consciousness is evoked by William James.

In *The Mental State of Hystericals* (1892), Pierre Janet's description of the phenomenon of post-hypnotic suggestion revealed how unconscious actions were "intelligent acts"—they indicated that some portion of the person was thinking and responding, but in a way that was split off from their normal consciousness.[58] Janet considered the unconscious to be "intelligent," "based on reasoning," and "purposeful."[59] From Janet to Morton Prince (1854–1929) and Joseph Jastrow (1863–1944), they all conceive the unconscious as a mechanism that contains a complex and rational element that is akin or even superior to conscious mental processes though it does not involve the thinker's awareness. This line of thinking is a key concept in the historical development of the study of the mind and unconscious mental processes.

The view that the unconscious is a reservoir of cognitive potential, often of greater scope than consciousness, was prototypically adopted by Frederic Myers (1843–1901) throughout the 1890s in his articles on the "subliminal consciousness." This view was also shared, to various degrees, by others in France and abroad. One of the main exponents of the intelligent unconscious in Britain, Myers asserted that the ordinary waking self was but one possibility among a multitude of thoughts, feelings and memories, which clustered subliminally in the self. The unconscious self, for him, was active albeit detached and hidden from empirical consciousness.

The developments in physiology also shaped to a large extent the newly emergent field of experimental psychology. For William James, a physiological angle was needed if psychology was to survive as a scientifically respected discipline.[60] As it becomes obvious from Hugo

Munsterberg's (1863–1916) description of the Harvard lab (founded by William James), these initial studies were packed with bodily terms: "a visit to a psychological institute would hardly suggest to the casual guest that it has anything to do with the mind."[61] After providing a brief description of the layout and equipment at Harvard, he went on to argue that "in short, everything suggests interest in bodily material processes, and nothing betrays the predominant activity of this scientific institute, the study of the mind."[62] James, as we will see in detail in the next chapter, adopted the idea of the intelligent unconscious from the British physiologists. These influences, along with his involvement with the psychical research, shaped an intricate view of the unconscious that played a formative part in many of his philosophical theories. The idea that James's psychology does not admit the "unconscious" in his thought and theory has arisen from a failure to take into consideration the specific undertones of the term at the dawn of psychology. But as Joel Weinberger has shown, the belief that James opposed postulating unconscious processes stems, primarily, from a misreading of a passage in his *Principles*, which lists ten refutations of unconscious mental states. But these, Weinberger notes, were concerned with disproving the metaphysical notion that mental states are composed of elementary mental units. In fact, Weinberger argues "James actually supported what we would now term unconscious processes."[63]

Between 1890 and 1930, the concept of the body was undergoing a transition. On the one hand, the human was figured as a machine composed of functional units. On the other hand, English physiologists proposed that the concept of an intelligent physiological unconscious should replace notions of mechanical materialism. The view of the mechanical body largely shaped the ways critics approached the body in modernism.[64] However, we should also acknowledge the counter-discourse of the intelligent physiological unconscious. Alfred T. Schofield (1846–1929), for instance, like many writers of the time, set out his book *The Unconscious Mind* (1908) against discourses that "degrade physiology and obscure the marvels of the body." In order to prove that the body is "more than blind material forces," he turns to the "ultimate governor and ruler of all actions and functions of the body, and in every way a most important factor in our psychical and physical life"—the unconscious mind.[65] Together, these developments in physiology produced an account of the existence of an intelligent unconscious which has the ability to respond to external stimuli and act independently of the mind. For 19th-century thinkers, the understanding of the intelligent unconscious facilitated an account whereby a series of apparent oxymorons, as we will see in Chapter 2, could be explained: thinking without thinking or memory without memory.

Chapter 2 of this book deepens into the ways in which psychologists and psychical researchers of the late 19th and early 20th centuries conceived of the unconscious as a cognitive agent, as a distinct hidden consciousness. More specifically, one can trace the experiments that established the independence of a secondary consciousness capable of full cognizance by means of a focus on the research conducted by members of the Society of Psychical Research. Special attention is given to the pivotal role of Frederick Myers, William James, Pierre Janet, Alfred Binet, Boris Sidis and Morton Prince in the development of the notion of the intelligent unconscious. This discovery emerged from observations on the tip-of-the-tongue phenomenon, cases of warning, the phenomenon of the two co-existing selves, hypnosis and automatic writing. After having established James's contribution to research on the unconscious, I analyse his ontological theory, wherein the unconscious is conceived of as capable of performing complicated forms of cognition even though it does not possess the conceptual apparatus of the discursive, conscious mind. The arguments of this chapter are anchored around James's writings for two main reasons. First, his theories cut right through the heart of contemporary psychology, physiology and spiritualism, allowing for the discussion to draw into its dragnet these varied fields of enquiry. And second, because of his highly influential oeuvre, on the period's psychologists, psychiatrists, philosophers and literary writers. In turn, this discussion provides new insights into James's theory of the unconscious and its relation to consciousness.

The physiological unconscious emerging from Jamesian psychology has many similarities with Lawrence's *Psychoanalysis and the Unconscious* (1921) and *Fantasia of the Unconscious* (1922). Chapter 3, "D.H. Lawrence on the Intelligent Unconscious and the Allotropic State of Being," builds on these connections and discusses how D.H. Lawrence developed his theory of the bodily unconscious as a reaction against the Freudian formulation of the unconscious and the increasing tendency in contemporary scientific thought to mechanize the body and its cognitive processes. Here, I consider the theme of industrialism in Lawrence's fiction and how his own theory of the unconscious, informed by contemporary developments challenged the mechanistic principle. This chapter, then, links Lawrence's philosophical thought to his literary practice; puts accounts of his theory of the unconscious under a different light; and demonstrates how a turn to his formulation of the notion of the intelligent unconscious can provide us with new interpretive tools to re-examine notions of character construction, gender and homosexuality in his work.

In "Virginia Woolf's Stream of (Un)Consciousness: The Ontology of Unconscious Androgyny," we delve deeper into the ways in which contemporary authors adopted the theory of the intelligent unconscious for their own literary, aesthetic and ideological purposes. Virginia Woolf occupies a central position in this narrative, as her literary writing was informed by her own theory of cognition. As in the case of Lawrence in the previous chapter, this chapter links Woolf's philosophical thought with her literary theory and practice. It reassesses our understanding of her theory of cognition and consciousness, and equipped with this conceptual apparatus, it studies how she channelled her theoretical work into her fiction. This approach opens up questions pertaining to her feminist aesthetics, notions of selfhood, subjectivity and gender identity. The chapter contends that Woolf envisions the demolition of gender identity through an internal, psychological revolution founded upon the premise of getting in touch with our androgynous and intelligent unconscious, which forges the paths of the streams of our consciousness. In a nutshell, this chapter studies Woolf's understanding of the connections between the stream of thought and unconsciousness, and explores the way in which her theory of the stream led her to technical developments and shaped her feminist project.

Chapter 5 studies how T.S. Eliot adopted, tested and reformulated contemporary theories of the unconscious and incorporated them in his poetry in order to convey to his readers inarticulable notions that can be communicated only once consciousness and its apparatus (language) are withdrawn. This cognitive phenomenon entails the fusion of feeling and thought in what Eliot referred to, following Bradley, "immediate experience," which can only be attained via a poetic language that effectively consumes or deconstructs itself in such a way as to convey to readers what remains in an embryonic state that cannot be delivered into the symbolic, discursive and conceptual mode of understanding. Like the previous chapters, this one begins by laying out T.S. Eliot's theory of the unconscious and by looking at the ways in which his conception of human cognitive psychology was shaped by his intellectual and literary predecessors. Following this account, the second main section turns to an exploration of how this cultural backdrop can help us to reassess his literary output, paying a particular focus on the *Four Quartets*. Reading Eliot's *Quartets*, this chapter argues, becomes a form of a prayer that gives rise to a mystical, inarticulate cognitive experience that liberates us from the finiteness of logocentric thinking and experiencing, of consciousness itself.

In Chapter 6 to this study, I argue that the ontology of the intelligent unconscious is not idiosyncratic to the authors discussed in the preceding chapters. Rather, it was a pervasive phenomenon that emerged in the works of a number of writers in different guises. This persistent return to unconscious cognitive abilities points at the need to draw out the genealogy of the intelligent unconscious, and to study the complex and shifting network of relations between power, knowledge and the unconscious which produced, and still produce, the historically specific forms of bi-subjectivity. Twenty-first-century cognitive theorists, philosophers and medical practitioners have called for a turn to the unconscious as an independent and intelligent cognitive agent. Today, bolstered by work in cognitive science on the central role of non-deliberate thought in complex as well as everyday decisions, the concept of the intelligent unconscious is gaining recognition.

This interdisciplinary study pulls into its net topics from such diverse fields as philosophy, physiology and psychology. In engaging the unconscious as an independent cognitive agent, literary writers trigger awareness of this multilayered significance. From fiction and poetry to letters, essays and diaries, the view of the unconscious as an autonomous thinking entity opens up new vistas of thought against which to reassess our perceptions of what literature can be thought and felt to do. This book seeks to analyse the complexity and importance of a hitherto understudied line of thought, one that influenced profoundly the modernist understanding(s) of the relation between conscious and unconscious, of self and subjectivity.

Notes

1 Alfred T. Schofield, *The Unconscious Mind* (New York: Funk and Wagnalls, 1908 [1901]), 413.
2 Alan Gauld, *A History of Hypnotism* (Cambridge: Cambridge University Press, 1995), 412.
3 Rainer Maria Rilke, Letter to Lou Andreas Salomé, 20 Jan. 1912, in *Rainer Maria Rilke and Lou Andreas-Salomé: The Correspondence*, ed. and trans. by Edward Snow and Michael Winkler (New York: Norton, 2006), 184.
4 Ezra Pound, "Letter to Wyndham Lewis, Jan. 1952," in *Pound/Lewis: The Letters of Ezra Pound and Wyndham Lewis*, ed. by Timothy Materer (London: Faber and Faber, 1985), 269.
5 Richard Ellmann, *James Joyce* (Oxford: Oxford University Press, 1959), 538.
6 Richard M. Kain, "An Interview with Carola Giedion-Welcker and Maria Jolas," *James Joyce Quarterly*, 11: 2 (1974): 120.
7 Luke Thurston, *James Joyce and the Problem of Psychoanalysis* (Cambridge: Cambridge University Press, 2004), 126.
8 Wyndham Lewis, *The Art of Being Ruled* (London: Chatto & Windus, 1926), 400.
9 Thomas Mann, "Freud and the Future," *International Journal of Psychoanalysis*, 37 (1952): 106, 111.
10 Pound, *Letters*, 347.
11 D. H. Lawrence, *Mr Noon*, ed. by Lindeth Vasey (Cambridge: Cambridge University Press, 1984), 99.
12 Rilke, *Correspondence*, 184.
13 Carolyn Burke's biography of Loy gives some detail on this series of meetings, though we have little information directly from either Loy or Freud about the content of their discussions. Burke notes these were not psychoanalytic consultations but rather discussions about artistic expression. See Carolyn Burke, *Becoming Modern: The Life of Mina Loy* (New York: Farrar, Straus, and Giroux, 1996), 313.
14 Mina Loy, *Stories and Essays of Mina Loy*, ed. Sara Crangle (Champaign: Dalkey Archive Press, 2011), 228.
15 Ibid., 229.

16 Burke, *Becoming Modern*, 144.
17 Matt Ffytche, "The Modernist Road to the Unconscious," in *The Oxford Handbook of Modernisms*, ed. by Peter Brooker, Andrzej Gasiorek, Deborah Longworth, Andrew Thacker (Oxford: Oxford University Press, 2010), 416.
18 See, for instance, Lancelot Law Whyte, *The Unconscious Before Freud* (London: Friedmann, 1979), Frank Tallis, *Hidden Minds: A History of the Unconscious* (New York: Arcade Publishing, 2002), and John Hendrix, *Unconscious Thought in Philosophy and Psychoanalysis* (Basingstoke: Palgrave Macmillan, 2015).
19 Elke Völmicke, *Das Unbewußte im Deutschen Idealismus* [*The Unconscious in German Idealism*] (Würzburg: Königshausen and Neumann, 2005), 11.
20 For some representative works on psychoanalytical criticism, see Kylie Valentine, *Psychoanalysis, Psychiatry and Modernist Literature* (Basingstoke: Palgrave Macmillan, 2003), Gavriel Reisner, *The Death–Ego and the Vital Self: Romances of Desire in Literature and Psychoanalysis* (London: Fairleigh Dickinson University Press, 2003), Maud Ellmann, *The Nets of Modernism: Henry James, Virginia Woolf, James Joyce, and Sigmund Freud* (Cambridge: Cambridge University Press, 2010), Tony E. Jackson, *The Subject of Modernism: Narrative Alterations in the Fiction of Eliot, Conrad, Woolf, and Joyce* (Ann Arbor: University of Michigan Press, 1994), Leonard Jackson, *Literature, Psychoanalysis and the New Sciences of Mind* (Harlow: Longman, 2000), Peter Collier and Judy Davies, *Modernism and the European Unconscious* (New York: St Martin's Press, 1990).
21 Mark S. Micale, *The Mind of Modernism: Medicine, Psychology, and the Cultural Arts in Europe and America, 1880–1940* (Stanford, CA: Stanford University Press, 2004), 7.
22 Henri F. Ellenberger, *The Discovery of the Unconscious: The History and Evolution of Dynamic Psychiatry* (London: Penguin Press, 1970).
23 Ffytche, "The Modernist Road to the Unconscious," 416.
24 Vanessa Ryan, *Thinking without Thinking in the Victorian Novel* (Baltimore, MD: Johns Hopkins University Press, 2012).
25 Markus Iseli, *Thomas De Quincey and the Cognitive Unconscious* (Basingstoke: Palgrave Macmillan, 2015).
26 See, for instance, Helen Sword, *Ghostwriting Modernism* (Ithaca, NY: Cornell University Press, 2002), Leigh Wilson, *Modernism and Magic Experiments with Spiritualism, Theosophy and the Occult* (Cambridge: Cambridge University Press, 2013), Simone Natale, *Supernatural Entertainments Victorian Spiritualism and the Rise of Modern Media Culture* (Pennsylvania: Pennsylvania State University Press, 2016), Janet Oppenheim, *The Other World: Spiritualism and Psychical Research in Victorian Britain, 1850–1914* (Cambridge: Cambridge University Press, 1985), Alex Owen, *The Darkened Room: Women, Power and Spiritualism in Late Victorian England* (London: Virago Press, 1989), Roger Luckhurst, *The Invention of Telepathy 1870–1901* (Oxford: Oxford University Press, 2002), Marlene Tromp, *Altered States: Sex, Nation, Drugs, and Self-Transformation in Victorian Spiritualism* (Albany, NY: State University of New York Press, 2006) and Shane McCorristine, *Spectres of the Self: Thinking about Ghosts and Ghost-Seeing in England, 1750–1920* (Cambridge: Cambridge University Press, 2010). These works, while a partial and not exhaustive list, are representative of the kinds of connections between the unconscious and occult that contemporary scholars have brought to our attention for the past 35 years.

27 As Eugene Taylor points out the phrase "French experimental psychology of the subconscious" is from the foreword to Binet's *On Double Consciousness* (1890). See Taylor, "The New Jung Scholarship," *Psychoanalytic Review* 83: 4 (1996): 584.

28 Eugene Taylor, *William James on Consciousness Beyond the Margin* (Princeton, NJ: Princeton University Press), 185.

29 Roger Smith, "The Background of Physiological Psychology in Natural Philosophy," *History of Science*, 11: 2 (1973): 83–4.

30 Graham Richards, *Mental Machinery: The Origins and Consequences of Psychological Ideas* (London: Athlone Press, 1992), 361.

31 Thomas Laycock, "Further Researches into the Functions of the Brain," *The British and Foreign Medico-Chirurgical Review* 16: 31 (1855): 168–9.

32 Jonathan Miller, "Going Unconscious," in *Hidden Histories of Science* (New York: New York Review of Books, 1995), 28–9.

33 Smith, "Background of Physiological Psychology," 85.

34 Leslie Spencer Hearnshaw, *The Shaping of Modern Psychology* (London: Routledge and Kegan Paul, 1987), 151.

35 Miller, "Going Unconscious," 28.

36 Ibid., 19.

37 William Benjamin Carpenter, *Principles of Human Physiology* (Philadelphia, PA: Blanchard and Lea, 1853), 832.

38 Laycock, "Further Researches," 157.

39 On this point, see also Laura Salisbury and Andrew Shail (eds.), *Neurology and Modernity: A Cultural History of Nervous Systems, 1800–1950* (Basingstoke: Palgrave Macmillan, 2010), 21.

40 Lewes juxtaposed his theory to the current mechanical interpretations of organic processes insisting instead that sensibility was inherent in nervous substance: "I am a conscious organism, even if it be true that I sometimes act unconsciously. I am not a machine." In George Henry Lewes, *The Physiology and Common Life* (Edinburgh: W. Blackwood, 1879), 76.

41 Ibid., 234–5.

42 Ibid., 48.

43 Ibid.

44 Ibid., 194.

45 Ibid., 131.

46 Edwin Clarke and L. S. Jacyna, *Nineteenth-Century Origins of Neuroscientific Concepts* (Berkeley: University of California Press, 1987), 212–20.

47 Wilhelm Max Wundt, *Beitrage zur theorie der Sinnes Vermehrung* (Heidelberg: C. F. Winter'sche, 1862), 439, 438.

48 George Henry Lewes, *Problems of Life and Mind* (Boston, MA: Houghton, 1879), 161.

49 Charles Sanders Peirce, *Reasoning and the Logic of Things: The Cambridge Conferences Lectures of 1898*, ed. by K.L. Ketner (Cambridge, MA: Harvard University Press, 1992), 182.

50 Charles Sanders Peirce, *Collected Papers of Charles Sanders Peirce*, Vols. 1–6 ed. by Charles Hartshorne and Paul Weiss, Vols. 7–8 ed. by Arthur W. Burks (Cambridge, MA: Harvard University Press, 1992), 5, 181.

51 Léon Dumont, "A New Phase of German Thought: Hartmann's Philosophy of the Unconscious," in *Popular Science Monthly: Volume 2* (New York: Popular Science Publishing Company, 1872), 312.

52 Joseph John Murphy, *Habit and Intelligence in Their Connexion with the Laws of Matter and Force: Vol. 2* (London: Macmillan, 1869), v.

53 Ibid.

54 Ibid., 4.
55 Ibid., 5, 27.
56 Ibid.
57 Ibid., 162.
58 Pierre Janet, *The Mental State of Hystericals; A Study of Mental Stigmata and Mental Accidents* (London: G. Putnam's sons, 1901), 254.
59 Adam Crabtree, "The Transition to Secular Psychotherapy: Hypnosis and the Alternate- Consciousness Paradigm," in *History of Psychiatry and Medical Psychology*, ed. by Edwin R. Wallace and John Gach (New York: Springer, 2008), 576.
60 William James, "A Plea for Psychology as a Natural Science," *Philosophical Review* 1 (1892): 146–53.
61 Frank Landy, "Hugo Munsterberg: Victim or Visionary," *Journal of Applied Psychology* 77 (1992): 788.
62 Ibid., 789.
63 See also Joel Weinberger, "William James and the Unconscious: Redressing a Century-Old Misunderstanding," *Psychological Science*, 11: 6 (2000): 439.
64 See, for instance, Beatrice Monaco, *Machinic Modernism: The Deleuzian Literary Machines of Woolf, Lawrence and Joyce* (Basingstoke: Palgrave Macmillan, 2008), Evelyn Cobley, *Modernism and the Culture of Efficiency: Ideology and Fiction* (Toronto: University of Toronto Press, 2009), Edward Comentale, *Modernism, Cultural Production, and the British Avant–garde* (Cambridge: Cambridge University Press, 2009), Pamela Thurschwell, *Literature, Technology and Magical Thinking, 1880–1920* (Cambridge: Cambridge University Press, 2001), Nicholas Daly, *Literature, Technology, and Modernity, 1860–2000* (Cambridge: Cambridge University Press, 2004), Mark Seltzer, *Bodies and Machines* (London: Routledge, 1992), Tim Armstrong, *Technology, and the Body: A Cultural History* (Cambridge: Cambridge University Press, 1998).
65 Schofield, *The Unconscious Mind*, 411, 412, xi.

2 The Psychology of Unconscious Consciousness

The Intelligent Unconscious: Automatic Reactions or Cognitive Actions?

William James's *The Principles of Psychology* marked the beginnings of scientific psychology at a time when it was barely distinguished from philosophy and physiology.[1] James's impact on both the literary imagination of the period and its intellectual framework has been repeatedly stressed, some going as far as to conclude that his theories helped shape not only physiology, philosophy, psychology and literature but modernism itself.[2] Yet, aspects of James's contribution to the psychology of the unconscious remains relatively understudied. It is also often the case that critics who deal with James's contribution to the rise of psychotherapy in the 19th century tend to treat it as a Freudian prelude,[3] placing him in a psychoanalytic context. Eugene Taylor, however, has reconstructed and made available a new and important addition to the body of James's work on the psychology of the unconscious. This material bears witness to James's preoccupation with the unconscious. Taylor offers his account as an effort to correct the historical record, a record of lost possibilities within the history of psychology and physiology. One of the reasons for this neglect, according to Taylor, is the shadow Freud has cast over depth psychology.[4]

A number of people closely associated with the James family were engaged with the study of the unconscious, providing him with ideas and material that would become a lifelong preoccupation.[5] Emerson, his godfather, turned to the unconscious in his journals, presenting its underground stream as flowing like a river, and set self-realization and God-consciousness as its destination.[6] James John Garth Wilkinson, the Swedeborgian translator, homeopath and pastoral psychiatrist to the James family, expanded on the stream of consciousness as a technique for writing, drawing and speaking that influenced both young William and Henry.[7] Henry James Sr., William's father, also acknowledged the reality of the unseen,[8] and William's famous younger brother, Henry, became a master in the fictional representation of the interior landscape of his characters, exposing their subliminal thoughts and desires.[9]

William James wrote extensively on the unconscious, studied its processes in experimental psychopathology, practised psychotherapeutic treatment on several patients, investigated the medium Mrs Piper throughout the 1890s,[10] and through his writings, demonstrations and experiments he was one of the main founders of the modern fields of personality theory and psychotherapeutics.[11] James was involved with the two main strands of research, on hysteria and spiritualism, which set the stage for the new concept of the unconscious. The former focussed primarily on hypnotism, and it was represented mainly by the French Experimental Psychology of the Subconscious. James was one of its key interpreters and corresponding regularly with Pierre Janet and Théodule Ribot on issues relating to pathology.[12] The latter was the Society for Psychical Research established with the purpose of scientifically examining psychical phenomena. The SPR played a crucial role in formulating and disseminating the idea of the intelligent unconscious. James became a member of SPR shortly after its formation, serving as Vice-President from 1890 to 1910 and as President in 1894–1895. He also founded the American branch in 1884. James was the first to introduce the work of Breuer and Freud to the American psychological public, and a major influence on the formulation of Jung's personality types. He ardently defended the psychotherapeutic treatment of the American mental healers against attacks by medical doctors; and between 1893 and 1896 he taught an advanced graduate seminar on psychopathology at Harvard, which influenced future researchers in psychotherapy.[13] His interest in exceptional mental states, including trances and automatic writing, led to his widely acclaimed study of the psychology of religion, *Varieties of Religious Experience* (1902). In addition, through his research in depth psychology, he defined the direction that the study of mysticism would take for the next one hundred years,[14] and he proposed an entirely new direction for scientific psychology based on his metaphysics of radical empiricism.[15]

The discovery of the existence of a secondary self was for James "the most important step forward that has occurred in psychology [...] because, unlike the other advances which psychology has made, this discovery has revealed to us an entirely unsuspected peculiarity in the constitution of human nature."[16] This peculiarity consisted in the discovery of the existence of a separate thinking mechanism that is located "outside of the primary consciousness altogether."[17] James conceived of the unconscious as a cognitive mechanism that possessed "a set of memories, thoughts, and feelings which are outside of the primary consciousness altogether."[18] This mechanism could take the form of a distinct and hidden consciousness that shapes, controls and initiates conscious thinking. Research into the unconscious represented for James a promise of uncovering its hidden cognitive potential, which would mark an "epoch, not only in medical, but in psychological science, because it brings in an entirely new conception of our mental possibilities."[19] For James, the unconscious shaped our behaviour and judgements: "in these crepuscular depths of personality the sources of all our outer deeds and decisions take their rise."[20] He used several new phrases to describe unconscious thinking, including "fields of consciousness," "below the threshold," "subconscious mental operations" and "beyond the margin." James described the unconscious as possessing "masses of truth" to which consciousness has a limited access.[21] Moreover, although we are not aware of the unconscious, "it is nevertheless there, and helps both to guide our behavior and to determine the next movement of our attention."[22] The ability of the unconscious to direct our attention places it at the core of cognition. According to James, the unconscious can relate instantly new stimuli with material from the "whole past store of memories [...] the entire mass of residual powers, impulses, and knowledges that constitute our empirical self."[23]

From 1893 to 1896, abnormal psychology was the main topic in James's research and teaching. He taught it as a course four times, presented three public talks on it in February 1895 and gave a series of eight lectures on it twice in 1896. However, after this, his focus shifted; he did not publish the Lowell lectures or write a book on the subject. Pathological cases were only one way of approaching the unconscious but there was, for James, another way not covered by Janet, Breuer and Freud.[24] This way was indicated by his friend F.W.H. Myers, whom James had singled out as the most important author on the subject as well as the originator of the idea of the unconscious mind. Thus, primarily influenced by Myers, James expanded on the idea of the intelligent unconscious, which he conceived of as able to perform higher cognitive processes than our "daylight" consciousness. In his article "What Psychical Research Has Accomplished," James adopted Myers's comparison of the unconscious with light beyond the visible spectrum:

> The ordinary consciousness Mr. Myers likens to the visible part of the solar spectrum; the total consciousness is like that spectrum prolonged by the inclusion of the ultra-red and ultra-violet rays. In the psychic spectrum the "ultra" parts may embrace a far wider range, both of physiological and of psychical activity, that is open to our ordinary consciousness and memory.[25]

This passage captures James's belief in the unconscious as the mental part that has the ability to comprehend a far wider range of material than consciousness.

The appeal that Myers's approach had for James was coupled with his interest in phenomena that exemplify the existence of the intelligent unconscious. Many such events triggered James's attention and prompted him to call for a different approach to the unconscious. For example, he considered instances that demonstrate the ability of the unconscious to recollect what the conscious mind has forgotten. He described the following cases:

> A lady accustomed to taking salicylate of soda for muscular rheumatism wakes one early winter morning with an aching neck. In the twilight she takes what she supposes to be her customary powder from a drawer, dissolves it in a glass of water, and is about to drink it down, when she feels a sharp slap on her shoulder and hears a voice in her ear saying, "Taste it!" On examination, she finds she has got a morphine powder by mistake. The natural interpretation is that a sleeping memory of the morphine powders awoke in this quasi-explosive way. A like explanation offers itself as most plausible for the following case: A lady, with little time to catch the train, and the expressman about to call, is excitedly looking for the lost key of a packed trunk. Hurrying upstairs with a bunch of keys, proved useless, in her hand, she hears an "objective" voice distinctly say, "Try the key of the cake-box." Being tried, it fits. This also may well have been the effect of forgotten experience.[26]

Many such examples point to the existence of a distinct mental level which stores information that can re-emerge in case of need. The existence of the unconscious in these instances is described in terms of a separate consciousness, an "'objective' voice" that can remind, advise and warn. James concludes by suggesting that these examples may not be fully explained by forgetfulness. Rather, they constitute the most primary instances of a number of cases that reveal more and more prominently the existence of an intelligent, goal-oriented and purposeful unconscious.

James also turned to the "tip-of-the-tongue phenomenon," which was a classic example employed by the physiological psychologists to characterize the nature of the "gap" in our consciousness. He described it as a sudden emergence of the unconscious in consciousness:

> You know how it is when you try to recollect a forgotten name. Usually you help the recall by working for it, by mentally running over the places, persons, and things with which the word was connected. But sometimes this effort fails: you feel then as if the harder you tried the less hope there would be, as though the name were *jammed*, and pressure in its direction only kept it all the more from rising. And then the opposite expedient often succeeds. Give up the effort entirely; think of something altogether different, and in half an hour the lost name comes sauntering into your mind, as Emerson says, as carelessly as if it had never been invited.[27]

James's choice of the "tip-of-the-tongue phenomenon" to illustrate the powerful sway of the unconscious over consciousness is significant, for it describes a process that is not simply cognitive but exceeds the abilities of consciousness. The unconscious in this passage is described as working with consciousness towards achieving a common goal. The workings of each component are nevertheless radically different. The unconscious "may consequently be actually interfered with (*jammed*), by voluntary efforts slanting from the true direction."[28] Reversing the common belief in the superiority of consciousness, James saw consciousness as obstructing the process which can only be completed once the "voluntary effort" ceases and the unconscious is free to operate. Similarly, Herbert Spencer believed that thinking which takes place without "conscious intention" or "appreciable effort" is more likely to yield better results than would discursive reasoning.[29] "An effort to arrive forthwith at some answer to a problem," he noted, "acts as a distorting factor in consciousness and causes error," whereas "a quiet contemplation of the problem from time to time, allows those proclivities of thought which have probably been caused unawares by experiences, to make themselves felt, and to guide the mind to the right conclusion."[30] For Spencer, deliberate thinking is relegated to a secondary position, especially in cases that require demanding thinking processes like problem solving and innovative thinking. In these cases conscious reasoning should be abandoned by relinquishing control and knowledge of our thoughts. This form of thinking does not involve the combination of ideas present within consciousness; rather, it produces complex and original creative products.

Similar experiences had been related by Frances Power Cobbe, William Carpenter and George Meredith. They captured something of Oliver Wendell Holmes's idea of feeling the internal movement of thought. James was aware of theorists who expanded on this phenomenon and specifically on the ways that it has been related to the unconscious. As he noted:

> sir William Hamilton and Professor Laycock of Edinburgh were among the first to call attention to this class of effects; but Dr. Carpenter first, unless I am mistaken, introduced the term "unconscious cerebration," which has since then been a popular phrase of explanation.[31]

This phenomenon is related to unconscious problem solving, which can emerge in the form of insight and incubation processes taking place on the subliminal *fringe* of consciousness. For example, Henri Poincaré insisted that he gained a fundamental mathematical insight without conscious processing,[32] while August Kekulé is reputed to have solved the problem of the structure of benzene upon waking from a dream.[33] These are cases whereby a decision or recognition takes place while the mind is not aware and does not register the process. Such sudden realizations are what is commonly known as a "eureka" moment. In his *Principles of Human Physiology*, Carpenter provided examples of artists experiencing their creative process within the context of unconscious cerebration. He cited experiences of authors like William Blake and Charlotte Brontë, who expressed the development of a story or character as occurring without any conscious effort and arising suddenly as a striking revelation. Carpenter argued that composers, too, go through similar unconscious processes in the creation of their works. Referring to Mozart, Carpenter wrote,

> The whole of a Symphony or an Overture would develop itself in his mind, its separate instrumental parts taking (so to speak) their respective shapes, without any *intentional* elaboration. In fact, the only exercise of Will that seemed to be required on his part, consisted in the noting-down of the composition when complete.[34]

James's studies into the flight of time during sleep is another example of the cognitive unconscious: "How can this knowledge of the hour (more accurate often than anything the waking consciousness shows) be possible without mental activity during the interval?" (*PP* 199). As James explained,

> It wakes them at a preappointed hour; it acquaints them with the moment when they first awake. It may produce a hallucination—as in a lady who informs me that at the instant of waking she has a vision of her watch-face with the hands pointing (as she has often verified) to the exact time.

As a solution to this mystery, he proposed the "existence of a highly developed consciousness in places where it has hitherto not been suspected at all" (*PP* 200). James proposed the presence of an "unconscious consciousness" that works parallel with the upper consciousness, and has "one essential function that of 'intelligent action'" (*PP* 85).

His attribution of foresight and understanding to dreams bears further testimony to James's interest in thinking processes that evade our consciousness. He used a hypothetical example of a man who dreams of death and simultaneously dies, and he poses the question: "Is the dream a mere coincidence, or a veritable cognition of the death?" If the death in the dream and in reality were identical, then James held that "his dreams in an inscrutable way knew just those realities which they figured" (*PP* 214). This example demonstrates his belief in the cognitive capacities of an unconscious which can comprehend the physical condition of a person and represent these realities through dreams. While the conscious self lies dormant, the unconscious self is awake and active.

James criticized the scientific community and its materialist bias, which "is identified with a certain fixed belief—the belief that the hidden order of nature is mechanical exclusively."[35] The Cartesian assumption of a perfectly self-transparent view of consciousness results in the refusal to acknowledge the existence of an intelligent unconscious. The traditional scientific approach to physiology is thereby portrayed as law-governed and mechanical. According to this viewpoint, for James, "non-mechanical categories are irrational ways of conceiving and explaining even such things as human life."[36] He attacked the proponents of scientific objectivity who dismiss any theory that challenges the mechanical principle and treat it as antithetical to logic. James's assertion also reminds us that even researchers who take the unconscious into account mainly identify it with the illogical, with the irrational. For James, the fact that "we do not yet know the full extent" of the workings of human cognition should not lead us to presumptions.[37] James aimed to expose the fallacy of the scientific approach. His stress lies in the need to recognize how much unconscious forms of thinking "have been, and even still are, outside of well-drilled scientific circles, the dominant forms of thought."[38] He regarded the science of the time as reductive and unable to comprehend the entire fabric of psychic life. In lieu, James believed in the existence of the unconscious "*in the form of a secondary consciousness* entirely cut off from the primary or normal one, but susceptible of being tapped and made to testify to its existence in various odd ways" (*PP* 201). He derived his idea of the "secondary consciousness" mainly from the empirical work of Janet (1859–1947) and Binet (1857–1911) as well as from the theoretical works of Myers (1843–1901). The concept of a secondary consciousness refers to the existence of separate conscious centres (variously called "secondary selves," "secondary personalities," "subconscious personalities" and "new psychological existences") operating outside the field of ordinary consciousness.[39]

James bequeathed his theory of the unconscious to his Harvard graduate student Boris Sidis, in a way that encouraged Sidis's interest in hypnotism and the launching of the Boston School of Abnormal Psychology. In the Preface James wrote to Sidis's *The Psychology of Suggestion*, he offered a generous tribute to his student's work, which testifies to their shared ways of thinking about the unconscious. James found the focus of this book to be the superior ability of the unconscious to discern aspects of reality unavailable to the conscious mind: "By other ingenious experiments Dr. Sidis tries to show that the 'subliminal' or 'ultramarginal' portions of the mind may in normal persons distinguish objects which the attentive senses find it impossible to name" (*PS* vi). This conception of the unconscious is aptly described in Sidis's *Symptomatology, Psychognosis, and Diagnosis of Psychopathic Diseases*:

By the subconscious is meant all processes of intelligence which are subjectively known as conscious, but which under special conditions fall outside the range of awareness, or of the knowledge of the individual. The subconscious is essentially a consciousness, a consciousness other than the personal consciousness.

(*SPD* 14)

In this context, the waking state and the subliminal consciousness work in perfect harmony, with the former only representing a small portion of mental operation while the subliminal guides thought in the background.

In the phenomenon of the two coexisting selves, the primary personality can enter into a discourse with the unconscious self. This is exemplified in the phenomenon of automatic writing. The unconscious self gradually emerges as the writer begins his practice on the planchette, starting with disjunctive memories and thoughts. The unconscious self, as Sidis commented, "gathers more intelligence and reason, attains even some degree of self-consciousness, gives itself a name, becomes at times eloquent, pouring forth flat discourses on metaphysics and religion" (*PS* 141). Automatic writing betrays a phenomenon whereby the unconscious self reaches independence from the primary consciousness. It is a case of coexistence of the two selves without the one interfering with the other.

Sidis, in his interpretation of Binet's research into psychological automatism and automatic writing in particular, found evidence in support of the coexistence of two consciousnesses: "the one, the waking consciousness, the waking self; the other, the subwaking consciousness, the subwaking self" (*PS* 91). In limb anaesthesias, to cite an instance, an anaesthetic hand adjusted itself correctly to an unseen object, for example, a pencil, the fingers seized and placed it in a position as if the hand were going to write. Similarly, when scissors were placed in the anaesthetic hand, the hand got hold of the instrument in the right way, ready for cutting. For all these adaptive movements to occur, the anaesthetic hand has to "recognise" the object. Boris Sidis analysed the cognitive implications that govern these movements of adaptation. He asserted that

recognition requires a complex mental operation: it requires that the object should be perceived, should be remembered, and should be classed with objects of a certain kind and order. The very fact of the adaptation movements indicates the presence of some kind of embryonic will.

(*PS* 92)

These experiments demonstrated the "presence of a hidden agency that works through the anaesthetic hand; an agency that possesses perception, memory, judgment, and even will" (*PS* 92). All these operations, being "essentially characteristics of consciousness, of a self," led Sidis to the conclusion that "it is a conscious agency that acts through the insensible hand of the hysterical person" (*PS* 92). These cases exemplify the activity of a consciousness unknown to the subject and expressed through the anaesthetic hand; hence, "it is quite clear that there is present within him a secondary consciousness standing in no connection with the primary stream of personal consciousness" (*PS* 92). The secondary consciousness is autonomous, it "perceives and knows facts hidden from the upper consciousness or primary self" (*PS* 94).

For Janet "psychological automatism" refers to the result of the dissociation between behaviour and consciousness, when spontaneous physical acts are performed with no conscious control. He postulated that, in "psychological automatism," consciousness does not belong to the personal consciousness and it is not connected to the personal perception. The term "psychological automatism" had been used before by French psychologist and physician Prosper Despine (1812–1892), who defined subliminal processes as "very complex and intelligent acts reaching a goal which is perfectly specific and adjusted to circumstances; acts exactly similar to those which the ego commands in other occasion through the same apparatus."[40] There is, however, a fundamental difference between Janet's (and James's) conception of the secondary consciousness and Despine's. For Janet, the secondary personality is an unconscious intelligence characterized by its own consciousness, but for the latter, although the unconscious is intelligent and its cognitive processes resemble those of the ego, they nevertheless lack consciousness.[41] The very term "automatism" acquires different meanings in Despine's and Janet's work. For the former, it implies an intellect albeit mechanical unconscious because it lacks consciousness, whereas for the latter it suggests that the unconscious is intelligent with a consciousness of its own, the processes of which appear to personal consciousness as automatisms. Janet's use of the term "automatism" is thus closer to the Greek terms *autos* (self) and *maiomai* (to strive for), which give the sense of a separate consciousness possessing the ability for independent action and separate from the personal consciousness.[42]

For Binet, the existence of a secondary consciousness is manifested in automatic writing. Even though the phenomenon has been observed in spiritists and normal individuals it is more commonly demonstrated, as Binet remarked, in hysterics. In the following experiment performed by Binet, the secondary personality demonstrates its ability to arrive at more precise conclusions, when confronted with insufficient information, than the primary consciousness:

> We place, the hysterical subject before a scale of printed letters, and tentatively seek the maximum distance from the board at which the subject is able to read the largest letters. After having experimentally determined the maximum distance at which the subject can read

the largest letters of the series, we invite him to read certain small letters that are placed below the former. Naturally enough, the subject is unable to do so; but if at this instant we slip a pencil into the anaesthetic hand, we are able by the agency of the hand to induce automatic writing, and this writing will reproduce precisely the letters which the subject is in vain trying to read. It is highly interesting to observe that during the very time the subject is repeatedly declaring that he does not see the letters, the anaesthetic hand, unknown to him, writes out the letters one after another. If, interrupting the experiments, we ask the subject to write of his own free will the letters of the printed series, he will not be able to do so; and when asked simply to draw what he sees, he will only produce a few zigzag marks that have no meaning.

(PS 95–6)

In his comments on Binet's experiment, Sidis argued that it proves that "the secondary consciousness sees the letters or words, and directs the anaesthetic hand it possesses to write what it perceives" (*PS* 96). What is nevertheless more tantalizing to observe is that the experiment revealed an even higher cognitive act, namely, the ability to estimate a result even when insufficient information was provided. In the same experiment, when "the subject was removed at too great a distance, so that the letters are altogether out of the range of vision of the secondary consciousness, the automatic writing begins to make errors writing, for instance, 'Lucien' instead of 'Louise.'" In other words, as Sidis remarked, "it tries to guess" (*PS* 96). The ability to guess is a complex cognitive act suggestive of the existence of a reasoning mechanism that in many cases exceeds the abilities of consciousness. According to Sidis, "Now if anything plainly shows the presence of a hidden intelligence, it is surely this guessing of which the subject himself is totally unconscious, for guessing is essentially a characteristic of consciousness" (*PS* 96). Sidis's conclusions regarding the experiment echo those of Binet's. Binet treated his results as a clear proof of the existence of an intelligent unconscious: "An automaton, does not mistake; the secondary consciousness, on the contrary, is subject to errors because it is a consciousness, because it is a thing that reasons and combines thoughts" (*PS* 96). Guessing is therefore an obvious mark of a reasoning process, since it requires the ability to relate the provided stimuli and make an effort to draw a conclusion. Binet's experiments provided proofs for an unconscious and intelligent guessing—a guessing tied to a rational process. "There are patients," wrote Binet "(St. Am., for example), whose hand spontaneously finishes the word they are made to trace. Thus I cause the letter 'd' to be written; the hand continues and writes 'don.' I write 'pa,' and the hand continues and writes 'pavilion.' I write 'sal,' and the hand writes 'salpetriere'" (*PS* 96–7). The unconscious synthesizes the information it receives to concoct a result that follows naturally and logically from the available data, however incomplete. According to Sidis, "Here it is still more obvious that we are in the presence of a hidden agency that can take hints and develop them intelligently" (*PS* 96).

Gurney also used automatic writing to tap the intelligence of the unconscious self. He gave the hypnotic subject arithmetical problems to solve, and immediately had the subject awakened. When put to the planchette, the subject gave the solution to the problem without being conscious of what s/he was doing. As Sidis commented on this experiment: "It was the hypnotic self who made the calculation, who solved the arithmetical problem" (*PS* 105). Just like his predecessors, Sidis concluded, "decisively the intelligence of the secondary, subwaking, hypnotic self," suggests not "a physiological automaton, but a self, possessing consciousness, memory" (*PS* 105).

These observations led Sidis to hypothesize that "this hidden intelligence may be of still higher organization; it may possess even some degree of self-consciousness, which may grow and develop" (*PS* 129). To probe this possibility, Sidis referred to Janet's well-known case of Madame B. (Leonie), also quoted by William James in *Principles*. The case on Leonie, published serially between 1886 and 1889, provided the first experimental evidence for the existence of a secondary self. The phenomenon occurs when the unconscious self acquires self-consciousness and becomes "so much individualized as to lead a perfectly independent life from that of the waking self" (*PS* 138). The two consciousnesses in this case can run parallel, so that they "may be totally ignorant of each other" (*PS* 138). Thus, Janet's subject Leonie B., when hypnotized, assumed a different name, Leontine. Crystallizing the unconscious as a distinct self, Leontine assumed independence and took control of the conscious self, blaming and ridiculing the primary personality (Leonie). Leontine would call Leonie "that stupid woman" and threatened to eliminate her (*PS* 132). Janet received a letter in which the first page was signed with the subject's real name, while another page followed in a very different tone under the name Leontine, who complained about the ills afflicted upon her by the primary self.

William James, too, conducted numerous experiments on automatic writing as a way to study the nature of the unconscious. This technique was known to James early in his life, as it was in vogue in Europe and America since the mid-19th century.[43] He was to retain this interest throughout his life, an interest which shaped his conception of the unconscious. "Planchette writing," James wrote in his 1896 notes, "makes Myers' notion [of an independently operating, intelligent, secondary consciousness] more plausible [...] I have a whole drawer full" of writings of "all varieties-mirror script, hieroglyphics, even the gift of tongues."[44] He also taught this technique to Gertrude Stein, who was one of his Radcliffe undergraduates. Stein studied the technique experimentally and then used it to form a new style of writing.[45] In *The Principles*, James quoted the case of Sidney Dean, a very advanced case of automatic writing who exhibited a high level of intelligence and even the ability to tackle philosophical and religious questions. As Dean wrote to James:

> When the work is in progress I am in the normal condition, and seemingly *two* minds, intelligences, persons, are practically engaged. The writing is in my own hand, but the dictation not of *my own mind and will*, but that of another, upon subjects of which I can have no knowledge, and hardly a theory; and I myself consciously criticise the thought, fact, mode of expressing it, etc., while the hand is recording the subject-matter, and even the words impressed to be written [...] Sentences are commenced without knowledge of mine as to their subject or ending.
>
> *(PP 373)*

Through this process, Dean wrote 24 chapters on scientific features of life, moral and spiritual. He treated metaphysical questions and, remarkably, each chapter was signed off either by people he was acquainted with or by historical figures (*PP* 374). Dean reported that he had no knowledge either of the authorship of each chapter until it was recorded on paper, or of the philosophical and metaphysical subjects treated. He characteristically described his experience of automatic writing in the following terms: "It is not myself; of that I am conscious at every step of the process" (*PP* 374). Dean experienced this process as a separate self, capable of performing complex thinking processes: "It is an intelligent *ego* who writes" (*PP* 374).

In *Principles*, James cited Janet's experiments that were tasked to induce automatic writing. In these experiments, to exemplify the ways the unconscious is capable of full cognizance without the awareness of the primary consciousness, Janet used a method called "suggestion by distraction." According to this method, the attention of the patient would be totally distracted and the secondary self would accept motor suggestions of which the primary self was totally unaware. For example, James tells us that Janet stood behind his subjects while they were engaged in a conversation with a third party. While conversing, Janet addressed his subjects in a whisper, asking them to perform simple acts like raising their hand. The subjects obeyed "the order given but the *talking* intelligence was quite unconscious of receiving it" (*PP* 201). They responded in writing and through the use of other signs to Janet's demands, while the primary consciousness "went on with the conversation, entirely unaware of these performances on the hand's part" (*PP* 201). These were acts that, according to Janet, demonstrated a partial somnambulism whereby the intelligence of the unconscious can easily be discerned.

Likewise, in his own examples, James referred to two consciousnesses (primary and secondary): the first one is "the talking intelligence," which is involved in the conversation; the latter is the unconscious intelligence, which exists independently and executes orders without the awareness of the primary consciousness. Another way in which James conceptualized the topography of double consciousness is as follows: "*consciousness may be split in two parts which coexist but mutually ignore each other* [...] More remarkable still, they are *complementary*" (PP 204). In other words, since the talking and unconscious intelligences are complementary, they are both responsible for our cognitive actions and behaviour. This portrays an autonomous unconscious that contributes equally to the cognitive process and can rightfully be called a form of consciousness rather than a mechanical reaction. As James put it, "It is therefore in no 'automatism' in the mechanical sense of the word that such acts are due" (PP 206). His conception of the secondary consciousness involves a cognitive sphere possessing high intelligence, a conception diametrically opposed to Descartes's view, which traced the thinking processes only in the conscious mind and viewed the unconscious, physical operations as mechanical.

Hypnosis provided contemporary psychologists and physiologists with a fertile field of enquiry in their attempts to unravel the processes of cognition. Janet and Edmund Gurney (1847–1888) conducted extensive experiments on deferred or post-hypnotic suggestion which showed, as Sidis commented, "clear, valid, and direct evidence of the reality of a secondary consciousness, of an intelligent, subwaking, hypnotic self concealed behind the curtain of personal consciousness" (PS 99–100). Janet further explained that "suggestions were made during a well-established hypnotic sleep, then the subject was thoroughly wakened, and the signals and the actions took place in the waking state" (PS 101). While Lucie was in a state of genuine somnambulism, Janet gave her suggestions like "At the third blow you will raise your hands, at the fifth you will lower them, at the sixth you will look foolish, at the ninth you will walk about the room, and at the sixteenth you will go to sleep in an easy-chair" (PS 101). Then, Janet woke her up. The forgetfulness of everything that had happened during the hypnotic state was complete. Other individuals surrounded Lucie, who was replying to their questions, yet she still performed all the actions in the order required. And it was thought provoking to realize that she "was not aware that she counted the noises, that she looked foolish, or that she walked about" (PS 101). Following the same method, Janet used some variations on the experiment. He asked Lucie to become rigid when she repeated the same letter in succession. After Lucie awoke, Janet whispered the letters "a," "c," "d," "e," "a," "a," and Lucie instantly became motionless and perfectly rigid. This experiment manifests another aspect of the intelligent unconscious, that of judgement of resemblance. Following examples that involved suggestions like: "'You will go to sleep when I pronounce an uneven number,' or 'Your hands will revolve around each other when I pronounce a woman's name'" draw attention to an unconscious judgement of difference (*PS* 102). When Janet whispered even numbers or men's names, Lucie didn't react, but when the right signal was given, she performed the suggestion. Lucie listened unconsciously, compared and discerned between differences. Janet complicated the experiment to see "to what lengths this faculty of an unconscious (subconscious) judgment would go" (*PS* 102). Suggestions were therefore carried out in a manner that involved independent thought. He would ask the subject to perform an act, not upon waking, but at the end of a specified time. He gave the following suggestion: "'When the sum of the number which I shall pronounce amounts to ten you will throw kisses'" (*PS* 102). Lucie then awoke and started chatting with other people who disturbed her as much as possible. Janet took a distance from her and whispered "'Two, three, one, four,'" and Lucie performed the suggestion. More complicated numbers and operations followed: "'When the numbers that I shall pronounce two by two, subtracted from one another, leave six, you will make a certain gesture'—or multiplication, and even very simple divisions" (*PS* 102). These experiments demonstrate that Lucie could be attentive, count and judge without being able to recall any of these incidents. The results provided Janet with evidence for the existence of a separate consciousness able to perform complex mental operations while remaining hidden from the waking consciousness. An unconscious faculty measuring time works in parallel to consciousness and counts the days and hours intervening between the suggestion and its performance, even though the suggestion is altogether forgotten by the waking consciousness. The unconscious involves, in Janet's words, "a memory that persists, an attention always on the alert, and a judgment perfectly capable of counting the days, as is shown by its being able to make these multiplications and divisions" (*PS* 103).

In his lecture on "Automatism," James turned to Gurney's research on hypnotism. A subject referred to as "P-11" was "given a letter and told to mail it on the 123rd day." The subject subsequently had "no memory [of the command], but when returned to the hypnotic trance," it was revealed that he had been keeping an unconscious "record of the days that had passed" with such an accuracy that he could specify the number of hours and minutes left.[46] James stressed the fact that even when a "sovereign was offered" to the subject when not under hypnosis to account for the elapsed days, the subject was still unable to recall the suggestion. In another instance, Gurney commanded P-11 under hypnosis: "You will get up and poke the fire in six minutes." The subject was then awakened and after being induced again into the hypnotic condition, s/he was able to report: "three and a half more, poke the fire."[47] These experiments, according to James, reveal the existence of a "secondary intelligence" independent of the waking consciousness.[48]

Another way to study the existence of an unconscious self below the waking consciousness was post-hypnotic negative hallucinations and systematized anaesthesia. Experiments were conducted by Hippolyte Bernheim and M. Jules Liegeois, which were quoted by Binet in his monumental *The Alternations of Personality*. The hypnotic subject would receive a suggestion like, "When you wake you will no longer see me: I shall have gone."[49] The subject, after awaking, communicated normally with other people but did not see or interact with the hypnotizer, who "shouted in her ear, stuck a pin in her skin, her nostrils, under the nails, and thrust the point of the pin in the mucous membrane of the eye. She did not move a muscle."[50] The subject would then be hypnotized again and given the suggestion that the hypnotizer should "be there" after awakening. The subject followed this suggestion and, after the hypnotizer's probing, she was able to recall everything the hypnotizer had done to her while she was unable to see him. As Bernheim commented: "she saw me with her bodily (subconscious) eyes, but she did not see me with the eyes of the mind (upper consciousness). All sensorial impressions emanating from me were distinctly perceived, but remained unconscious for her (upper consciousness)."[51]

Liegeois's experiments in suggestion led him to similar conclusions. The subject, following his suggestions upon wakening, would follow every command he gave. For instance, "I said that she was cold, and she shivered; that she ought to go to the stove in which there was no fire and there she went; until I told her that she was warm, and then she was all right."[52] However, she had no sense of his presence, and when asked by the assistants if he was there, she said he was absent. Liegeois concluded, "It is her unconscious ego that causes her to act, and the conscious ego has not the slightest idea of the impulse that she receives from without."[53] Sidis concurred: "The facts of hypnotic memory alone strongly indicate the intelligent nature of the subconscious" (*PS* 118). The ability to remember and follow the suggestions of the hypnotizer requires the existence of an intelligent mechanism. However, this is not the only manifestation of cognitive ability: "the subject during hypnosis not only acts, moves, but he also speaks, answers questions intelligently, reasons, discusses" (*PS* 119). The unconscious can understand suggestions, follow them and even formulate logical arguments.

Along with Boris Sidis, Morton Prince was another major American psychiatrist practising hypnotism to examine the role of buried experiences. He was also influenced by Janet and James, and partly by Myers. A friend of both Sidis and James, Prince was influential in his time. He was a physician and active member of the "Boston school of abnormal psychology and psychotherapy," and a central figure in the establishment of psychology as an academic discipline. After graduating from Harvard medical school, he visited Europe in the early 1880s and met Jean-Martin Charcot. Prince was fascinated by the work of Charcot and Janet, using it as a foundation that shaped his own experimental work.[54] He wrote about the importance of the unconscious in studies of hysterical symptoms at the same time as Freud, but he was critical of psychoanalysis. Prince emphasized the role of the unconscious as the causal factor in hysterical symptoms and developed an experimental scientific methodology for the application of hypnosis to the understanding of unconscious processes.[55] These experiments culminated in the publication of his 1914 book *The Unconscious*, which, in Alan Gauld's words, marks "both the climax and the end of the golden age of the subconscious."[56]

One of the questions that Prince sets out to answer in *The Unconscious* is as to whether the unconscious can "perform the same functions as are ordinarily performed by conscious *intelligence* [...] that is to say memory, perception, reasoning, imagination, volition, affectivity, etc." (*U* 163). In order to provide an answer to this overarching question, Prince took into consideration cases that range from hypnotic suggestions, hallucinations and dreams to diurnal experiences. In hypnotic suggestions, for example, he found that the subjects, while unconscious, were able to exhibit a series of actions involving complicated behaviour, including mathematical calculations. The conditions of the experiments suggested that such processes "must not only be subconscious but must be a more or less complicated succession of processes" (*U* 165). To cite one example, a subject was given, while awake, a mathematical problem to solve. The subject dutifully performed the calculations in the usual manner. The same subject was then presented under hypnosis with a very similar mathematical problem of addition and multiplication. Quite tantalisingly, the subject performed the calculations but in a different way, which was imagistic in nature. Although it took the subject more time to arrive at the correct solutions, it was interesting to observe that the numbers were visualized and arranged in all sorts of ways. Finally, nevertheless, the result was obtained. This indicated to Prince that there exists in human subjects a "secondary consciousness, i.e., the subconsciousness," wherein

> the numbers kept coming and going [...] until the problem was solved and then they ceased to appear. It is to be understood of course, that the *principal or personal consciousness was not aware of these coconscious figures, or even that any calculation was being or to be performed.*
>
> (*U* 170–1).

These findings prompted Prince to investigate how our secondary consciousness works in such a way as to provide solutions to unsolved moral or social problems that may cause unease. And so Prince continues to give an account of how one of his subjects utilized the cognitive powers of his subconsciousness in order to arrive at what he felt as a *"spontaneous* subconscious solution of problems" (*U* 171). In one of the examples that the subject provides, he tells us that when he is trying to translate a difficult passage from Virgil and he encounters an impasse for some time, he decides to "put it out of" his mind. However, the subject interestingly interjects to note that

> it is a mistake to say you put it *out* of your mind. What you do is, you put it *into* your mind [...] by putting it into your mind I mean that, although the waking consciousness may have put it aside, the problem still remains in the secondary consciousness
>
> (*U* 172)

That is, the subject puts it out of his conscious mind and into his unconscious mind in order to allow for his unconscious to come up with what might appear in consciousness to be a spontaneous solution.[57] This, the subject concludes, is suggestive of the fact that the secondary consciousness has a memory where it retains persistently all sorts of information. Then, the secondary consciousness is able to recall memories and thoughts associated with the passage under question in order to provide a satisfactory solution. Although the translation itself is not performed by the secondary consciousness, it nevertheless stores and incubates the problematic passage and retrieves the necessary information that is associated with the passage in order to enable the conscious mind to translate the passage. And so, the subject admits, "with this information I complete the translation" (*U* 173). This solution may seem "to come in a miraculous sort of way," but it is explicable in terms of what Prince referred to as "subconscious incubation" (*U* 173).

Complex associations, memory, the ability to retrieve the necessary information to solve a problem, calculations and logical and sequential thought are characteristics of unconscious intelligence. But in order to further mine the cognitive wealth of our unconscious mind, Prince continues to offer his observations on an experiment with yet another subject. This subject was able to distinguish in her mental processes an upper and a lower stratum. The former pertains to thoughts that are at the forefront of consciousness, while the latter consists of perceptions and thoughts that are not in the focus (*U* 174). The lower stratum is also called the "background of the mind" and corresponds to the fringe of consciousness, where thoughts and perceptions are pushed and we are no longer aware of their presence. Admittedly, Prince observes, there is nothing unusual in the spontaneous emergence of what rests in the fringe into the upper stratum. What is unusual is that this particular subject was able, after long practice, to recall the contents of the fringe at will. And she discovered that these contents, once recalled, are far richer in thoughts than ordinary attention would show. This phenomenon led

Prince to the conclusion that "It is indeed a veritable coconsciousness in which there goes on a secondary stream of thoughts often of an entirely different character and with different affects from those of the upper stratum" (*U* 174–5). Prince speaks here of a double consciousness or, in his own terminology, of a "coconsciousness," a type of consciousness that works in parallel with our personal consciousness and of which we are oblivious. This entails a secondary stream of thoughts that runs in parallel to the primary stream of thoughts, each one of them yielding different effects, associations and results.

Based on his analysis of the cases mentioned above, Prince concluded that our unconscious exhibits a series of cognitive capabilities that resemble closely those of the personal consciousness. To begin with, Prince observes that the calculative phenomena indicate an intellectual character that requires "*reasoning* and the cooperation of mathematical *memory*" (*U* 177). Unconsciousness also exhibits personal will or volition. All these characteristics are the markings of "intelligent appreciation [...] Each step was adapted to an end, ceased as soon as it accomplished that end, and was followed by another in logical sequence, the whole taking place as if performed by an intelligence" (*U* 178). To dig a bit further into what he refers to as "subconscious intelligence," Prince also turns to the phenomena of spontaneous hallucinations, which exhibit "constructive intelligence" (*U* 188). These phenomena indicate that "the subconscious link must be of considerable complexity and equivalent to logical processes of reasoning, volition, and purposive intelligence" (*U* 188). To illustrate this exposition, Prince provides the example of an experimental case where the subject, apparently automatically and without self-conscious awareness, finds what she was unable to find for days. In the meantime, the subject had a vision, which repeated the pattern of a series of visions she had as a young child. After waking from the vision, the subject was led immediately to the discovery of the lost object. Prince observes here that between the primary causal factor, which is the anxiety to find the missing object, and the seemingly automatic phenomenon of retrieving that object, rests a connecting link, *viz.*, unconscious intelligent cognitive processes that are aim-oriented and bent on achieving a certain purpose. In Prince's words

> *between the two as connecting links were subconscious processes of an intelligent, purposive, volitional character which first fabricated a visual symbolism as a message to consciousness and then made use of the conserved knowledge of her previous absent-minded act to solve her problem.*

(*U* 191)

Prince explains here that the hallucinations sprang from the unconscious and the symbolism implicated therein was processed by the unconscious.

And this "is an excellent example of intelligent subconscious process indicative of judgement and purpose" (U 191).

The same process, according to Prince, applies to dreams as types of hallucinatory phenomena. Having considered a series of experimental cases, Prince argues that dreams are fabrications of a subconscious intelligence that breeds and analyses their symbolizations "in the logical form of an argument" (U 202). Just as in the case of hallucinatory phenomena, between a wish or any type of anxiety and the manifestation of these anxieties in consciousness, lies the subconscious intelligence as a connecting link that processes a large complex of memories and diverse experiences in order to arrive at a resolution (U 202). In this, dream phenomena and their underlying mechanism become also analogous to the subconscious solution of mathematical problems (U 203). It is thus no surprise that the unconscious intelligence, having the characteristics of reasoning, memory, volition, purposiveness, constructive imagination, analytical skills and affectivity, is thought by Prince to closely resemble the cognitive abilities of personal consciousness: "I have suggested that the *subconscious intelligence* may be *comparable to the phenomenon of a coconscious personality.*" Prince alternatively refers to this phenomenon as a "secondary consciousness" (i.e. U 212). The processes taking place in this subconscious intelligence are referred to by Prince as "subconscious incubation," a term which he attributes to William James (U 224). Indeed, as we saw earlier in this chapter, James referred to the cognitive processes taking place in the unconscious as "incubation."

In a final twist of thought, Prince generalizes his findings on the phenomena of hallucinations and dreams to argue that in our everyday experience, when we confront "a novel and difficult question," we often say that we cannot decide such a question offhand and that we would need time for consideration. That is, we "take the matter 'under advisement,' to use the conventional expression." And here Prince insists that what we "undoubtedly do is to put the problem *into* our minds and leave it, so to speak, to incubate" (U 226–7). The problem goes through a "subconscious incubation" wherein the various associations and cognitive processes performed yield a solution which emerges in consciousness for deliberation (U 227).

Research into the notion of an unconscious intelligence did not restrict itself to visions, dreams, hallucinations and the silent processes that underpin the solutions to our everyday dilemmas. It leaped off the interpretation of depth psychology into sensorial perception, opening the door to the investigation of the physiological and neural processes that underpin unconscious intelligence. In the early days of hypnotic experiments, when it was known as "animal magnetism," somnambulist subjects indicated the existence of a certain kind of "intelligence." Alfred Binet and his collaborator Charles Féré began working for Jean Martin Charcot at Salpêtrière hospital. Their first experiments on hypnosis and hysteria probed such phenomena and traced back their source in a form of what they referred to as "unconscious reasoning." The execution of actions induced by suggestion undermined previous conceptions of the hypnotic subject as an automaton evacuated of any sense of cognition:

> When care is taken to suggest a somewhat complex act, whose performance necessitates some combination, we may observe that the subject thinks out such combinations although they have not been suggested to him. This inventive process shows that comparing him to an automaton does not explain everything.[58]

Based on these experiments, Binet's first book *The Psychology of Reasoning* (1886) proposes that the "unconscious reasoning" which occurs in perception is essentially the same as conscious, logical reasoning, for the function of both reasoning and perception is to establish relations between different terms. The mental process relating to perception and unconscious reasoning has the ability to form judgements based on "a relation of resemblance, co-existence or of sequence between two things."[59] As Binet concludes, "We have several times, in alluding to the psychological nature of perception, seen in it the result of unconscious reasoning."[60] According to Binet, it is the sense of touch and the visual images that it excites which allow us to cross a room in darkness among the furniture without stumbling. He finds "unconscious reasoning" to be "exceptionally developed in somnambulists, who usually walk with their eyes closed and can avoid obstacles of every kind by their hyper-aesthetic sense of touch."[61] This phenomenon exemplifies the reasoning of the senses as "the somnambulist does not see by his eyes, he sees by reasoning." Through association, Binet proposes that the guiding reason that leads the somnambulist can also help us "understand a multitude of improbable feats, how, for example, a certain somnambulist can write a page of manuscript, read it over and correct it exactly, without the cooperation of sight."[62] The actions of the hypnotic subject provided evidence of calculated movements that were ascribed to the existence of an unconscious memory and intelligence. Through further experimentation, Binet and Féré cemented their theory of the ability of "unconscious reason" to surpass conscious reason and even to provide rational explanations for the somnambulist's actions. The two researchers were assigned to study Blanche Wittmann, called Wit or simply W in their writings. In one of these experiments, they suggested to "W—," who was in the state of somnambulism, that "she should make a gesture of contempt at a bust of Gall." After being awakened, she made the gesture indicated and when asked to explain the motive of this suggested act, she responded: "'That bust is disgusting.'" The subject provided a reasoned conclusion, but one that "takes the form of a hallucination; the patient *sees* the bust under a disgusting aspect."[63] Other scenarios were suggested to subjects that were able to logically justify the action and "draw every possible deduction from the theme imposed upon it."[64] Binet concluded that the purpose of this reasoning is "to create a kind of *logical vision*, so much the more striking as under these circumstances, logical—or in other words, hallucinatory—vision surpasses actual vision in intensity" and "fills the gaps in actual vision; it constructs a new universe in our mind."[65] Accordingly, it is probably no coincidence that Binet and Féré chose to assign their subject the name Wit: it is a literary ploy suggestive that the hypnotic subject, although her waking consciousness rests dormant, her unconscious mind remains wide awake and demonstrates wit.

The acuteness of the senses that characterized subjects under hypnosis became a focal point of many experiments during the end of the 19th century. For Sidis, for example, "The senses of touch, pressure, and temperature are much more delicate in the hypnotic condition" (*PS* 148). James Braid also reported how "A patient could feel and obey the motion of a glass funnel passed through the air at a distance of *fifteen-feet*" (*PS* 149). The ability of a subject under hypnosis to walk in a room with bandaged eyes or in absolute darkness without striking against anything was also taken up by Moll, Braid, Poirault and Drjevetzky who ascribed it to an unconscious sensitivity which enabled the subject to recognize objects by the resistance of the air and by the alteration of temperature (*PS* 149). In Henri Bergson's extraordinary case of "visual hypersesthesia," the subject could read the image of a page reflected in the experimenter's cornea and discern with the naked eye details in a microscopic preparation (*PS* 150). Further experiments demonstrated the potency of smell in hypnosis. Braid's subject was able to recognize individuals by smell, locate objects, and restore them to the rightful owners (*PS* 151). Sidis conducted 3,000 laboratory experiments, concluding that there is "direct and conclusive proof of the presence of the subwaking, subpersonal, hyperaesthetic self in our normal state" (*PS* 158). Another insight Sidis gained from these experiments—some of which were conducted in collaboration with William James—was that when the conscious self is completely absorbed with a task, it fully disregards features not necessary for it because they would distract his/ her attention (*PS* 159–60). One of the conclusions of these experiments was that the figure "still impressed the sense organ, reached the secondary self, which took it as a suggestion, sending it up as a message to the primary self or personality and influencing the latter's choice" (*PS* 174). For these researchers, this was a clear indication that the unconscious within us "perceives things which the primary waking self is unable to get at" (*PS* 171).

James's conclusion from such experiments was that the main feature of hypnotic subjects is not "sensorial anaesthesia," not a simple "failure to notice," but a much more complex process, an "active counting out and positive exclusion of certain objects." In instances, for example, "when one 'cuts' an acquaintance, 'ignores' a claim, or 'refuses to be influenced' by a consideration," s/he is dealing with an unconscious judgement and exclusion (*PP* 209). For James, this unconscious cognitive process is autonomous and distinct from conscious ones: "But the perceptive activity which works to this result is disconnected from the consciousness which is personal, so to speak, to the subject, and makes of the object concerning which the suggestion is made, its own private possession and prey" (*PP* 209). The attribution of independent perceptive activities to the bodily substrata elevates the status of the sense organ from a mere passive receptor to an independent cognitive mechanism. The latter functions in parallel to those of conscious mentality, influencing it without its being aware of the control placed upon it. James also provides us with the example of "mothers of infants, who will sleep through much noise of an irrelevant sort, but waken at the slightest stirring [...] of the babe" (*PP* 199). In this case, the auditory sensibility functions independently, awaking the conscious mind in case of need. There is a whole process at work regarding what seems to go unnoticed, involving an unconscious decision making. Therefore, *"we must never take a person's testimony, however sincere, that he has felt nothing, as proof positive that no feeling has been there"* (PP 208). The feeling here represents the existence of the consciousness of a secondary personage of which the primary one is unaware.

The Physiology of the Intelligent Unconscious

Continuities and Discontinuities with the Victorian Physiological Psychologists

The independence attributed to the body and the senses by researchers like Sidis, Binet and James marks a continuity with a long tradition that started in the mid-19th century and its preoccupation with non-deliberate thoughts that were conceived as physiologically based. Physiologists discovered that most reflexes involve a simple nervous pathway, the "reflex arc." Nineteenth-century psychologists applied the concept of the reflex arc to the mind that allowed automatic and reflexive mental processes to take place independently of consciousness.[66] The concept came under an entire rubric of multiple terms, including "reflex thought," "latent thought," "latent consciousness," "obscure perception," "the hidden soul," "reflex action of the brain," "unconscious psychical activity," "unconscious psychical processes," and "unconscious sensual and volitional processes."[67] However, the main term to describe such cognitive actions was "unconscious cerebration," first used by William Carpenter (1813–1885) in 1854.[68] Carpenter's notion of "unconscious cerebration" was incorporated into most subsequent debates of the issue. In *Principles of Mental Physiology*, Carpenter noted that the unconscious mind can produce logical conclusions *"below the plane* of consciousness, either during profound sleep, or while the attention is wholly engrossed by some entirely different train of thought."[69] "When we have been *trying to recollect* some name, phrase, occurrence, etc," Carpenter asserted, "it will often occur *spontaneously* a little while afterwards, suddenly flashing (as it were) into our consciousness, either when we are thinking of something altogether different, or on awaking out of profound sleep."[70] Expanding on the physiological model of the mind, Carpenter not only attributed thinking to bodily processes but also treated them as the basis for our highest intellectual activity. "Our highest Mental Activity," in Carpenters's theory, is "the expression of the *automatic* action of the Cerebrum."[71] Carpenter elaborated on the unconscious processes:

> we seem justified in proceeding further, and in affirming that the Cerebrum may act upon impressions transmitted to it, and may elaborate results such as we might have attained by the purposive direction of our minds to the subject, without any consciousness on our own parts; so that we only become aware of the operation which has taken place, when we compare the result, as it presents itself to our minds after it has been attained, with the materials submitted to the process.[72]

His description of the dynamic role of the unconscious in the thinking process stressed its active and transformative powers: it does not merely transmit stimuli for consciousness to process; it also "acts upon impressions," filtering and analysing their content. This is a fluid process that can only be known through its results. The unconscious is active throughout conscious reasoning, and it can "elaborate" on its results to form new conclusions. The concept of "unconscious cerebration" covered a wide range of unconscious manifestations. It included the recall of forgotten words, the production of solutions to intellectual problems while one is sleeping, and even the emergence of fully formed literary or musical creations constructed without the conscious efforts of the artist.[73] Carpenter's doctrine that all unconscious processes result from the reflex action of the brain gained many supporters.

The concept, however, was often misunderstood, as certain terms used by Carpenter, such as "reflex" and "automatic," appeared to imply mechanical reactions devoid of any notion of a thinking process. Such approaches were criticized by some of the most prominent authors of the period, including James, Myers and Sidis. Myers, for instance, refused to acknowledge any link between unconscious cerebration and mechanical forms of information processing:

> I wish to protest against the undue extension of such phrases as "unconscious cerebration," and to insist that we have as good ground for attributing consciousness to some at least of these subliminal

operations in ourselves as we have for attributing consciousness to the intellectual performances of our neighbours.[74]

Myers proposed that the unconscious does not lack any of the properties associated with intelligence, since it, too, has the ability to think and reason. His conception of latent forms of thinking as cognitive led him to dismiss the terms "'Unconscious' or even 'subconscious,' [as] directly misleading" fearing that they suggest a mechanism that runs counter to consciousness. He favoured instead the words "supraliminal" and "subliminal," respectively for consciousness and unconsciousness.[75] Myers believed that the term "unconscious," by definition, is placed in opposition to consciousness as its negative side. The substituting terms he proposed signify instead a differentiation in the mode of consciousness, "subliminal" consciousness being characterized as superior to "supraliminal" consciousness:

> at the superior or psychical end, the subliminal memory includes an unknown category of impressions which the supraliminal consciousness is incapable of receiving in any direct fashion, and which it must cognize, if at all, in the shape of messages from the subliminal consciousness.[76]

Reiterating his former point, Myers asserted that "There seems no reason to assume that our active consciousness is necessarily altogether superior to the consciousnesses [or processes] which are at present secondary, or potential only."[77]

In the second of his Lowell Lectures, "Exceptional Mental States," James examined the concept of "unconscious cerebration." He criticized Arthur H. Pierce's and Samson Landmann's arguments against the existence of a secondary intelligent consciousness.[78] In "Subliminal Self or Unconscious Cerebration?" Arthur Pierce had rejected the results and implications of Gurney, Janet, Binet and others.[79] For him, such phenomena do not merit any special attention because they are nothing more than habitual repetitions of simple behaviours by the lower brain centres. Similarly, Landmann theorized that the brain functions on three levels: consciousness; ideation and association without self-consciousness; and the "sub-cortical centers," also referred to as the unconscious.[80] Like Pierce, Landmann argues that the lower centres are limited to habitual tasks and simple reflexes. In both Peirce and Landmann, waking consciousness is superior to other states of consciousness which can only be illuminated when consciousness sheds light on them. James rejected these theories, concluding that they did not provide any new contribution to the subject.[81] For him, Pierce and Landmann's view that secondary consciousness is an inferior derivative of the primary one "is disproved by cases where a command given has to be intellectually worked out."[82] James stressed that experiments had provided irrefutable evidence of the existence of an intelligent unconscious. It is in this spirit that he provides a series of experiments that testify to his conclusions. Thus, James tells his readers,

> Gurney has given his subjects problems in addition and multiplication. He has commanded them to write backwards; to count letters in a sentence; or to give an anecdote from their childhood. Meanwhile the subject might be either reading aloud, talking, or engaged in a conversation.[83]

Janet's empirical approach, too, had favoured the existence of "two simultaneous conscious systems."[84] James prompted his reader to consider "Janet's case of Lucie, who counts signals up to 43" and then falls asleep, and "multiplies 739 times 42."[85] James's reference was to Janet's experiment on Lucie, who, under hypnosis, had been commanded to fall asleep when the hypnotizer's knocks reached 43. After being awakened to perform various tasks, the hypnotizer began signalling irregularly. At precisely 43, she fell asleep in an armchair. She consequently asserted that during her period of activity she had heard the hypnotizer knock only once. Janet concluded that Lucie had been counting the remaining knocks unconsciously. In another experiment, Janet commanded the subject while under hypnosis to multiply, in writing, 739 times 42. Upon awakening her right hand was performing the computation and stopped when it was finished. In the meantime, she was relating to the hypnotist her daily activities, oblivious of her right hand writing automatically.[86]

William James Sidis (1898–1944) inherited from his father (Boris Sidis) and Godfather (William James) not only their names, but he synthesized their complementary, on many levels, theories to arrive at what he referred to as "unconscious intelligence." The child prodigy was the youngest Harvard graduate of the time at the age of 16. In 1914, the year of his graduation, James Sidis published his first essay, "Unconscious Intelligence," which was included as an appendix to his father's *Symptomatology, Psychognosis and Diagnosis of Psychopathic Diseases*.[87] The essay champions the idea of unconscious cognition invested with logical thinking. Already a competent mathematician, he applied the method of isomorphism in his analysis of the relationship between conscious and unconscious thinking. The method depends on the supposition that when we are confronted with two hypotheses, the consequences of which are the same, then they must be considered as identical. Building on this method, James Sidis continues to provide examples from personal experience which show that "there is no essential difference between the properties of unconscious intelligence and those of consciousness" (*SPD* 433). Accordingly, he concludes, it would be illogical, on the premises of isomorphism, to draw a distinction between an unconscious intelligence that is not conscious of itself and a conscious intelligence that is conscious of itself. The characteristic instances that he provides include the ability of our unconscious intelligence to read and remember. After glossing the abilities to remember and to reason as "the two properties most characteristic of consciousness" (*SPD* 434), James Sidis is led to the conclusion that "such an 'unconscious intelligence' differs in no way from a normal consciousness; except that *I* only know of it through circumstantial evidence. But the same can be said of the consciousness of another person" (*SPD* 434). Here, James Sidis postulates the existence within us of a separate, alter ego, rendering the human subject essentially bi-subjective. The logic of isomorphism tells us that since intelligence and consciousness are practically identical, it is unnecessary to differentiate between the two. To corroborate his thesis James Sidis evokes Isaac Newton for whom, one should not differentiate, for example, between a terrestrial reflection of light and other planetary light reflections. Just as Newton finds no justification for a difference in explanation with regards to this physical phenomenon, James Sidis contends that we should approach the two forms of consciousness in the same manner. Next, James Sidis embraces the Victorian concept of "unconscious cerebration" while questioning its terminological implications to insist that "it follows from the principle enunciated by Newton that their unconscious intelligence must be conscious. That is to say, the phenomena of the subconscious are due to a consciousness [...], which is the same physiologically as normal consciousness" (*SPD* 436). In each one of us there is a second, hidden consciousness of which we are not aware, other than by inferential evidence about its cognitive processes. In James Sidis's words "I must infer that there is one more consciousness existent in me" (*SPD* 437). It is in this spirit that James Sidis chose to conclude his chapter on unconscious intelligence with his adage "*subconscious processes are conscious*" (*SPD* 439).

Body of Wisdom: Neural Action and Sensory Cognition

James was writing in a period when psychology was transitioning from philosophy to the laboratory, to a new alliance with physiology. As Gerald Myers suggests, "unlike B.F. Skinner's concept of psychology today, physiological psychology in James's day required going 'under the skin' [...] James saw its task as improving our knowledge of mind-body relationships by drawing upon the new science of human physiology."[88] As was a common practice among psychologists, James started his *Principles* with an analysis of the physical aspect of man. As we have seen, under the rubric of "unconscious cerebration," William Carpenter had maintained that a large proportion of mental activity took place automatically.[89] In biology, notions of organic memory arose, based on Jean Baptiste Lamarck's (1744–1829) theory of the inheritance of acquired characteristics and Ernst Haeckel's (1834–1919) biogenetic law according to which ontogeny recapitulated phylogeny. As Laura Otis wrote,

> The theory of organic memory placed the past *in* the individual, *in* the body, *in* the nervous system; it pulled memory from the domain of the metaphysical into the domain of the physical [...] it equated memory with heredity, arguing that just as people remembered some of their own experiences consciously, they remembered their racial and ancestral experiences unconsciously, through their instincts.[90]

Hermann Ebbinghaus's (1850–1909) work, which James characterized as "a really heroic series of daily observations of more than two years duration," demonstrated that "association is subtler than consciousness, and that a nerve-process may, without producing consciousness, be effective in the same way in which consciousness would have seemed to be effective if it had been there" (*PP* 636, 638).

In the "The Functions of the Brain," James sheds light on the nervous centres and their relation to consciousness. At first sight, his insistence on neural action as an unconscious process seems to contrast sharply with his assertion that the nervous centres are "organs of consciousness" (*PP* 85). We are caught in what might sound like a contradiction because, on the one hand, neural action is regarded as unconscious, but on the other, it is seen as an organ of consciousness. Nevertheless, rather than a contradiction or inconsistency, James suggests that the unconscious processes performed by the nervous centres possess a form of reasoning and intelligence through which a type of unconscious consciousness emerges, as per, for example, Janet's, Myers's, Binet's and Sidis's conclusions. According to James, the human neural system is capable both of choosing certain beneficial sensations and of retaining a memory of them in order to reactivate them in their absence: "They [nerve centres] feel, prefer one thing to another, and have 'ends'" (*PP* 85). Having specific "ends," the neural system demonstrates personal volition or a will of its own, a characteristic traditionally attributed to consciousness. Nerve centres "identify in memory any motor discharges which may have led to such ends, and associate the latter with them, then these motor discharges themselves may in turn become desired as *means*" (*PP* 85). The nerve centres that can perform these cognitive processes pass on to the more intellectually developed hemispheres and, accompanied by consciousness, they perform the operations of thought. James stated that in more developed animals, like humans and monkeys, the neural system mainly executes the thinking processes, with only a small contribution by the basal ganglia (cerebral hemispheres that are involved in the regulation of voluntary movement). In less cognitively evolved species, the thinking process is predominantly done by the basal ganglia. The nervous centres are also responsible for "the education of our human hemispheres" in that they regulate "the acquisition of memories and associations which may later result in all sorts of 'changes of partners' in the psychic world" (*PP* 86). For example, the original tendency of the baby to touch a candle is inhibited by the image of the burn, left in the cortex, that excites the tendency to withdraw the next time a candle is perceived. This is exemplary of the education the nerve centres offer through an association of pain with the candle. The memories and associations the neural system forms in order to attain specific ends are paradigmatic of an autonomous intelligence. Thus, early on in his *Principles*, James drew attention to the cognitive dimensions of the neural centres that have the capacity to formulate intentions. What may seem to be a mechanical reaction is, for James, in fact a volitional cognitive act.

A central thematic section which clarifies James's understanding of the unconscious is his "Automation Theory," which focusses on the autonomy and role of the nervous system. From the beginning of the chapter, James explicitly stated his anti-Cartesian stance. Descartes attributed an intelligent, self-sufficing nervous mechanism to animals but in man, he claimed, the higher acts are performed by the rational soul, a distinction that James condemned as a "singularly arbitrary" (*PP* 134). The role of the physical aspect is so defining that James suggests that even our conscious intelligence itself is the product of neural processes:

> What is there to hinder us from supposing that even where we know consciousness to be there, the still more complicated neural action which we believe to be its inseparable companion is alone and of itself the real agent of whatever intelligent deeds may appear?
>
> (*PP* 133)

The Corporeal Roots of Thinking: From Percept to Concept

James's distinction between percepts and concepts provides significant insight into the notion that intelligence is primarily the product of somatic cognitive processes. He differentiated between the discursive intellect with its separating, categorizing functions and the percept, which accesses the "passing pulses of our life" (*SPP* 110). James described percepts as a flow, profusion, the full self, a "much-at-once," and he asserted that instead of percept he will "often speak of sensation, feeling, intuition, and sometimes of sensible experience or of the immediate flow of conscious life" (*SPP* 49, 48). This mechanism, formed by sensory data, is not a passive receptor of the experiential multiplicity, but it is a locus of novelty: "The percepts are singulars that change incessantly and never return exactly as they were before. This brings an element of concrete novelty into our experience" (*SPP* 98). Percepts, by accessing a pluralistic flux in which disparate realities coexist in loose relations, open up a space where genuine novelty can "leak in" (*SPP* 132). Through percepts we can engage the full potentialities of our experiential life and open up to our cognitive abilities. Percepts, James argued, are more expansive and dynamic than concepts, for the latter offer only "post-mortem" reconstructions and build on the already known (*SPP* 99). They gather sensations and yield results, which are not simply a plenum of data, but information invested with a response. As James's language may have indicated, he appears to have struggled to give expression to the nature and function of the percepts. He seems to be wrestling to give language to the body without turning it into a duplicate of the language of the conscious mind. James's ecstatic over-writing seems to be his attempt to put the body on the wrack until it reveals how it speaks. Exploring further the development of the discursive mind from primarily bodily reactions, James asserted that:

> Some parts of the stream of feeling must be more intense, emphatic, and exciting than others in animals as well as in ourselves; but whereas lower animals simply react upon these more salient sensations by appropriate movements, higher animals remember them, and men react on them intellectually, by using nouns, adjectives, and verbs to identify them when they meet them elsewhere.
>
> (*SPP* 48)

What the discursive mind chooses to single out and turn into an abstraction is the natural outgrowth of a bodily selective process. The object of abstraction and conceptualization is defined by the result of the perceptual flux. Percepts form what James called a "sensible muchness," which "shows duration, intensity, complexity or simplicity, interestingness, excitingness, pleasantness or their opposites" (*SPP* 50, 49). It is percepts and their selective character that define the object of investigation of the mind. The mind picks out and abstracts elements based on the bodily criteria and responses like "excitingness, pleasantness or their opposites" (*SPP* 49).

Since concepts emerge after singling out and isolating what is provided by percepts, they cannot bring about any originality: "This novelty finds no representation in the conceptual method, for concepts are abstracted from experiences already seen or given, and he who uses them to divine the new can never do so but in ready-made and ancient terms" (*SPP* 98–9). To support his belief in the primacy of the percept, James demonstrated "1. That concepts are secondary formations, inadequate, and only ministerial; and 2. That they falsify as well as omit, and make the flux impossible to understand" (*SPP* 79). Concepts are presented as passive recipients of the products of a complicated physiological process, "[they] are fixed, even though they designate parts that move in the flux; they do not act" (*SPP* 82). James asserted that concepts are "sufficient only for retrospective understanding; and when we use them to define the universe prospectively we ought to realize that they can give only a bare abstract outline or approximate sketch, in the filling out of which perception must be invoked" (*SPP* 99). He thereby criticized the overreliance on concepts and stressed the damaging effect it can have in philosophy: "instead of seeing that the fault is with the concepts, it blames the perceptual flux" (*SPP* 84). Western thought, he argued, overvalues the concept, forgetting or missing its secondary, derivative, necessarily reductive nature and treats senses as "organs of wavering illusion that stand in the way of 'knowledge,' in the unalterable sense of that term. They are an unfortunate complication on which philosophers may safely turn their backs" (*SPP* 75). Thus, James inverted the order of "The Platonizing persuasion," which assumes "that the intelligible order ought to supersede the senses rather than interpret them" (*SPP* 75). Intellectualism conceives of knowledge as distinct from the experiential domain and tries to conceive percepts by defining them. The inevitable result of this approach is that "the more we learn *about* our subject of discourse," the farther away we have moved from "the perceptual type of experience" (*SPP* 83). James described the way intellectualism undermines its own purpose: "Intellectualism draws the dynamic continuity out of nature as you draw the thread out of a string of beads" (*SPP* 86). Instead, he proposed that philosophy should "Use concepts when they help, and drop them when they hinder understanding; and take reality bodily and integrally up into philosophy in exactly the perceptual shape in which it comes" (*SPP* 95). Concepts, as less adequate means of grasping reality than percepts, should only be used as tools since they only touch the surface of the fullness of perceptual reality.

James's main thesis is that we should not abandon concept for percept but rather grasp, in the complexities of our cognitive processing, their imbricated, reciprocal relations. He asserted that both concepts and percepts are indispensable to the thinking process, which is determined by their interaction: "Percepts and concepts interpenetrate and melt together, impregnate and fertilize each other. Neither, taken alone, knows reality in its completeness. We need them both, as we need both our legs to walk with" (*SPP* 53). Concepts, according to James, have practical advantages, as their function is to "*harness* perceptual reality [...] in order to drive it better to our ends" (*SPP* 65). He formulated his "pragmatic rule" that becomes a criterion to judge the advantage of a concept according to which "the better we understand anything the more we are able to *tell about it*." The only valuable criterion to judge a concept is whether it makes us understand our percepts better, by "knowing *what* these are, we can tell all sorts of farther truths about them, based on the relation of those whats to other whats" (*SPP* 65). The conceived order is therefore based on and theoretically explains the perceived order; it "is only a system of hypothetically imagined *thats*, the *whats* of which harmoniously connect themselves with the *what* of any *that* which we immediately perceive" (*SPP* 66). Accordingly, for James, the foundation of cognition lays with percepts, which concepts theorize and abstract. Concepts are therefore derivative abstractions: "All conceptual content is borrowed: to know what the concept 'color' means you must have *seen* red or blue, or green" (*SPP* 79–80). James gave primacy to perceptual knowledge, which becomes the locus of immediate apprehension that evades conscious reason. Consequently, for James, "Conceptual knowledge is forever inadequate to the fullness of the reality to be known" (*SPP* 78).

James's friend and colleague, C.S. Peirce (1839–1914) located the difference between his and James's pragmatism in the way they understand the term percept.[91] In his attempt to clarify the "meaning" of a concept or the "ultimate logical interpretant," Peirce distinguished his pragmatism from that of James: "he does not restrict the 'meaning,' that is the ultimate logical interpretant, as I do, to a habit, but allows percepts, that is, complex feelings endowed with compulsiveness to be such."[92] For James, meaning is ingrained in percepts while for Pierce habit is the "ultimate logical interpretant." Boris Sidis swayed the other way, corroborating James's thesis. He asserts that sensations awaken unconscious processes which are synthetized into a percept. In *The Psychology of Suggestion*, after numerous experiments on the nature of the unconscious in normal individuals, Sidis concluded that sensory stimuli ignored by the waking self were still impressed on the sense organs, and were present in the unconscious self. This is suggestive of the higher possibilities of the unconscious that has a wider range of knowledge than the primary consciousness and is able to reach information that the conscious self is unable to recognize and process. The experiments also suggested an interrelation between the two spheres as the secondary self sends messages to the primary self so that "an inhibited particular idea still reaches the primary self as an abstract idea" (*PS* 171). Sidis characteristically remarked that "*An abstract general idea in the consciousness of the waking self has a particular idea as its basis in the subwaking self*" (*PS* 171). He related the source of an idea to the unconscious with only a generalized sense reaching the waking consciousness. Locating the roots of concepts to percepts has the potential to solve "The great contention of nominalism and conceptualism over the nature of abstract general ideas" (*PS* 171). The conceptualists argue that an abstract idea may exist in consciousness apart from the particular idea or perception perceived, "but they do not say that this consciousness is that of the waking self" (*PS* 172). Nominalists, however, assert that a concept has a particular idea or percept as its basis; but as Sidis noted, "they do not add that this percept may be totally absent from the waking consciousness and only present in the subwaking consciousness" (*PS* 172). Sidis therefore furthered the nominalist approach to account for the separate existence of the unconscious self, its ability to store, contain and send information to the primary self. His experiments provided proof that messages are first perceived by the unconscious and are then sent to the waking self, showing in this way the interrelation between the two spheres: "*No general abstract idea without some particular percept as basis*" (*PS* 172). He also explained the phenomena of synaesthesia and hallucination through the workings of percepts (*SPD* 143–64).

James also contrasted the fixed, stationary nature of the concept or abstract thought with the transience, fluidity and mobility of the percept. Concepts, he stated, in substituting truth for reality, selectively map and reductively circumscribe the fullness of our experience. Our conceptual understanding, which explains by "deducing the identical from the identical," can name new forms, but only in the terms of the already known, so that "if the world is to be conceptually rationalized no novelty can really come" (*SPP* 152). In contrast, percepts have a separate and distinct function; through their connection with the perceptual flux they "yield a perfect effervescence of novelty all the time" (*SPP* 151). James reversed the primacy that the intellect has received and places the wisdom of the body at the core of cognition and foundation on which the mental domain is founded.

Beyond "The Stream of Thought": Transitive and Substantive Parts

James's theory of the "The Stream of Thought" constitutes another important thematic section through which we can gain deeper insight into his understanding of the unconscious and its effects on consciousness. James extended his theory of unconscious reasoning to explore the ways that it shapes conscious thought through relations that are *felt* and not just conceived. This theory, as we will see later in this book, had significant influence on the literary writers of the period. For the time being, it is important to clarify James's distinction between substantive and transitive parts.

The substantive parts constitute the resting-places of our thoughts, where they "can be held before the mind for an indefinite time." The transitive parts are the thoughts of relations that act as passages or transitions between our more stable thoughts. They are the ones that "lead us from one substantive conclusion to another" (*PP* 236). The transitive parts are rather impossible to arrest and analyse, as focussing on them is to annihilate them. To grasp them is tantamount to turning them from flights to a conclusion, to substantive parts. They are essentially felt, but they are non-imagistic relations, and the only way to identify them is through an empirical reality of relations of "every sort, of time, space, difference, likeness, change, rate, cause."[93] This distinction is fundamental to our understanding of James's theory of the primary consciousness's processes of cognition.

The master metaphor for James's conceptualization of consciousness is that of a stream or a river. This is drawn from his famous contention that

> Consciousness, then, does not appear to itself chopped up in bits. Such words as "chain" and "train" do not describe it fitly as it presents itself *in the first instance*. It is nothing jointed; it flows. A "river" or a "stream" are the metaphors by which it is most naturally described.
>
> (emphasis added, *PP* 233)

Here, James drives a wedge between a phenomenal, surface "*first instance*" and a deeper, stealthier and imperceptible "instance." In the first instance, consciousness feels a continuous, unified flow of thinking, and therefore terms such as "chain" or "train" appear to be inaccurate. Such terms entail disconnected parts being linked together. To phenomenal consciousness, however, these links are absent, thought is unified, it forms a "river" or a "stream" and they are, as a result, more natural metaphors to describe the phenomenon. However, this is only a phenomenal, surface reality, James contends. It is only in the first instance that words like chain or train seem inappropriate. But a closer look shows that "chain" and "train" are actually better metaphors for explaining and clarifying the notion of the stream of thought. The continuity that has been attributed to consciousness is made possible by the transitional parts of thought, which are unconscious. At this point, James invents yet another metaphor, which he contends elucidates how the chain or the train of thought is held together by a very particular kind of connecting link. The stream of consciousness is more accurately captured by the following metaphor: "Like a bird's life, (the stream of consciousness) seems to be made of an alternation of flights and perching" (*PP* 236). Ralph Barton Perry (1876–1957), James's student and first commentator, adopted James's metaphor, explaining that: "The practically habituated mind flies from perch to perch, and is aware of the perch rather than of the passage."[94] This is a call to account for the diversified contents of consciousness which are "discrete and discontinuous; they do pass before us in a train or chain" forming a unity of jointed parts: "The transition between the thought of one object and the thought of another is no more a break in the *thought* than a joint in the bamboo is a break in the wood" (*PP* 233, 234). This account brings James's theory of the transitive and substantive parts to bear on his understanding of the workings of the stream of consciousness. The stream contains two distinct activities: flying and perching. The former is congenial to James's explanation of the transitive parts and the latter to his theory of the substantive parts. The substantive parts form a "chain" or a "sequence of differents," as James's predecessors claimed, rather than a stream (*PP* 224). The overall impression that consciousness is a stream is rendered possible because of the transference of the transitive parts into the substantive mode of cognition. There is no essential "break" in thought but a continuous interplay of flying and perching, of transitions to substantive parts. The metaphor of the stream or the river steers clear of the nuances of this process: Perry's bamboo, on this metaphor, would be stripped off of its "joints" and James's bird of its "perchings."

However vague and ungraspable, the transitive stages forge the paths of our thinking processes, leading to "the attainment of some other substantive part" (*PP* 236). They are the ones that "lead us from one substantive conclusion to another" (*PP* 236). They perform the cognitive process that decides what will emerge to occupy our thoughts and what will remain lower in the stream. It's a selective process that chooses the thought to be presented before the conscious mind. Thoughts may seem to be impulsive, leaving us with "the conclusion before we can arrest it" (*PP* 237). But unconscious cognitive processes have been at work, which define actively the flow of thought. The transitive parts, the processes by which we transition from one conclusion or cognitive object to the next, remain ever elusive and imponderable, as they are in a constant flux. And yet again, James resorted to a metaphor as the most appropriate means to flesh out the elusiveness and imponderability of the transitive parts: "a snowflake caught in the warm hand is no longer a flake but a drop" (*PP* 237). Instead of comprehending the inner feeling of relations that bring forth the next term, we end up with a "substantive part," but its "function, tendency, and particular meaning in the sentence quite evaporated" (*PP* 237).

James expanded on the teleological nature of the unconscious, which he related to how it furthers practical needs by providing purpose and direction to the stream of consciousness. The attempt to recall a forgotten name is an example of this sense of *telos* characterizing this peculiar state of consciousness. As James noted, this is "no mere gap. It is a gap that is intensely active," it approves or negates proposed names (*PP* 243). The name in this case is "beckoning us in a given direction, making us at moments tingle with the sense of our closeness, and then letting us sink back without the longed-for term" (*PP* 243). Instant rejection of a term and the feeling of proximity of another are two very different states that we are unable to describe. Discussing our inability to express this difference, James asserted that "namelessness is compatible with existence" (*PP* 243). He treated language as a construct alienated from the deeper recesses of our being while he supported the existence of cognitive processes eluding our conscious awareness. James provided further examples of unconscious thinking located under the stream:

> Everyone must know the tantalizing effect of the blank rhythm of some forgotten verse, restlessly dancing in one's mind, striving to

be filled out with words. Again, what is the strange difference between an experience tasted for the first time and the same experience recognized as familiar, as having been enjoyed before, though
we cannot name it or say where or when? A tune, an odor, a flavor
sometimes carry this inarticulate feeling of their familiarity so deep
into our consciousness that we are fairly shaken by its mysterious
emotional power.

(*PP* 244)

This sign of direction is manifested in every word as well as in large
tracts of human speech as felt meaning. This sense of direction is related
to the flights or the transitive states which are so elusive that "If we try to
hold fast the feeling of direction, the full presence comes and the feeling
of direction is lost" (*PP* 245).

The way grammatico-syntactical constructions are embedded in our
thought is yet another example of the cognitive processes taking place
under the stream:

How comes it about that a man reading something aloud for the first
time is able immediately to emphasize all his words aright, unless
from the very first he have a sense of at least the form of the sentence
yet to come, which sense is fused with his consciousness of the present word, and modifies its emphasis in his mind so as to make him
give it the proper accent as he utters it?

(*PP* 245)

The ability to read with "the most delicately modulated expression of intelligence" even if the reader is unable to understand any of the ideas expressed in the text, is a good example of the instrumental role played by
the unconscious in thought (*PP* 245). James provided further instances
of our inability to grasp ideas directly:

What is that shadowy scheme of the "form" of an opera, play, or
book, which remains in our mind and on which we pass judgment
when the actual thing is done? What is our notion of a scientific or
philosophical system?

(*PP* 246, 247)

James referred to ideas formed by laws of association under the stream,
a phenomenon that also explains sudden revelatory manifestations. Genius also lies in the ability to make novel associations: "Great thinkers
have vast premonitory glimpses of schemes of relation between terms,
which hardly even as verbal images enter the mind, so rapid is the whole
process" (*PP* 247).

The Birth of the Emotion and the Judgement of the Senses

In James's theory, emotions do not spring from any conscious centres in the brain, although once triggered and felt, they emerge in consciousness. What is of particular interest for James is precisely the triggering processes, that is, the processes taking place that yield any given emotion. These processes take place at an unconscious level. According to James, what has been axiomatically labelled as instinctual reaction, as opposed to cognitive action, is invested with qualities or faculties typically found in the sphere of conscious mentality. For James, the "seat" of emotions is located in motor and sensory processes of the same sort that underlie our perceptual experience (*PP* 235). He conceived of emotions, like perceptions, as afferent bodily processes, objecting to the idea of emotion as a primarily mental product:

> Common-sense says, we lose our fortune, are sorry and weep; we meet a bear, are frightened and run; we are insulted by a rival, are angry and strike. The hypothesis here to be defended says that this order of sequence is incorrect, that the one mental state is not immediately induced by the other, that the bodily manifestations must first be interposed between, and that the more rational statement is that we feel sorry because we cry, angry because we strike, afraid because we tremble, and not that we cry, strike, or tremble, because we are sorry, angry, or fearful, as the case may be. Without the bodily states following on the perception, the latter would be purely cognitive in form, pale, colorless, destitute of emotional warmth.
>
> (*PP* 1065–6)

In his famous example of the bear, James invites us to consider the emotion of fright. According to common sense and traditional psychology, the perception of the bear causes the feeling of fright, which is purely mental and independent of physiological events. Any associated physical changes, such as running, sweating, heightened blood-pressure, palpitations, or trembling, are called the expressions or effects of the bodiless emotion of fright. According to these accounts, the intellect, the conscious mind, induces an emotion and the corresponding physiological alterations. *Pace* these accounts, James stressed the impossibility to postulate an emotion without its bodily reverberations:

> *If we fancy some strong emotion, and then try to abstract from our consciousness of it all the feelings of its bodily symptoms, we find we have nothing left behind*, no "mind-stuff" out of which the emotion can be constituted, and that a cold and neutral state of intellectual perception is all that remains.
>
> (*PP* 1067)

To illustrate his thesis, James noted that it would be impossible to think of an emotion of fear if "the feeling neither of quickened heart-beats nor of shallow breathing, neither of trembling lips nor of weakened limbs, neither of goose-flesh nor of visceral stirring, were present" (*PP* 1067). Organic experience, therefore, emerges as the primary cause for the activation of emotions, not a conscious cognitive process:

> Our natural way of thinking about [...] emotions, is that the mental perception of some fact excites the mental affection called emotion, and that this latter state of mind gives rise to the bodily expression. My theory on the contrary, is that *the bodily changes follow directly the perception of the exciting fact, and that our feeling of the same changes as they occur* IS *the emotion.*
>
> (*PP* 1065)

Fear, for instance, feels different from anger or love because it has a different physiological signature. The mental aspect of emotion, the feeling, is a slave to its physiology, not vice versa: we do not tremble because we are afraid or cry because we feel sad; we are afraid because we tremble and are sad because we cry. Inherent therefore in James's theory of emotions is the idea that sense perception responds to stimuli at a pre-conceptual stage, that is, before conscious cognitive processes have been involved. This response indicates that a form of reasoning or evaluative process has been at work even though it does not fall within the bounds of discursive thought.

For James, what is of particular interest is the physiological response to stimuli. He stressed that the word "run" must "stand for what it was meant to stand for, namely, for many other movements in us, of which invisible visceral ones seem by far the most essential [...] Whatever the fear may be in such a case, it is not constituted by the voluntary act."[95] So emotion is some feeling of bodily, organic change which is performed independently of consciousness. James placed the emotional process in the motor-sensory system attributing their origin to a physiological mechanism similar to the one used by ordinary perception:

> An object falls on a sense-organ, affects a cortical part, and is perceived; or else the latter, excited inwardly, gives rise to an idea of the same object. Quick as a flash, the reflex currents pass down through their preordained channels, alter the condition of muscle, skin, and viscus; and these alterations, perceived, like the original object, in as many portions of the cortex, combine with it in consciousness and transform it from an object-simply-apprehended into an object-emotionally-felt. No new principles have to be invoked,

nothing postulated beyond the ordinary reflex circuits, and the local
centres admitted in one shape or another by all to exist.

(PP 1087)

James analyses here the way that bodily processes respond to the environment and the way that ideas and consciousness rise out of this
process. These internal bodily changes cause responses like running or
crying, and without them no emotion of fear or sorrow can occur. One
of James's central aims is to support the theory that the origin of the
emotion rests in neural cognitive processes that precede conscious mental
contents: "An emotion of fear, for example, or surprise, is not a direct
effect of the object's presence on the mind, but an effect of that still earlier effect, the bodily commotion which the object suddenly excites."[96]
He stated that feelings in general are caused by the continuous flow of
visceral, sensorimotor and affective responses: "whatever moods, affections, and passions I have are in very truth constituted by, and made up
of, those bodily changes which we ordinarily call their expression or consequence" (PP 1068). Enabling our adjustment to the environment, emotions are not only a proof of the way embodied cognition can influence
conscious activity and initiate thought on its own, but also of the way
mental life is "knit up with our corporeal frame" (PP 1082). Within this
framework, thought is only the end result of complicated physical processes: "cognition in this view is but a fleeting moment, a cross-section at
a certain point of what in its totality is a motor phenomenon" (PP 941).

James's analysis of the processes that produce emotions is instrumental
to our understanding of his philosophy of aesthetics, where he grounds his
views in the processes that underpin artistic creation and appreciation. As
we have seen, James conceived of "our very senses themselves [as] organs
of selection" that shape experience by choosing only certain ranges of
stimuli and turning them into sensations (PP 273). James asserted that we
only notice stimuli which "happen practically or aesthetically to interest
us, to which we therefore give substantive names, and which we exalt to
this exclusive status of independence and dignity" (PP 274). The mind
shapes, uses and combines the "data chosen" from the lower levels (PP
277). "In the senses," he explained, "an impression feels very differently
according to what has preceded it; as one color succeeding another is mod-
ified by the contrast, silence sounds delicious after noise, and a note, when
the scale is sung up, sounds unlike itself when the scale is sung down" (PP
228). Aesthetic selective shaping is what enables the transformation of
sensations into perceptions and then of perceptions into object properties.
James further held that aesthetic and practical factors shape our reality:

*Out of all the visual magnitudes of each known object we have se-
lected one as the REAL one to think of and degraded all the others*

> *to serve as its signs.* This "real" magnitude is determined by aesthetic and practical interests. It is that which we get when the object is at the distance most propitious for exact visual discrimination of its details.
>
> *(PP* 817)

The real properties of things are therefore based on both aesthetic and practical characteristics as a way to categorize and distinguish certain objects out of the perceptual multitude. Similarly, *"when two sensorial sense-impressions, believed to come from the same object, differ, then* THE ONE MOST INTERESTING, *practically or æsthetically,* IS JUDGED TO BE THE TRUE ONE" (*PP* 818). Processing innumerable impressions, the senses engage in a process of elimination in order to distinguish the most aesthetically and practically appealing characteristics of an object. For instance,

> The real color of a thing is that one color-sensation which it gives us when most favorably lighted for vision. So of its real size, its real shape, etc.—these are but optical sensations selected out of thousands of others, because they have aesthetic characteristics which appeal to our convenience or delight.
>
> *(PP* 934)

What defines certain properties as practical or convenient are aesthetic qualities like clearness or vividness, which allow us to turn to these objects that bear the specific properties when needed. This principle, however, does not only apply to this primary classification. Aesthetic qualities, according to James, also determine the choice of scientific theories: *"That theory will be most generally believed which, besides offering us objects able to account satisfactorily for our sensible experience, also offers those which are most interesting, those which appeal most urgently to our aesthetic, emotional, and active needs"* (PP 940). Building on this initial selection process performed by the senses, the aesthetic principle defines "our intellectual as well as our sensuous life" (*PP* 943).

In addition to the first aesthetic principle that James singled out as clarity, he distinguished between "the two great aesthetic principles, of richness and of ease." According to James, theories that are widely acceptable are "rich, simple, and harmonious" (*PP* 943). "The richness," James continued, "is got by including all the facts of sense in the scheme; the simplicity, by deducing them out of the smallest possible number of [...] primordial entities." Simplicity provides the aesthetic "law of least effort" because it tends to make things as "definite as possible" (*PP* 944). Accordingly, the aesthetic criteria overlap with the practical ones. James's definition of simplicity as the "law of least effort" also amounts to a practical criterion. In other instances, however, the two are clearly distinguished. Philosophy, for example, emerges from an aesthetic drive of "scientific curiosity" or "metaphysical wonder" with which "the practical [...] has probably nothing to do [...] The philosophic brain responds to an inconsistency or a gap in its knowledge, just as the musical brain responds to a discord in what it hears" (*PP* 1046). The pleasures of philosophical thinking are therefore like "many other aesthetic manifestations, sensitive and motor" (*PP* 1046). For James, philosophy springs from a feeling of pleasure or discord which is the initial, bodily response which the philosopher consequently elaborates and expresses in discourse. The Jamesian conception of the aesthetic is distanced from the abstract theorizing of fine art or the appreciation of beauty. He noted that "no good will ever come to Art as such from the analytic study of Aesthetics, harm rather, if the abstractions could in any way be made the basis of practice."[97] For James, discourse is unable to represent adequately aesthetic impressions. He is thus particularly critical of German philosophers and their conceptual theorizations: "Why does the *Aesthetik* of every German philosopher appear to the artist like the abomination of desolation?" he asks, and notes that the error of such an approach is that it distances itself from the sensational terms that aesthetics spring from and rather relies on an abstractive "system of categories" of inert, "gray monotony."[98]

The very same experience, for James, could be rational, practical and aesthetic. The aesthetic in James's cognitive psychology comes to signify the ability of the body to respond to its environment according to what it deems to be agreeable. James reformulated the mind/ body problem by giving primacy to the somatic and treating the mental sphere as posterior, since it responds and builds on the choices made by the somatic. Rather than relating the sensational terms with the subjective element in experience, James associated them with objectivity and asserted that it is an aesthetic process that shapes our experience and defines objects as "REAL." In "The Sentiment of Rationality," James related logic with the affective dimension, making sentiment the "mark" of rationality. Aesthetic selection shapes experience and its marks include a "strong feeling of ease, peace, rest," and a "feeling of the sufficiency of the present moment," a "loyalty to clearness and integrity of perception."[99] The aesthetic is not simply conceived as facilitating logic; it becomes a principle used to judge what is logical: "of two conceptions equally fit to satisfy the logical demand, that one which awakens the active impulses, or satisfies other aesthetic demands better than the other, will be accounted the more rational conception, and will deservedly prevail."[100] The feeling of rationality is maintained by a bodily selective process whereby objects are "approved or rejected by our aesthetic and practical nature."[101]

James distinguished between the "coarse" and "subtler emotions" (*PP* 1082). The former, which include the emotions of rage, fear and love, are characterized by an overt physiological manifestation. The latter, which include the "aesthetic emotions," are characterized by a physiological activity which is not as distinctly felt as in the case of the coarse emotions. James analysed aesthetic emotions to demonstrate that their source lies in the "widespread bodily effects by a sort of immediate physical influence, antecedent to the arousal of an emotion or emotional idea."[102] In asserting that the body produces an "emotional idea," James reverses the commonly held notion that an idea can only be a mental product. He further distinguished between "primary" and "secondary" aesthetic emotions. The former are defined as the "simple primary and immediate pleasure [caused by] certain pure sensations and harmonious combinations of them" (*PP* 1083). The "primary pleasure" is caused by the direct impact that the object has on the optic receptors and/ or auricular receptors: "[T]he pleasure given us by certain lines and masses, and combinations of colors and sounds, is an absolutely sensational experience, an optical or auricular feeling that is primary" (*PP* 1082). The "primary" emotions originate in an optical or auricular perception which causes instant bodily changes. According to James, what makes art so aesthetically appealing is the pleasing effect it has on "the bodily sounding board."[103] The response to art forms, like poetry, drama or music, should not rely, according to James, on critical reflection, which is based on an elevated class of abstractions. Instead, he asserted that our response to art involves physical modifications which precede our conscious response. An aesthetic judgement is primarily a somatic response, the result of perception that causes pleasure or displeasure.

The "secondary" aesthetic emotions involve a more complicated, subtle response that builds on the "primary" aesthetic emotions. They occur through a "repercussion backwards [to the physiological level] of other sensations elsewhere consecutively aroused," by an emotion pure and simple (*PP* 1083). These secondary pleasures are rooted in physiological processes, causing "a glow, a pang in the breast, a shudder, a fullness of the breathing, a flutter of the heart, a shiver down the back, a moistening of the eyes, [...] and a thousand unnamable symptoms besides, may be felt the moment the beauty *excites* us" and fills us with pleasure (*PP* 1084). The "*added* secondary pleasures" involve a more complicated bodily response and play a great part in formulating "the practical enjoyment of works of art by the masses of mankind" (*PP* 1083). In James's words,

> In listening to poetry, drama, or heroic narrative, we are often surprised at the cutaneous shiver which like a sudden wave flows over us, and at the heart-swelling and the lachrymal effusion that unexpectedly catch us at intervals. In listening to music, the same is even more strikingly true.
>
> (*PP* 1072)

These physiological responses are felt, but still not as strongly as the feelings that characterize the coarser emotions, as an addition upon the feelings of the immediate, purely perceptual response.

The Intelligent Unconscious and the Psychoanalytic Unconscious

Although recent studies on Freud's writings have shown that his theory entails an unconscious characterized by thinking processes,[104] the period's psychologists viewed psychoanalysis primarily as promoting a mechanical, irrational unconscious that stands in conflict with consciousness. This discrepancy notwithstanding, what is of particular interest for the historical purposes of this chapter is how contemporary psychologists and physiologists perceived Freud's theory.

James's conception of subconscious awareness differed in significant ways from Freud's view of the unconscious.[105] As G.E. Myers pointed out, "Freud, who explicitly opposed his own view to Janet's, saw the unconscious as an impersonal realm in which opposing mental forces are in conflict." Myers referred to the main differences between James and Freud:

> The idea that an item experienced unconsciously must be conscious to a secondary or subconscious self struck Freud as paradoxical. "Anyone who tried to push the argument further and to conclude from it that one's own hidden processes belonged actually to a second *consciousness* would be faced with the concept of a consciousness of which one knew nothing, of an 'unconscious consciousness'—and this would scarcely be preferable to the assumption of an 'unconscious mental.'" Could James have replied, he would presumably have denied such a paradox, insisting that the secondary consciousness is indeed not known or recognized by the primary, but knows or recognizes itself in the way that any of us is acquainted with our own consciousness. Thus the notion of a secondary or subconscious personality does not saddle us with an unintelligible "unconscious consciousness." James would have shifted the burden of proof upon Freud, as many others have, by asking what can be the point of calling something both unconscious and mental if it is not felt or experienced to some degree, that is, if it is not impressed upon someone's consciousness at least a little bit.[106]

Thus, whereas Freud postulated the existence of one consciousness, James asserted the existence of an unconscious that shares all the characteristics of consciousness. Freud acknowledged the possibility that ideas can split from consciousness and constitute a "consciousness apart," which has become estranged from "the bulk of conscious activity."[107]

He recognized that this view is supported by cases of dual personality, such as that described by Eugène Azam, but he argued that we are not justified in using the word "conscious."[108] He proposed that instead of a "splitting consciousness," we should be talking about a "shifting of consciousness," expressing thus a unitary consciousness theory.[109] However, Freud's contemporaries contested that his proposition could not explain cases in which two apparent intelligences communicate simultaneously. As we have seen, observation from experiments led Myers, James, Janet and Prince, among others, to advocate the view of an intelligent unconscious that is independent of the waking consciousness. In his presidential address to the Medical section of the British Psychological Society, Bernard Hart criticized Freud and psychoanalysis for failing to account for the phenomena of dissociation in their theoretical construction.[110]

Boris Sidis also criticized psychoanalysis on many fronts. As he asserted, "Psychoanalysis is a conscious and more often a sub-Conscious or unconscious debauching of the patient. Nothing is so diabolically calculated to suggest sexual perversion as psychoanalysis" (*SPD* vii). He further accused psychoanalysts of explaining away psychical phenomena: "The representatives of this tendency are not satisfied unless they read some meaning, conscious or unconscious, into the various phenomena of abnormal mental life" (*SPD* vii). This view was not idiosyncratic to Sidis. As he noted, his view of psychoanalysis was also shared, among others, by William James:

> When Freud's *Psychopathologie des Alltagslebens* was published I discussed the examples, so ingeniously worked out by Freud, with the late Professor James of Harvard. James laughed at the puerility of Freudian associations; he threw up his hands at the psychoanalytic absurdities, and characterized Freudian *Psychopathologie* as "silly and nonsensical." Some similar opinion is maintained by Wundt, Ziehen, Oppenheim, Aschaffenburg and others.
>
> (*SPD* viii)

The intelligent unconscious is able to make judgements and, accordingly sets certain aims which it attempts to achieve. It is this conception that Sidis juxtaposed to Freud's notion of the irrational unconscious. According to Sidis, it is precisely this lack of purpose that characterizes pathological phenomena. As he noted,

> I lay special stress on the fact that the phenomena of abnormal mental life do not present any purpose in the present; they are repetitions, recurrences of a past, but they have no aim, no purpose, no meaning in the present life existence of the patient.
>
> (*SPD* viii)

Psychoanalytic symptoms are also, according to Sidis, "*pathological, just because they have no purpose, no meaning in the life of the patient*" (*SPD* viii). Similarly, symptoms which are characteristic of a pathological condition have "essentially no meaning in the present, although the patient especially with the help of the physician may find some meaning as do the insane when trying to account for their pathological state" (*SPD* xii). Symptoms are "*survivals, relics from a previous epoch of the life existence of the patient*" and this is what renders them meaningless. Their origin "from a stage of experience the meaning of which is gone" is precisely what makes them "entirely *irrational*" (*SPD* xii). Sidis proposed an altogether different approach to these phenomena; he suggested that "It is only when we come to realize the irrationality and lack of adaptation, inner and outer, of such pathological, meaningless systems [...] that we begin to understand the psychopathic character of the symptom complex" (*SPD* xii).

Sidis also questioned the validity of the association method used in psychoanalysis, characterizing it as arbitrary and superficial. He asserted that psychoanalysts themselves are the best illustration of their own thesis, namely, that "one may be duped by their own wishes" (*SPD* ix). Since pathological phenomena lack meaning, the methods used to extract it by psychoanalysis are futile and amount to nothing more than a wish-fulfilment. "In fact, the very methods of free association and oneiromantic interpretations," he noted, "are of such a character that any associations may be formed, according to the wish of the physician" (*SPD* ix). He sarcastically added that "In this respect the Freudian does live up to his theory that everything can be explained by wish and its ideal fulfilment" (*SPD* ix). The reason for this is that the unconscious in pathological phenomena and its corresponding system-complexes are "survivals of a former period of mental activity; they are atavistic systems which keep on recurring [...] under appropriate circumstances and favorable conditions, but which are now irrational, without meaning and purpose" (*SPD* xiv). Sidis suggests that "We may lay it down as a law that *psychopathic life* lacks meaning. I lay special stress on this principle, —*lack of meaning is characteristic of psychopathic affections*" (*SPD* xvii). Sidis's stress on this "principle" is because he is convinced that psychoanalysis has been founded on a misguided premise. He proposed that the "absence of meaning is the key to a right comprehension of the facts of psychopathology and of the methods of psychotherapy" (*SPD* xvii).

The classic psychoanalytic approach was that unconscious forces, like drives, instincts and defence mechanisms, disrupted thought processes to serve basic needs.[111] By contrast, a number of contemporary cognitive psychologists contented that the intelligent unconscious is characterized by a cognitive apparatus, which can open up new vistas of thought rather than produce merely the heat and irrationality of the psychoanalytic drives and conflicts. For example, the idea of non-deliberate thought as a moral compass sets the intelligent unconscious apart from what many have come to identify as the Freudian unconscious, namely, a sort of dungeon of the mind that threatens reason and control. While Freud emphasized the sexual and taboo aspects of unconscious impulses, wishes and desires, James devoted his *Varieties* to maintain the purity of that inner world. The intelligent unconscious was described as the source not only of some of our most sophisticated thinking but also of some of our most moral behaviour.

The central concern here is that focussing solely on the Freudian conception of the unconscious does not do full justice to the complexity of the psychological ideas that surrounded this concept in modernism. We need a fuller appreciation of the period's belief that the unconscious is connected to intelligence, rather than to private drives and instincts. Freud's work certainly had a profound influence upon the literature and art of the modernist period, and upon past and current critical scholarship in modernist studies. Much has been written about this impact. However, much less has been written on the influence of Freud's predecessors and contemporaries. As Patricia Rae noted, this is an unfortunate oversight because the "new psychology" emerging in the 1870s and 1880s had wide-ranging consequences for the way writers and artists conceived of themselves and their art.[112] The notion of an unconscious consciousness or of the intelligent unconscious was not a marginal ontological outlook, but one that represents a formative and hitherto understudied moment in the history of the unconscious and its relation to consciousness.

Notes

1 Michael Goeffrey, Johnson and Tracy, B. Henley, eds., *Reflections on The Principles of Psychology: William James after a Century* (Hillsdale, NJ: Lawrence Erlbaum Associates Inc., 1990), 2.

2 See David H. Evans, *Understanding James, Understanding Modernism* (London: Bloomsbury, 2017) and Robert D. Richardson, *William James: In the Maelstrom of American Modernism* (Boston, MA: Houghton Mifflin, 2006).

3 Dorothy Ross, "American Psychology and Psychoanalysis: William James and G. Stanley Hall," in *American Psychoanalysis: Origins and Development*, ed. by J. M. Quen and E. T. Carlson (New York: Brunner, 1975), 38–51; John C. Burnham, *Psychoanalysis and American Medicine, 1894–1918: Medicine, Science, and Culture* (New York: Intl. Universities Press, 1998); Nathan G. Hale, *Freud in America: The Beginnings of Psychoanalysis in America, 1876–1917* (New York: Oxford University Press, 1971).

4 Eugene Taylor, *William James on Exceptional Mental States: The 1896 Lowell Lectures* (Amherst: University of Massachusetts Press, 1984) and *William James on Consciousness beyond the Margin* (Princeton, NJ: Princeton University Press, 2011), 13.

5 For an analytical account of James's psychical research, see Krister Dylan Knapp's *William James: Psychical Research and the Challenge of Modernity* (Chapel Hill: The University of North Carolina Press, 2017).

6 Gay Wilson Allen, *Waldo Emerson: A Biography* (New York: Viking, 1961).

7 Saul Rosenzweig, "The James's Stream of Consciousness," *Contemporary Psychology*, 3 (1958): 250–7.

8 Henry James Sr., *Substance and Shadow* (Boston, MA: Ticknor and Fields, 1863).

9 Leo B. Levy, "Henry James's Confidence and the Development of the Idea of the Unconscious," *American Literature*, 28: 3 (1956): 347–58.

10 Taylor, *William James*, 32.

11 William James, "Person and Personality," in *Johnson's Universal Cyclopedia* (New York: D. Appleton, 1895), 538–40 and "Notice of A.H. Pierce's Subliminal Self; F. Podmore's Reply; F. Von Schrenk-Notzing's *Uber Spaltung der Personlichkeiten*, and S. Landmann's *Die Mehrheit geistiger Personlichkeiten*," *Psychological Review*, 3 (1896): 682–4.

12 William James, *The Letters of William James* (Boston, MA: The Atlantic Monthly Press, 1920).

13 Robert H. Wozniak, *Mind and Body: René Descartes to William James (Bethesda, MD; National Library of Medicine, Washington, DC: American Psychological Association, 1992)*, 54.

14 William Barnard, *Exploring Unseen Worlds: William James and the Philosophy of Mysticism* (Albany: State University of New York Press, 1997).

15 Eugene Taylor and Robert Wozniak, *Pure Experience: The Response to William James* (Bristol: Thommess Press, 1996).

16 William James, *The Varieties of Religious Experience*, ed. by Matthew Bradley (Oxford: Oxford University Press, 2012 [1902]), 182–3.

17 Ibid., 184.

18 Ibid., 182.

19 William James, *Essays in Psychical Research*, ed. by Frederick Burkhardt and Fredson Bowers (Cambridge, MA: Harvard University Press, 1986).

20 William James, *The Will to Believe and Other Essays in Popular Philosophy* (New York: Longmans Green, 1912 [1896]), 80.

21 James, *Varieties*, 181.

22 Ibid., 182.

23 Ibid.

24 Richardson, *William James*, 348.

25 James, *Essays in Psychical Research*, 98.

26 James, *Essays in Psychical Research*, 102–3.

27 James, *Varieties*, 162.

28 Ibid., 165.

29 Herbert Spencer, *An Autobiography* (London: Williams and Norgate, 1904), 401.

30 Ibid.

31 James, *Varieties*, 163.

32 Joseph Marie Montmasson, *Invention and the Unconscious* (London: Routledge, 1999), 24.

33 August Kekulé, "Address to the German Chemical Society," in *Literature and Science in the Nineteenth Century*, ed. by Laura Otis (New York: Oxford University Press, 2002), 431–3.

34 William Carpenter, *Principles of Human Physiology* (Philadelphia: Blanchard and Lea, 1853), 790.

35 William James, *William James on Psychical Research*, ed. by Gardner Murphy and Robert O. Ballou (London: Chatto and Windus, 1961), 44.
36 Ibid., 45.
37 Ibid., 44.
38 Ibid.
39 Kelly Edward and Kelly Williams, *Irreducible Mind: Toward a Psychology for the 21st Century* (Lanham, MD: Jason Aronson, 2007), 310.
40 Prosper Despine, *Psychologie Naturelle* (Paris: Savy, 1868), 490–1.
41 Giuseppe Craparo, Francesca Ortu, Onno vander Hart, eds., *Rediscovering Pierre Janet* (New York: Routledge, 2019), 10.
42 Onno van der Hart and Rutger Horst, "The Dissociation Theory of Pierre Janet," *Journal of Traumatic Stress*, 2: 4 (1989): 397–412.
43 Anita M. Muhl, *Automatic Writing* (Germany: Kessinger Publishing, 2003 [1930]).
44 Taylor, *William James*, 50.
45 Michael J. Hoffman, "Gertrude Stein and William James," *The Personalist: An International Review of Philosophy, Religion, and Literature*, 47:2 (1966): 226–33.
46 Edmund Gurney, "Some Peculiarities of the Post-Hypnotic Trance," *Proceedings of the English Society for Psychical Research*, 4 (1886–1887): 290–2.
47 Ibid., 296.
48 Taylor, *William James*, 39.
49 Alfred Binet, *Alterations of Personality* (New York: D. Appleton and company, 1896), 305.
50 Ibid.
51 Ibid., 308.
52 Ibid., 311.
53 Ibid.
54 Alan Gauld, *A History of Hypnotism* (Cambridge: Cambridge University Press, 1992), 410.
55 Robert W. White, "Who Was Morton Prince?," *Journal of Abnormal Psychology* 101: 4 (1992), 604.
56 Gauld, *A History*, 412.
57 As we will see later into this chapter, William James in his *Principles* had already, along very similar lines of thought, argued that genius is rooted in such unconscious cognitive processes.
58 Alfred Binet and Charles Féré, *Le magnétisme animal*, 4th ed. (Paris: Félix Alcan, [1887] 1890), 286.
59 Alfred Binet, *The Psychology of Reasoning* (Chicago, IL: Open Court Publishing, [1886] 1912), 79.
60 Ibid., 80.
61 Ibid., 166.
62 Ibid.
63 Ibid., 167.
64 Ibid., 171.
65 Ibid., 171–2.
66 Victorian physiological psychologists represented the most advanced psychological thought of their time, flourishing from 1850 to 1880. They include William B. Carpenter (1813–1885) and George Henry Lewes (1817–1878), Benjamin Collins Brodie (1783–1862), Robert Dunn (1799–1877), Henry Holland (1788–1873), Thomas Laycock (1812–1876), John Daniel Morell (1816–1891), Daniel Noble (1810–1885) and Henry Maudsley

(1835–1918). For more on British psychology, see Rick Rylance, *Victorian Psychology and British Culture 1850–1880* (Oxford: Oxford University Press, 2000) and Robert M. Young, *Mind, Brain, and Adaptation in the Nineteenth Century: Cerebral Localization and Its Biological Context from Gall to Ferrier* (Oxford: Clarendon, 1970).

67 See Oliver Wendell Holmes, "Mechanism in Thought and Morals," in *The Writings of Oliver Wendell Holmes* (Cambridge: Riverside, 1891), VIII, 284–5; James Sully, *Outlines of Psychology* (London: Longmans, 1884), 74, 75; and George Henry Lewes, *The Study of Psychology* (London: Trübner, 1878), 18.

68 Carpenter, *Principles of Human Physiology.*

69 William Carpenter, *Principles of Mental Physiology* (London: H.S. King & Co, 1876), 516.

70 Ibid., 519.

71 Ibid., 607.

72 Ibid.

73 Ibid., 606–7.

74 Frederic William Henry Myers, "The Subliminal Consciousness," in *Proceedings of the Society for Psychical Research*, VII (1892), 327.

75 Myers, "The Subliminal Consciousness," 305.

76 Ibid., 306.

77 F.W.H. Myers, "Automatic Writing, or the Rationale of Planchette," *The Contemporary Review*, 47 (1885): 234.

78 Taylor, *William James*, 39.

79 Arthur H. Pierce, "Subliminal Self or Unconscious Cerebration?," *Proceedings of the Society for Psychical Research*, 11 (1895), 317–25.

80 Samson Landmann, *Die Mehrheit geistiger Personlichkeiten in einem Individuum: Eine psychologische Studie* (Stuttgart: Enke, 1894).

81 William James, "Notice of A.H. Pierce's *Subliminal self*; F. Podmore's *Reply*; F. von Schrenk-Notzing's *Uber spaltung der personlichkeiten*; and S. Landmann's *Die mehrheit geistger personlichkeiten*," *Psychological Review*, 3: 6 (1896), 682–4.

82 William James, *Manuscript Lectures* (Cambridge, MA: Harvard University Press, 1988), 67.

83 Taylor, *William James*, 40.

84 Ibid.

85 James, *Manuscript Lectures*, 67.

86 Reference to Janet's 1886 article, "Unconscious Acts and the Division of Personality under Induced Somnambulism."

87 Amy Wallace, *The Prodigy: A Biography of William James Sidis* (New York: E.P. Dutton, 1986), 103–4.

88 Gerald E. Myers, *William James: His Life and Thought* (New Haven, CT: Yale University Press, 1986), 54.

89 Carpenter, *Principles of Mental Physiology.*

90 Laura Otis, *Organic Memory: History and the Body in the Late Nineteenth & Early Twentieth Centuries* (Lincoln, NE and London: University of Nebraska Press, 1994), 3.

91 For more see Evelyn Vargas, "Perception as Inference," in *Peirce on Perception and Reasoning*, ed. by Kathleen A. Hull, Richard Kenneth Atkins (New York: Routledge, 2017), 14.

92 Charles Sanders Peirce, *The Collected Papers of Charles Sanders Peirce: Pragmatism and Pragmaticism*, vol. 5 (Cambridge, MA: Harvard University Press, 1974), 494.

93 William James, "The Continuity of Experience" (1909) in *The Writings of William James*, ed. by John J. McDermott (Chicago, IL: University of Chicago Press: 1977), 293.

94 Ralph Barton Perry, *In the Spirit of William James* (New Haven, CT: Yale University Press, 1938), 81.

95 William James, *Collected Essays and Reviews* (New York: Russell and Russell, 1969), 352.

96 William James, *The Heart of William James*, ed. by Robert Richardson (Cambridge, MA: Harvard University Press, 2010), 131.

97 William James, *The Correspondence of William James*, 8 vols. (Charlottesville: University of Virginia Press, 2004), 475.

98 William James, *Collected Essays and Reviews* (New York: Russell and Russell, 1969), 122–3.

99 William James, *The Will to Believe and Other Essays in Popular Philosophy* (New York: Longmans, 1897), 63, 64, 66.

100 Ibid., 75–6.

101 Ibid., 76.

102 William James, "What Is an Emotion?," *Mind* 9 (1884): 196.

103 Ibid., 202.

104 See for example, Vesa Talvitie, *The Freudian Unconscious and Cognitive Neuroscience: From Unconscious Fantasies to Neural Algorithms* (London: Routledge, 2018), James Phillips, "Freud and the Cognitive Unconscious," *Philosophy, Psychiatry, & Psychology*, 20: 3 (2013): 247–9, and Mathieu Arminjon, "The Four Postulates of Freudian Unconscious Neurocognitive Convergences," *Frontiers in Psychology*, 2: 125 (2011).

105 For the differences between Freud's and James's conception of the unconscious, see also Gerald E. Myers, "James and Freud," *The Journal of Philosophy*, 87: 11 (1990): 593–9. For their radically different philosophical epistemologies and historical origins, see Eugene Taylor, "William James and Sigmund Freud: 'The Future of Psychology Belongs to Your Work,'" *Psychological Science*, 10: 6 (1999): 465–9.

106 Myers, *William James: His Life and Thought*, 60.

107 Sigmund Freud, "A Note on the Unconscious in Psychoanalysis," in *Proceedings of the Society for Psychical Research*, 26 (1912), 315.

108 Eugène Azam, *Hypnotisme, double conscience, et altérations de la personnalité* (Paris: J.B. Baillière et Fils, 1887).

109 Ibid.

110 Bernard Hart, "The Conception of Dissociation," *British Journal of Medical Psychology*, 6 (1926): 253–6.

111 See, for instance, Anna Freud, *The Ego and the Mechanisms of Defense* (New York: International Universities Press, 1937) and Sigmund Freud, *A General Introduction to Psychoanalysis* (New York: Washington Square Press, 1952).

112 Patricia Rae, "Modernism, Empirical Psychology and the Creative Imagination," in *Modernism*, ed. by Astradur Eysteinsson, Vivian Liska, and Anke Brouwers (Amsterdam: John Benjamins, 2007), 405–18.

3 D.H. Lawrence on the Intelligent Unconscious and the Allotropic State of Being

This chapter seeks to establish that, according to Lawrence, human nature is a conjunction of two distinct cognitive components: the mental and the bodily, each of which is capable of performing complicated reasoning processes. Integral to this view is his notion of the bodily unconscious, which he conceived of as an autonomous and intelligent thinking agent. The first part of this chapter explores how Lawrence developed this theory as a reaction against the Freudian formulation of the unconscious and the increasing tendency in contemporary scientific thought to mechanize the body and its cognitive processes. The second part brings Lawrence's theory of the unconscious to bear on his literary theory. And the third puts his literary theory in practice through an analysis of *Women in Love*, which provides a fertile field of enquiry to study his attitude towards technology and industrialization in relation to human behaviour and perception. Here, I focus primarily on the gladiatorial scene through the lens of Lawrence's appropriation of the scientific concept of allotropy to describe the constituent elements of human nature. More than a battle that surreptitiously betrays the gladiators" histrionic resistance to their homosexual drives (the traditional interpretation of the scene's main symbolic import), Lawrence describes a battle between two conflicting worldviews: between Birkin, on the one hand, who stands for the spontaneous, the dark and the unconscious and is associated with the industrial element of coal, and Gerald, on the other, who embodies the spirit of industrialization and mechanization, and is associated with the diamond, that is, with the world of light and consciousness. This battle, I maintain, is an allotropic gladiatorial whereby the hostility of the one against the other is juxtaposed to an inner and subtle unity between them in the form of an organic connection.

Lawrence's ontological outlook has been the subject of rigorous and often conflicting interpretations. Critics tend to view Lawrence either as a monist or, conversely, as a dualist. Despite their different inflections on the particulars of Lawrence's theory, critics argue that Lawrence is a monist because he assumes a cellular basis of life according to which mind and body are composed of the same material. In his discussion of *Fantasia of the Unconscious*, for instance, David Ellis supports a monist view. He identifies the mental processes with the bodily ones and concludes that in Lawrence's theoretical works "the Freudian distinctions between consciousness and its opposite are redundant."[1] Similarly, Michael H. Black asserts that Lawrence argues for a fusion of mind and body.[2] Even though Robert Montgomery is careful not to use the term "monism" "because of its associations with Spinoza and later thinkers, like Haeckel from whom Lawrence must be distinguished," he nevertheless views Lawrence as a kind of a monist: "the opposites which seem to sunder life into an irreconcilable dualism are in fact polar opposites, the two forces of a single power, like the positive and negative poles of a magnet."[3] The main problem that arises from monist readings is that they fail to account for such radical forms of dualism as expressed, for example, in Lawrence's insistence that "My great religion is a belief in the blood, the flesh, as being wiser than the intellect. We can go wrong in our minds. But what our blood feels and believes and says, is always true" (1LD 503). Lawrence, moreover, expressed his opposition towards "torturing crude Monism," noting that he "cannot be a materialist," thus voicing his aversion towards monism's reification of materialism (1LD 147, 40).

On the other end of the spectrum, critics who view Lawrence as a dualist often support their position by tracing affinities between the terminology used by Lawrence in his psychology books and the sciences of the time. Katherine Hayles, for instance, portrays Lawrence as an ambivalent fellow traveller to the new scientists.[4] Her focus on the scientific advancements of the time, however, may lead to the inaccurate conclusion that, for Lawrence, the body is governed by laws in the same way that the science of the time suggested. Indeed, a number of critics have asserted that the penetration of this discourse in Lawrence's thought led him to the conclusion that the body is governed by mechanical laws. Michael Wutz, for example, locates Lawrence's *Psychoanalysis and the Unconscious* and *Fantasia of the Unconscious* in the Victorian field of thermodynamics, and uses it to explain the gender dynamics in his fiction.[5] Nicholas Crawford also conceives of the mental and the bodily within the same framework, and concludes that it is representative of "the drama of duality" that forms Lawrence's vision.[6] Jeff Wallace reads Lawrence's ontology through the lens of late 19th-century materialism, and argues for a blurring of boundaries between the organic and the mechanical in Lawrence.[7] The main problem arising from this trend is that it may give the impression that Lawrence understood the body as a law-governed and mechanical component. In sharp contrast to this conclusion, Lawrence articulates a theory wherein the body's activities cannot be reduced to mechanical reactions. He advocates a body that is an intelligent cognitive agent capable of performing complicated cognitive actions of which the conscious mind is unaware. This line of thought registers a somatic, biological basis for unconscious cognitive processes, one which literary scholars have not failed to notice. Tracing Lawrence's philosophical outlook Spitzer, for example, sees a "strategic inversion of Cartesian dualism, by which the body is elevated over the mind as the primary site of consciousness."[8] Michael Bell also traces Lawrence's radical reassertion of the body:

> As part of his radical anti-Cartesianism, consciousness in Lawrence is always more than a cerebral process: it is a bodily manifestation. And by the same token, the unconscious is an emanation of the body asserting a tangible, although not articulate, presence.[9]

The Industrial Human Motor

The modernist fascination with machines triggered a new interest in the material nature of the human body and its relationship to the mind. The use of the machine metaphor to describe bodily operations was a common practice in the popular physiological and anatomical texts of the time. Following the Cartesian ontological outlook, Thomas Lambert (1819–1897), for instance, suggested that the body is a clock, a "piece of mechanism of exceeding beauty, and with most wonderful perfection intended to fulfil certain duties."[10] Likewise, Wendell Holmes (1809–1894) asserted that "levers, pulleys, and even the wheel and axle, play their usual part in the passive transfer of the forces that move the living machinery."[11] William A. Alcott (1798–1859), one of the leading health reformers of the period, identified the hand as an intricate machine: "Is there in the wide world a factory containing a tenth part as much curious and complicated machinery as the hand?"[12] The same materialistic conception of the human body was expressed by John H. Griscom (1809–1874), who explicitly called the body "a machine, composed of apparatus of various kinds," the hand "an *instrument* which, for *perfection of mechanism* and *variety of uses*, surpasses every other yet known to man," and the heart a "powerful and complicated machine" for pumping blood.[13] The sheer objectification of the body as passive matter is reflected in Thomas Lambert's statement that the body is "merely a machine [...] without something to use it, it can do nothing."[14] As Charles Caldwell (1772–1853) maintained, physical education cultivated "a better piece of machinery, for mind to work with." Within this framework, the physical aspect of man "constitutes the machinery, with which alone his mind operates, during their connection, as soul and body."[15] As we read in Worthington Hooker's (1806–1867) work,

> our bones and muscles are like a machinery of a steam-boat or railroad-car [...] but as the machinery of a boat will not move without steam, so the bones and muscles [...] will not move, when we wish to do anything, without the aid of the mind.[16]

It is thus no surprise to find that another metaphor used to describe the human body was that of a factory comprised of various machine parts. Referring to human organs, Thomas Lambert noted that "a general idea of the use of them can be gained by noticing what is necessary in a common factory."[17] This notion of the mind as overseeing the processes performed by the body entails a social discourse that justifies the manager (mind), who oversees the mechanical labour performed by the workers (body). Alcott stressed the importance of learning the physiological laws governing the body. These laws would dictate rules for how, when and what to eat, how to sleep and dress, along with numerous other activities. This physiological discourse specified the "laws of health" that should be obeyed in order to keep the body healthy and efficient.[18]

Historians have argued that the emergence of this discourse was a response to the changing social environment brought about by industrialism.[19] Stephen Nissenbaum, for instance, suggested that the reformist Sylvester Graham (1794–1851) tried to control the body in order to provide stability in the face of the emergent instability caused by industrialism.[20] According to Martha Verbrugge, the reformer's call for self-governance "made particular sense to a middle-class audience, who hoped to check the turmoil of the outside world by regulating the internal one."[21] Relating the attempts to regulate the body with the attempts of the middle class to impose social order, Joan Burbick wrote that

> prescriptions about health often became a way to critique the society at large, and to offer specific remedies that on the surface appeared less threatening to the stability of the nation since they were veiled in the language of the flesh.[22]

Depicting the body as a machine subject to specific laws, these health reformers made their rules sound more pertinent than ever. As Stephen Rice asserted, "in calling the body a machine, popular physiology writers and lecturers helped to naturalize the work of machine-tending, since all human bodies were, by design, like machines that required operatives to work well."[23] In this way, they transformed manual labour from a mental to a mechanical task. Such theories placed mind over body, drawing a replicating symmetry between mind/body and manager/worker.

The industrial efficiency propounded by Frederick Winslow Taylor (1856–1915) created a shift of control from workers to management, and consequently formulated a qualitative distinction between mental (planning work) and manual labour (executing work). Taylor's theory emerged from a continuously increasing group of psychologists and physiologists who presented the body as a complex machine. This discourse was not a new development; it can be found in the late 18th and early 19th centuries, when industrial efficiency dictated that workers' bodies follow the pace of the clock and the rhythm of machines.[24] The metaphor of the mechanical body intensified in the years around the First World War. Anson Rabinback demonstrates the prevalence of thermodynamics as the model that was used to establish the metaphor of the "motor" to describe the human body at the end of the 19th century.[25]

The physiologist Jean-Marie Lahy (1872–1943) recognized the fact that Taylor's insistence on productivity prompted him to assimilate the human bodies to machines and to disregard the "human factor."[26] Lahy researched the issues of endurance and fatigue and the ways that energy expenditure, like wasted motions, could be reduced.[27] The physician and physiologist Etienne-Jules Marey (1830–1904) advocated the need for science to separate the worker's body into distinct components in order to establish the laws that could increase energy and consequently transform work. His consistent stress on the mechanical function of the heart and vascular system led to the invention of many instruments like the "sphygmograph."[28] His approach to the human body is characteristically summed up by one of his students, who commented that Marey was "never really a physiologist or a doctor in the usual sense of those terms, but above all, an engineer of life."[29] Marey applied the principle of the conservation of energy to the human organism by equating heat and mechanical work in order to understand the workings of the muscles. His strategies were founded on his belief that "the laws of mechanics are applicable to animated motors as well as other machines."[30] Marey thought and worked under the principle that there is no distinction between bodies and machines. His aim was to make the body the perfect machine. As he concluded, the "animal organism is no different from our machines, except for their greater efficiency."[31] He was convinced that if he could grasp the chemical and physical relationships of the body, he could reduce fatigue and maximize productivity.[32] The industrial physiologists at the Research Laboratory on Professional Muscular Work used laws of mechanics to draw conclusions on the human machine in different contexts, like mechanics or public speaking.[33] The "ergographe" invented by Angelo Mosso (1846–1910) measured the effects of many complex variables and their impact on muscular strength.[34] Jules Amar's *The Human Motor* illustrates the application of laws of physics to the human body. The materialist approach of this work is evident in its focus on energy expenditure.[35] By the beginnings of the First World War, these industrial psychologists and physiologists had circulated their theories on an international level through journals and conferences. Charles Labriffe's work on apprenticeship, *L' apprentissage dans l' industrie textile* (1945), reflects the extent to which half a century of industrial physiology had shaped the ways of thinking about the body.[36] He proposed exercises to train weavers in order to attune the "human motor" to the automatic loom.[37] The psychotechnicians Alfred Binet (1857–1911), Charles Henry (1859–1926) and Édouard Toulouse (1865–1947), working in the same framework and realizing that fatigue was inevitable, propounded the need to develop methods of gender and racial selection in order to apply physiological laws in the service of industrial productivity.

These developments did not pass unchallenged. Some of the consequences of the tendency to separate mental from manual labour were addressed by Catharine Beecher (1800–1878) in *Letters to the People on Health and Happiness*:

> By this method of dividing the labour of life one portion of the world weaken their muscular system, either by entire inaction of both brain and muscle, or by the excess of brainwork and the neglect of muscular exercise. Another large portion having all the work that demands physical exercise turned off upon them, overwork their bodies and neglect their brains.[38]

The mind-body split that was enacted in the workspace through the introduction of machinery not only atrophied the body but also reduced its creative potentials to the performance of repetitive, mechanical tasks. Thus, Francis William Bird (1809–1894) declared that "the separation of the interests of man's physical nature from those of his intellectual and spiritual natures is as impossible as it is unnatural."[39] Working with a machine made the body itself a machine, and this was perceived by some contemporary thinkers as posing a serious threat to human well-being. Despite these counter arguments, for the most part, contemporary physiologists and psychologists embraced the Corps-Machine Doctrine, which presented the body as a mere clock that performs the mind's dictates.

The Organic Function and Thinking of Lawrence's Biological Psyche

Lawrence was particularly vocal in his reaction to mechanization and his interest in the consequences for the body and mental life, which are exemplified throughout his essays and fiction.[40] Even though Lawrence's *Psychoanalysis* and *Fantasia* hold a central place in his philosophy, they have suffered great critical neglect. Critics who reviewed them when they were first published characterized them as "bizarre, illogical, or incomprehensible; a handful of reviewers questioned Lawrence's sanity."[41] Nonetheless, the books enjoyed favourable treatment in the hands of literary authors. The poet and playwright Don Marquis commended the book so lavishly in the *New York Tribune* that he was quoted on the dust-jacket to *Fantasia*:

> Lawrence, because he is a poet, sees deeper and more clearly than Freud and Jung: he is simpler and freer of their obsessions and absurdities. This essay is a brave clutch at the fundamental reality of human life. It is an outline, a sketch, that may be the beginning of nothing less than an original system of philosophy.[42]

Another review quoted on the dust-jacket to *Fantasia* was that of short-story writer B.F. Ruby: "Everyone who is interested in psychoanalysis, everyone, indeed, who is interested in life, must read this book [...] One cannot help finding it a powerful stimulus to thought."[43] T.S. Eliot, despite his general antipathy towards Lawrence, also spoke in defence of *Fantasia*:

> Against the living death of modern material civilisation he spoke again and again. And even if these dead could speak, what he said is unanswerable. As a criticism of the modern world, *Fantasia of the Unconscious* is a book to keep at hand and re-read.[44]

Their eccentricity notwithstanding, these psychology books deserve a closer examination as they provide us with access into Lawrence's philosophical outlook and literary theory. The importance of *Psychoanalysis and the Unconscious* for our understanding of Lawrence's thought and literary art was also raised in the beginning and ending of the first review by the eminent and influential Chicago critic Llewellyn Jones: "Indeed his novels and poems cannot be fully understood by anyone who has not read it" (*PFU* xlviii). As Fiona Becket noted, these essays underscore the importance of "Lawrence's value to the young intelligentsia of the day as a cultural critic, tuned in to the wider significance of the psychoanalytic as a mode of human understanding beyond the confined [...] clinical space."[45] These books are indeed indispensable to our understanding of Lawrence's literary work, as they represent the lengths Lawrence went to challenge the mechanistic conception of the body as well as advocate, explicate and justify his conception of the intelligent unconscious.

The science propagating the utopian ideal of a body without fatigue was grounded on one fundamental assumption: the body is a complicated machine. Lawrence attempted to undermine this hypothesis and expose the weaknesses that lie at the core of these theories. He located the unconscious or non-mental consciousness in the human nervous system. Faced with the automatizing effects of industrialism, Lawrence embarked on an extensive account of the thinking processes performed by the unconscious. He started the description of the unconscious by referring to it as the "first consciousness" (*PFU* 21). By proposing a psychological theory based on the physiology of the human body, Lawrence insisted that the somatic consciousness is temporally and existentially prior to "mental understanding."[46] The unconscious emerges from the doubly polarized interrelationships of the two pairs of the primary nerve centres of consciousness. The first polarity is formed between the solar plexus associated with the navel and the lumbar ganglion, located at the back. The second pair is formed by the cardiac plexus, associated with the breast or heart, and the thoracic ganglion located in the shoulders. The pairs are separated by a diaphragm dividing the body "psychically as well as organically" into two "planes": "the first, the lower, the subjective unconscious [plane] active beneath the diaphragm" (*PFU* 27), and "the second, the upper, objective plane, active above the diaphragm" (*PFU* 27). In addition to the polarity formed between the two planes of consciousness, Lawrence presented an opposition that takes places within each plane: the positive "sympathetic centres," the plexuses located at the anterior surface of the body and oriented towards other individuals, and the negative "voluntary" centres, the ganglia present posterior to the body and concerned with self-definition. In Lawrence's words, "the vertical division between the voluntary and sympathetic systems, the line of division between the spinal system and the great plexus-system of the front of the human body" (*PFU* 39), forms the main duality of dynamic consciousness: "It is the great difference between the soft, recipient front of the body and the wall of the back. The front of the body is the live end of the magnet. The back is the closed opposition" (*PFU* 39).

Lawrence traced the beginning of the dynamic consciousness in the solar plexus, which provides a pre-mental sense of the self, the knowledge that "*I am I, all is one in me*" (*PFU* 83). This "creative-productive centre, the quick, both of consciousness and of organic development" (*PFU* 19) is located beneath the navel of the foetus. It belongs to the "sympathetic" centre, since it signifies a fusion of self and other in a state of unified indifferentiation. In a grown-up, the centre of the unconscious is still located "within the solar plexus of the nervous system" (*PFU* 20). The subjective plane is chronologically formed first, before the infant has any clear idea of itself or others. Located in the lower plane, the navel establishes a "direct, unspeakable effluence and intercommunication, sheer effluent contact" with the mother (*PFU* 22). This centre is negatively polarized by the back which "stiffens" against this flow and facilitates the individuality of the infant: "In the lumbar ganglion the unconscious now vibrates tremendously in the act of sundering" (*PFU* 23). The lumbar ganglion provides "volitional knowledge" by creating a sense of separation and differentiation of self from other: "*I am myself, and these others are not as I am*;—there is a world of difference" (*PFU* 83). As Lawrence asserted, the lumbar ganglion makes the individual conscious that "because I am set utterly apart and distinguished from all that is the rest of the universe, therefore *I am I*" (*PFU* 80).

The individuation exemplified by the differentiation of the child from its mother naturally aligns the lumbar ganglion with the "voluntary" centre of separateness. The upper objective plane of the unconscious develops next. It enables "apprehension" (*PFU* 36), which is made possible through the polarity formed between the positive pole of the cardiac plexus and the negative pole of the thoracic ganglion. This negative pole exerts "a strong rejective force, a force which, pressing upon the object of attention, in the process of separation, succeeds in transferring to itself the impression of the object to which it has attended" (*PFU* 34). The "objective" plane is not concerned with one's own self, but with the immersion of the subject in the social sphere. As Lawrence noted, in this plane "I know no more of myself. Here I am not. Here I only know the delightful revelation that you are you" (*PFU* 82). The polarity between the sympathetic and voluntary centres is felt in the upper plane as a shift of the cardiac plexus towards the Other, and felt as a sense of wonder polarized by the reserved approach of the thoracic ganglion responding to the Other in a mode of inquisitiveness. Thus, through the polarity formed between the heart and the shoulders, we achieve "perfect *knowledge* of the beloved" (*PFU* 34). (See the polarity of the centres, marked as + and – in Figure 3.1.)

VOLUNTARY CENTRES OF SEPARATENESS (Posterior of the body)	SYMPATHETIC CENTRES OF THE BODY (Anterior of the body)		
Cervical Ganglion (neck) (H)	Cervical Plexus (throat) (G)	SOCIAL RELATIONS	
Thoracic Ganglion (shoulders) (D) –	Cardiac Plexus (breast/heart) (C) +		UPPER OBJECTIVE PLANE
DIAPHRAGM			
Lumbar Ganglion (back) (B) –	Solar Plexus (navel) (A) +		LOWER SUBJECTIVE PLANE
Sacral Ganglion (F)	Hypogastric Plexus (E)	SEXUAL RELATIONS	

Figure 3.1 A Graphic Representation of Lawrence's Eight Primary Nerve Centres of Dynamic Consciousness.

Following the development of the individual, Lawrence added four more centres activated in puberty: the hypogastric plexus and the sacral ganglion, located in the subjective plane, "deep in the lower body" (*PFU* 132), below the solar plexus and the lumbar ganglion and the second pair, the cervical plexus and the cervical ganglion, which is located at the objective plane, above the cardiac plexus and the thoracic ganglion "in the region of the throat and neck" (*PFU* 132). These additional nerve centres form the "sensual comprehension," enabling the development of sexual relations at the lower plane and the "spiritual" system of "dynamic cognition" (*PFU* 143). This system makes extended social interaction possible at the upper plane. According to Lawrence's chronological development of the individual, it is the energy of the newly formed subjective plane that brings forth the objective plane. A similar process unravels with the emergence of the second dynamic consciousness in puberty, when the sensual force of the lower plane enables the development of the upper, spiritual plane. (See the chronological development of the centres, marked as A–H, in Figure 3.1.)

Lawrence draws our attention to an unconscious mode of knowing facilitated by the first centre of consciousness, the solar plexus. The ability of a newly born baby to find the maternal breast indicates, according to Lawrence, the existence of a somatic consciousness. It is "this centre [that] directs the little mouth which, blind and anticipatory, seeks the breast" (*PFU* 21). The mouth "needs no eyes nor mind" to direct it because it has instead "the great first-mind of the abdomen," from which "it moves direct, with an anterior knowledge almost like magnetic propulsion, as if the little mouth were drawn or propelled to the maternal breast by vital magnetism, whose centre of directive control lies in the solar plexus" (*PFU* 21). Note here Lawrence's terminology, which draws attention to the body as a material organism invested with a "mind" and "knowledge." "Mind" is not to be perceived, according to Lawrence, as referring only to the mental mode of cognition, but to the mind of the unconscious as an independent cognitive agent. Raising the rhetorical question "How could it find the breast, blind and mindless little mouth?" (*PFU* 21), Lawrence invites us to recognize the existence of a separate, minded, and intelligent unconscious, one that can think autonomously, without any influence from the conscious mind. For, since the child "does not see with the eyes, it cannot perceive, much less conceive" (*PFU* 22). Thus, although the child does not have the ability to "perceive" and "conceive" through the conscious mind, it is nevertheless capable of an intuitive and perfected form of knowledge:

> Here the child knows beyond all knowledge [...] from the belly it knows, with a directness of knowledge that frightens us and may even seem abhorrent. The mother, also, from the bowels knows her child—as she can never, never know it from the head.
>
> (*PFU* 22)

The view that thinking processes are performed by nerve centres enables a dialectics where "we can quite tangibly deal with the human unconscious. We trace its source and centres in the great ganglia and nodes of the nervous system" (*PFU* 39). Organic function and organic thinking are so closely knit that "only by holding our breath can we realize their *duality* in identification [...] The two are two in one, a polarized quality. They are unthinkably different" (*PFU* 39). The expansion of the lungs is like an "aspiration, like a hope, like a yearning constant and unfailing," and when the heart dilates, it "opens its arms to the beloved. It dilates with reverent joy, as a host opening his doors to an honoured guest, whom he delights to serve" (*PFU* 83). This surge of the cardiac plexus is succeeded by a contraction of the lungs and heart, when the opposite motion of the thoracic ganglion is enacted. Creative vitality and materialism merge in a strange interdependence: "Functional and psychic at once, this is their first polar duality" (*PFU* 39). Lawrence turns the Cartesian doctrine on its head. For him, the mind represents idealism and everything that is static, it "is the dead end of life [...] It is a great dynamo of super–mechanical force" (*PFU* 42). Reacting against the corps-machine discourse of the physiologists, Lawrence maintained that it is the mind that has become a machine with the "*will* as accomplice" (*PFU* 42). Regulating the "machine-motions and automatizations over the whole of life," the mind channels its "mechanical force to the living unconscious, subjecting everything spontaneous to certain machine-principles called ideals or ideas" (*PFU* 42). In this way, every human being becomes an unnatural mechanism.

Lawrence counterpoised the mechanical mind with the cognitive capacities of the body by addressing the need to look beyond the automated body in order to "discover the relation between the functioning of the primary organs and the dynamic psychic activity at the four primary Consciousness-centres" (*PFU* 98). The nerve centres form a biological consciousness separate from the mental consciousness. One manifestation of the former is the five senses, along with the cognitive elements that are inherent in them, as they are rooted "in the four great primary centres of consciousness" (*PFU* 98). Their cognitive capability varies in the different planes and centres. For example, touch is mainly active in the sympathetic centre: "the breast is one great field of sympathetic touch, the belly is another" and in each field touch generates a different sense of organic thinking: "The breast touch is the fine alertness of quivering curiosity, the belly-touch is a deep thrill of delight and avidity. Correspondingly, the hands and arms are instruments of superb delicate curiosity, and deliberate execution" (*PFU* 98). This acuteness of touch at the sympathetic centre is polarized by the "two resistant fields behind from the neck to the heels," areas that are not sensory receptive for the sense of touch since the "voluntary centres act in resistance" (*PFU* 98). Our senses, Lawrence claimed, "are strictly sensations" enabling the "sensational *knowledge*," which wakes us into cognition (*PFU* 109). When we act according to the physical consciousness, it is a state wherein "our soul acts within us" through the objective circuit and the subjective circuit. The former includes the "circuits which are established between the self and some external object" (*PFU* 152). It involves an "affective connection," "a definite vital flow, as definite and concrete as the electric current" (*PFU* 153). The subjective circuit is formed within the individual "between the four primary poles" (*PFU* 154). When the sympathetic centres are polarized from the corresponding voluntary centre, "direct cognition takes place" (*PFU* 154). In short, the body takes precedence over the mind during a cognitive process, enabling thought and mental cognition. Yet, apart from enabling thought, the body is also capable of performing its own, independent forms of cognition.

Lawrence's redefinition of the mind-body dichotomy is summarized in his letter to Ernest Collings, where he stated his distinction between the conscious mind and blood consciousness (unconscious): "My great religion is a belief in the blood, the flesh, as being wiser than the intellect. We can go wrong in our minds. But what our blood feels and believes and says, is always true" (1*LD* 503). Through the use of the active verbs "feels," "believes" and "says," Lawrence stressed the autonomous and active role performed by the bodily unconscious. The intuitive nature of the unconscious makes it a better guide to life than intellect, since it generates knowledge that is innate, "always true" and anterior to mentality. He urged us to "depart from our old tenets of the mind" and "fathom our own *unconscious* sapience" (*PFU* 22). In a letter to Bertrand Russell, Lawrence stressed the fact that we are dealing with two separate forms of reasoning: "there is a blood-consciousness which exists in us independently of the ordinary mental consciousness" (2*LD* 470).

His reference to a bodily consciousness has important implications: to be able to be conscious of one's own self requires self-reflection and complicated cognitive processes, processes which cannot be reduced to mechanical, instinctual reflexes. Our inability to access directly the bodily consciousness should not restrain us from recognizing that "[t]he vast bulk of consciousness is non-cerebral" (*PFU* 19). The unconscious, in Lawrence's psychology, is another form of self, a corpo-*real* self. His theory on the ability of the body to know and make judgements is the product of intuition; experience and insights take place in the consciousness of the blood, not the mind. In a Jamesian vein, Lawrence maintained that

> in the body the great nerve centres are active, active both in knowing and in asserting [...] Now our first consciousness is seated, not in the brain, but in the great nerve centres of the breast and the bowels, the cardiac plexus and the solar plexus.[47]

The ability of the body to know and make assertions is part of a tradition embracing bodily knowledge, the ability of the body to make judgements that James expressed so aptly in his theory of the emotion (see Chapter 2). In *Phoenix*, Lawrence's adoption of the Jamesian theory of emotion becomes overt: "All the emotions belong to the body, and are only recognized by the mind."[48] Rather than originating in mental causes, emotions emerge as bodily judgements. As we saw in the previous chapter, on this theory, we do not run from a bear because we are afraid; we are afraid because we run. In other words, the decision to run is not made by the conscious mind; it constitutes an assertion of a bodily, unconscious judgement. According to Lawrence, human nature is a conjunction of two distinct consciousnesses. He endows the unconscious, like James before him, with characteristics traditionally attributed to conscious cognitive processes.[49] For Lawrence, every physiological process, from the most imperceptible ones, such as breathing or blinking, to the most intense and impactful, such as tachycardia or trembling, are forms of unconscious, somatic thinking. Breathing, for example, speaks a visceral language that can articulate the whole spectrum of human emotion, from fear, panic and grief to states of peace and tranquillity. It is a type of language, moreover, that causes an immediate aesthetic response in the audience, creating a network of sympathetic relations whereby a somatic, physiological form of communication triggers a corresponding visceral, physiological, emotional response in another human being. It is a primitive kind of language shared in common by everyone of us. The body speaks, and if we attune ourselves to its physiological language, we may listen an orchestrated polyphony of messages and emotions that are rooted in thinking processes that take place unconsciously. We may not be able to sense or feel the mental processes that cause alterations in the rhythms of our breathing, blinking or heart palpitations, but we cannot escape being swayed by the messages and emotions that these neural processes trigger.

Lawrence directed his theory of the mind and body against the prevailing physiological and psychological advances of his age. He drew attention, for instance, to the cognitive limitations imposed when "[t]he mind proceeds to assume control over every organic-psychic circuit" (*PFU* 43), and tried to dismantle the "[o]ne-and-allness which is attributed to it."[50] In his condemnation of the Cartesian mind-body dichotomy, Lawrence warned his readers that "[t]he mind as author and director of life is anathema" (*PFU* 43). Instead, he urged us to "descend too deep for our unpractised minds" (*PFU* 89), and acknowledge the existence of "a specific form of knowing that takes place at each of these [bodily] centres, without any mental reference at all."[51] Moreover, embracing conscious reason alone becomes "the death of all spontaneous, creative life" (*PFU* 14). To mechanize the body and the unconscious is to function by "the little, fixed, machine principle," a predicament that results in the human psyche working automatically. Lawrence asserted the direct connection between industrialism and the consequent mechanization of the body, which is the result of an idealist view of human nature: "Ideal and material are identical. The ideal is the god in the machine" (*PFU* 14). According to Lawrence, when ideas become "the machine-plan and the machine-principles of an automatized psyche," then "humanity proceeds to derange itself, to automatize itself from the mental consciousness" (*PFU* 43). In *Fantasia*, Lawrence argued against the reliance of science on intellectualism and the mechanical body:

> science is wretched in its treatment of the human body as a sort of complex mechanism made up of numerous little machines working automatically in a rather unsatisfactory relation to one another. The body is the total machine: the various organs are the included machines: and the whole thing, given a start at birth, or at conception, trundles on by itself.
>
> (*PFU* 95)

Lawrence attacked science and its underlying idealism as the shaping forces of industrialism, which enacted the view of the mechanical body.

Lawrence's Response to Psychoanalysis and the Jamesian Alternative

It is within this intellectual context that Lawrence placed psychoanalysis. He started his *Psychoanalysis* with an attack on the abstract intellect that characterizes the "psychiatric quack." Echoing Boris Sidis's accusation that Freudian explanations amount to little more than a wish-fulfilment of the psychoanalyst (see Chapter 2), Lawrence dismissed Freud's claims, stating that "when Freud makes sex accountable for everything he as good as makes it accountable for nothing" (*PFU* 15). He further linked the discourse of religion and science and their restriction of individual practices with psychoanalysis: "It is true that doctors are the priests, nay worse, the medicine-men of our decadent society. Psychoanalysis has made the most of the opportunity [...] It is time the white garb of the therapeutic cant was stripped off the psychoanalyst" (*PFU* 7–8). For Lawrence, psychoanalysis was a discipline identified with science and idealism, advocating a mechanical view of the body and mind. In his criticism of the Freudian "complex theory," for instance, we read:

> [t]he mechanism of the psyche could have its hitches, certain parts could stop working [...] This arrest in some part of the functioning psyche gave rise to a complex, even as the stopping of one little cog-wheel in a machine will arrest a whole section of that machine. This was the origin of the complex-theory, purely mechanistic.
>
> (*PFU* 10)

In broad terms, on Lawrence's understanding of psychoanalysis, Freud's "complex theory" deals with repressed ideas that compel habitual patterns of thought. This approach, according to Lawrence, is inherently flawed, because it applies a hydraulic model to the mind. It assumes that when ideas and anxieties put pressure on the unconscious part of the mind and burst through defences, they are released in consciousness.

It should be noted here that Lawrence never admitted to have read Freud's works: "I never read Freud, but I have learned about him since I was in Germany" (2LD 80). Fiona Beckett, nevertheless, points out that through the literary circles associated with Bloomsbury, Lawrence could have read or heard about *The Interpretation of Dreams,* which first appeared in English in 1913; "David Eder's translation of *On Dreams (1914)*; A.A. Brill's edition of *Psychopathology of Everyday Life* (1914); and Barbara Low's *Psycho-Analysis: A Brief Outline of Freudian Theory* (1920)."[52] His opportunities for hearing about Freud came not only from Barbara Low, Jones and the Eders, but also from the divorcee Frieda Weekley, who married Lawrence in 1914. Before meeting Lawrence, Frieda had had a long affair with the Austrian analyst Otto Gross, an important if eccentric figure in the early days of the psychoanalytic movement.[53] As David Ellis remarked, "That there are no records of Lawrence having read Freud cannot be conclusive, especially when he was quite often in houses where work by Freud, in either German or English, was available."[54] Particularly after 1914, it would have been very difficult for a British intellectual not to be informed about Freud's theories of introspection and sexuality, as they had become the vogue of the day. His theories were disseminated in both high and popular culture. Frederick J. Hoffman, in his study on Anglo-American modernism and psychoanalysis, describes the circulation of Freud's theories in the first decades of the 20th century:

> it is hardly likely that any thinking person who in any way associated himself with the world of letters failed to encounter the new psychology. It is more than likely that he was unable to escape getting too much of it. If he had not read any books on the subject, he was bound to come across it in almost any discussion; if he did not go out, he was just as likely to discover it in newspaper or magazine.[55]

From the first pages of *Psychoanalysis,* Lawrence contrasted the falsifying nature of the abstract intellect characterizing psychoanalysis with the psychology of William James. In his critique of Freud's theory, Lawrence contended that he "watched in frightened anticipation when Freud set out on his adventure into the hinterland of human consciousness," and continued to declare that all Freud made out of the "immortal phrase [stream of consciousness] of the immortal James!" was "nothing but a huge slimy serpent of sex, and heaps of excrement, and a myriad repulsive little horrors spawned between sex and excrement" (PFU 8, 9).

Lawrence levied a toxic critique against Freud for turning what he perceived as an insightful ontological outlook into a crude and poisonous account of human psychology. Freud, he thought, reduced James's theory of the stream of consciousness to mere sexual and repulsive physical impulses. However crude and simplistic Lawrence's understanding of Freud's work, it is nevertheless important for our understanding of his thought, which, as we will see, he injected into his literary theory and writing.

Lawrence noted that James's theory of the stream of consciousness had preoccupied him from a young age: "I felt it streaming through my brain, in at one ear and out at the other. And again I was sure it went round in my cranium, like Homer's ocean, encircling my established mind" (*PFU* 8). Lawrence seems to have understood the notion of the stream of consciousness as a source through which he could uncover the nature of the unconscious. What he found so appealing in James's work was his idea of the "belatedness" of thought, the primacy James attributed to the physiological states as preceding the conscious "I." In James's theories, Lawrence found the material to articulate his view of the unconscious, and he elaborated and expanded on it in an admirably intuitive manner. We could argue that the two psychology books constitute the answer to his adolescent preoccupation: "Whence did it come, and whither was it bound? The stream of consciousness!" (*PFU* 8) Contrasting his account of the unconscious with Freud's theory, Lawrence made it clear that the fountain of the stream of consciousness is the unconscious: "He [Freud] was seeking for the unknown sources of the mysterious stream of consciousness" (*PFU* 8). However, for Lawrence, the unconscious that Freud discerned is "the cellar in which the mind keeps its own bastard spawn," which results in "the horrid things that ate our souls and caused our helpless neuroses" (*PFU* 9). The affinities the Freudian unconscious has with neurosis are so great that, Lawrence noted, "the whole body of our repressions makes up our unconscious" (*PFU* 13). *Pace* Freud, Lawrence provided his definition of the

> true unconscious, where our life bubbles up in us, prior to any mentality. The first bubbling life in us, which is innocent of any mental alteration, this is the unconscious. It is pristine, not in any way ideal. It is the spontaneous origin from which it behoves us to live.
>
> (*PFU* 15)

Lawrence's awareness of James's work is also made manifest in the linguistic affinities between the two.[56] Using the metaphor of an underwater current to describe the "Binnenleben [hidden life, hidden self]," James asserted:

> As through the cracks and crannies of *caverns* those waters exude from the earth's bosom which then form the *fountain-heads* of

springs, so in these crepuscular depths of personality the sources of all our outer deeds and decisions take their rise.[57]

Adopting the word "cavern," Lawrence imagined Freud walking "straight through the wall of sleep [...] rumbling in the *cavern* of dreams" and finally "disappearing into the *cavern* of darkness" (*PFU* 8–9). Similarly, conceiving of the stream of consciousness as a product of the unconscious, he pictured it as emerging from an underground cavern: "It is the vast darkness of a *cavern's* mouth, the *cavern* of anterior darkness whence issues the stream of consciousness" (*PFU* 8). The unconscious is also portrayed in James as a "fountain-head" from which our judgements spring. In his psychology books, Lawrence repeatedly made the same lexical choice: "The true unconscious is *the well-head, the fountain* of real motivity" (*PFU* 12). In his analytic anatomical description of bodily consciousness, he further noted: "In the solar plexus is the first great *fountain* and issue of infantile consciousness" (*PFU* 25). Likewise, in *Women in Love*, the physiological unconscious becomes "the *fountain-head*" of thinking itself, "incorruptible and unsearchable" (*WL* 479).

James's notion of "unconscious consciousness" is also reflected in Lawrence's belief in the body as the primal consciousness. As Gerald E. Myers noted, William James's "special task" was to show "how a psychology, rooted in physiology, can avoid materialism and mechanism."[58] Lawrence's psychology books built on James's endorsement of "physiological psychology," and expanded on the notion of an intelligent physiological unconscious. George Johnson traced Lawrence's assimilation of the discourses of psychical research with a focus on his moral and religious views.[59] In his 1923 essay on Edgar Allan Poe, Lawrence showed an awareness of James's preoccupation with life after death. As he noted, "For it is true, as William James and Conan Doyle and the rest allow, that a spirit can persist in the after death. Persist by its own volition."[60] The subject personally preoccupied Lawrence and he turned to it in *Fantasia of the Unconscious*, his letters and fictional work. Chambers further suggests that *Pragmatism* "especially appealed" to Lawrence when he read it in the year of its publication, 1907. He also liked and recommended James's earlier work, *The Varieties of Religious Experience* (1902).[61] At Nottingham University College, Lawrence read *The Herbartian Psychology Applied to Education* by John Adams.[62] This book contains many references to James's work, which Adams mentioned with strong approval. He specifically stressed, for instance, James's reversal of "the usual view of the causal relation between emotion and its expression."[63] By contrast, for Lawrence, the Freudian unconscious is nothing more than a bundle of repressions: "the whole body of our repressions makes up our unconscious" (*PFU* 13). He formulated his own theory of an unconscious that promotes an intuitive, subjective knowledge and "repudiates a version of the unconscious charged with negative effects and impulses, a repository for everything 'which is bad, anti-social, sick in individual experience.'"[64] The subtle workings of unconscious reasoning are readdressed by Lawrence in his essay on Hawthorne (which appeared in the *English Review* in May 1919): "the great nerve-centres of the body are centres of perfect primary cognition [...] Each great nerve-centre has its own peculiar consciousness, its own peculiar mind, its own primary precepts and concepts, its own spontaneous desires and ideas."[65] Here, Lawrence developed his notion of "blood-consciousness," sharply contrasting his view of human psychology to Freudian psychoanalysis. Instead, like James, Lawrence insisted on an unconscious invested with a consciousness of its own, quite paradoxically but deliberately blurring the traditional meanings of the unconscious and the conscious aspects of human nature. Consciousness, in both James and Lawrence, does not refer only to what is readily recognized in the conscious dimension and reflected upon. It also refers to an ontological outlook whereby the unconscious is conscious of itself, allowing for the emergence of an alter ego characterized by qualities and cognitive faculties traditionally attributed to the conscious ego-self. Human nature is thus a conjunction of two separate and autonomous selves.

The Lawrencian unconscious is associated with the body and its processes. It emerges as an alien self with "its own peculiar mind, its own [...] concepts, its own [...] ideas." By using a vocabulary traditionally associated with mental consciousness, Lawrence stressed the cognitive nature of the unconscious. At the same time, he maintained the distinction of the two through the triple use of "own," a term that insists on the body's autonomy. It is this autonomy that makes the study of the unconscious cognitive processes difficult: "Do not ask me to transfer the pre-mental dynamic knowledge into thought. It cannot be done. The knowledge that *I am I* can never be thought: only known" (*PFU* 79). Along similar lines, Spitzer not only distinguishes the Lawrencian unconscious as a new theoretical conception, championing "a form of knowledge yielded by an alternative version of the unconscious," but she also places it in the larger context of his ontological view:

> Lawrence does not so much reinterpret the Freudian unconscious as offer a different model, one more consistent with his own theory of mind/ body dualism. To the "sack of horrors" of the Freudian unconscious, dominated by conflicts and complexes, Lawrence opposes his model of the "pristine unconscious."[66]

In contrast to what Lawrence saw as an irrational Freudian unconscious, he put forward a view of the unconscious as an intelligent cognitive agent. He insisted on an unconscious invested with a consciousness of its own, blurring the classic meanings of the unconscious and the conscious aspects of human nature. Consciousness does not only refer to what is readily recognized by the conscious mind and reflected upon, but also refer to the idea that the unconscious is conscious of itself.

Reconceiving Neurosis

Lawrence used his own theory to deconstruct Freud's theory of neurosis, which he places in the context of theories that shaped the science of work. Even though Freud's 1890s' writings on neurasthenia are divorced from the framework of fatigue, they still embrace the energy model, mentioning among other symptoms the inability to work. In February 1893, Freud wrote to Wilhelm Fliess that:

> sexual exhaustion can by itself alone provoke neurasthenia. If it fails to achieve this by itself, it has such an effect on the disposition of the nervous system that physical illness, depressive affects and over-work (toxic influences) can no longer be tolerated without [leading to] neurasthenia. Without sexual exhaustion, however, all these factors are incapable of generating neurasthenia. They bring about normal fatigue, normal sorrow, normal physical weakness.[67]

Freud's turn to a sexual aetiology of the condition is also evident in his remark: "I am now asserting that every neurasthenia is sexual."[68] He traced the cause to a waste of energy that is in this case libidinal: "Neurasthenia can always be traced back to a condition of the nervous system such as is acquired by excessive masturbation or arises spontaneously from frequent emissions."[69] In a similar spirit, neurasthenia was approached by psychophysiologists as an inverted work ethic or a resistance to the performance principle.[70] The causes of neurasthenia were subject to extensive debate, and they were frequently related to the theme of degeneracy and to a diminution of the will ("aboulia").[71] The New York physician George Miller Beard (1839–1883), father of the term neurasthenia, traced its causes in the cultural shocks of modernity.[72] In France, with the influence of Augustin Morel's theory of "degeneration" and Lamarck's theory of the inheritability of acquired characteristics, the prevailing view was that neurosis is a hereditary disorder.[73] The idea of a link between neurasthenia and degeneracy is related to the belief that disorder and dysfunction would overwhelm the increasingly threatened psychic and social order. Max Nordau's popular work, *Degeneration* (1892), is an extended description of the social dimensions of neurasthenia and its points of juncture with degeneration. In particular, Nordau focussed on "the confluence of two well-defined conditions of disease [...] viz. degeneration (degeneracy) and hysteria, of which the minor stages are designated as neurasthenia."[74]

The French neurologist and psychiatrist Jean-Martin Charcot (1825–1893) also argued for a hereditary predisposition to neurasthenia. He focussed on the weakness of energy as a characteristic symptom of neurasthenia, increasing in an analogous way to "what we call intellectual exhaustion among those pupils, anticipating a greater effort of the will."[75] Charles Féré (1852–1907), Charcot's assistant at La Salpêtrière, was also a leading proponent of the hereditary link between a nervopathic parentage and its propensity to neurasthenia.[76] In the physiological context, neurasthenia was understood in terms of energy. Physiologists of the time maintained that the nervous force was believed to be a limited resource being wasted due to an imbalance of the nervous system. In their study on 19th-century psychology, *Embodied Selves*, Jenny Bourne Taylor and Sally Shuttleworth discussed the dimensions that the preoccupation with neurasthenia had taken at the time, given the appearance of numerous books on the draining of the nervous force as an effect of overwork.[77] For Beard, neurasthenia was identified with a concept of modernity that required individuals to draw "on a limited store of nerve force."[78] Albert Deschamps, in his *Les Maladies de l'énérgie* (1908), summed up the widely held view that, despite its various symptoms, its cause was in essence one: a "diminution of the specific energy in an inverse ratio to the potential capital of energy."[79] Deschamps conceived the human body as a vast reservoir of energy carried along its pathways by "nervous waves" analogous to electromagnetic waves which created a "perpetual circulation of energy in the organism." The disorder was caused after excessive expenditure of energy, lack of supply or "a defective organisation in the energy reservoir."[80] Different factors, like trauma, heredity or sexual excess, were presented as causes of nervous exhaustion. What is common to all these justifications is the materialist conception of a human body which should moderate its energy expenditure. For example, Clifford Allbutt (1836–1925) described the condition as vital energy "clogged by the accumulation of waste products in the blood, or muscles, or both." [81] Applying an excremental terminology, Allbutt treated waste as a non-productive function of the nervous system that wastes energy in "molecular frictions and other invisible work."[82] This is another example of the materialist approach used at the time. Human processes are "work" and neurasthenia is the wasting of work.

Such an approach that treats organic processes as "work" is in sharp contrast to Lawrence's treatment of the physical as being both functional and psychic. Lawrence specifically mounted a critique on what he perceived to be Freud's energeticist model. Instead, he provided a radically different theory. The incest motive—being an inherently mental phenomenon—inevitably polarizes the lower sexual centres. Therefore, the "sexual or deeper sensual flow goes on upwards in the individual, to his upper, from his lower centres" (*PFU* 146). The result of this upward flow is an acute desire to gain "an intense consciousness in the upper self of the lower self [...] Then you get the upper body exploiting the lower body" (*PFU* 146). This is how masturbation occurs, by the desire of the hands (upper body) to "discover" the sensual part. This theory also explains "the pornographic desire to see the lower reactions" and the "lust for dirty stories" (*PFU* 146). It is the desire of the upper plane (eyes and ears) to gain knowledge in order to turn sexual drives into mental processes. As Lawrence observed, it is not a will to experience sex, but "the craving to feel, to see, to taste, to know, mentally in the head, this is insatiable" (*PFU* 146).

For Lawrence, Freud's theory constituted another example of the detrimental effects of idealism: socially constructed ideas are often presented as inherent and natural principles. He maintained that Freud's attempt to cure neurotic humanity through theories that revolved around an idealistic conceptualization of the mind resulted only in making "conscious a desire which previously was unconscious" (*PFU* 10). Freud's conclusion that "neurosis lies in some incest-craving" inevitably leads down the road of viewing incest-craving as "part of the normal sexuality of man" (*PFU* 10). Regarding incest-craving as "the cause of practically all modern neurosis and insanity," psychoanalysis leads mankind to an impasse whereby the complexity of human nature is reduced to a single disorder (*PFU* 11). The Freudian unconscious, as Lawrence understood it, "amounts practically to no more than our repressed incest impulses" (*PFU* 11). The notion of an unconscious craving incest is a false mental construct imposed on the pristine unconscious as its inherent characteristic. Incest-craving "is not inherent in the pristine psyche [...] it is nothing pristine or anterior to mentality" (*PFU* 11). In other words, it is the mind that "acts as incubus and procreator of its own horrors, *deliberately unconsciously*" (*PFU* 12). This is an example of the corrosive influence of the mind on the pristine unconscious, through the transference of "the idea of incest into the affective-passional psyche" that "keeps it there as a repressed motive" (*PFU* 12). The incest motive is simply a theoretical construct not inherent in the pristine unconscious: "Myself, I believe that biologically there is radical sex aversion between parent and child, at the deeper sensual centres" (*PFU* 145). This counter-claim is levied against Freud's theory of the Oedipal complex, and suggests an inherent sexual repulsion rather than attraction between parent and child. "The sexual circuit," Lawrence continued, "cannot adjust itself spontaneously between the two" (*PFU* 145). In other words, such an attraction occurs not spontaneously and naturally; it is imposed in retrospect by habitual modes of thinking. This is the way idealism is imposed unconsciously on the affective sphere, and becomes the guiding principle. The cause of neurosis, according to Lawrence, lies in the substitution of the spontaneous, creative source of unconscious motivity for the mechanical principle.

Fiona Becket has argued that Lawrence's focus on the body's centres of feeling in both *Psychoanalysis* and *Fantasia* bears testimony to his "anti-Cartesian stance" and attempts "to re-locate unconscious functioning, or feeling, in the *body*, challenging the psychoanalytic emphasis on *mind*."[83] Freudian interpretations of Lawrence's work started as early as with Alfred Booth Kuttner in September 1916. In his article *"Sons and Lovers*: A Freudian Appreciation," Kuttner argued that the novel has great value as evidence in support of Freud's theories of the Oedipus complex and the incest motive.[84] Lawrence's negative reaction to such approaches was made clear in his vitriolic response to Barbara Low: "My poor book: it was, as art, a fairly complete truth: so they carve a half lie out of it, and say 'Voila.' Swine!" (2LD 655). Not only did he disapprove of such Freudian interpretations of his work, but he also stated his view about the complexes as "vicious half-statements of the Freudians: sort of can't see wood for trees" (2LD 655). For Lawrence, Freudian concepts do not reach the source of psychic conflict, but remain on the surface; they turn a blind eye to the real cause of psychic illnesses: "When you've said Mutter-complex, you've said nothing—no more than if you called hysteria a nervous disease. Hysteria isn't nerves, a complex is not simply a sex relation: far from it" (2LD 655). John Turner has nevertheless argued that psychoanalysis after the 1950s in fact incorporated a number of aspects that are to be found in Lawrence's theory:

> it was not until the 1950s that psychoanalysis found its way towards the values that Lawrence held dear when Donald Winnicott, in language close to Lawrence's own, focused on the damaging effects of compliance on creative living and the importance of "the spontaneous gesture" to the process of personalisation, of feeling real as a person inhabiting a "body ego."[85]

The rise of the machine metaphor to dominance, along with the "Freudian craze" during the period, has shaped, to a significant extent, our approaches to reading and interpreting Lawrence. As a consequence, his own philosophy of the processes of human cognition has often been relegated to the margins, and this tendency has come at the cost of our understanding of Lawrence as a thinker and writer.

Lawrence's understanding of the physiological unconscious and its relation to the conscious mind pervades his literary writings. In "Why the Novel Matters," Lawrence encouraged his readers to acknowledge the existence of an intelligent physiological unconscious: "Why should I look at my hand, as it so cleverly writes these words, and decide that it is a mere nothing compared to the mind that directs it?" Instead, he proposed that the body is an independent cognitive mechanism that has "a life of its own," "learns" and "knows": "My hand is alive, it flickers with a life of its own. It meets all the strange universe in touch, and learns a vast number of things, and knows a vast number of things."[86] In Lawrence's fiction, the body repeatedly appears to possess a higher knowledge than the mind. The intuitive knowledge of the body proves to be potentially redemptive. In *Sons and Lovers* we read: "His hands were like creatures, living; his limbs, his body, were all life and conscious-ness, subject to no will of his, but *living in themselves*."[87] The body is a "thinking thing"; matter collapses into psychology, into a consciousness separate from the familiar ego consciousness. In another characteristic example, Lady Chatterley has difficulty understanding consciously her attraction to Mellors:

> In spite of herself she had a shock. After all, merely a man washing himself! Commonplace enough, Heaven knows [...] Yet in some cu-rious way it was a visionary experience: it had hit her in the middle of her body [...] It lay inside her. But with her mind she was inclined to ridicule.[88]

And in *Women in Love*, the sisters take up the question of the nature of voluntary and involuntary nervous control in their debate about Ger-ald's shooting accident, in which his brother died. Ursula suggests that it was the expression of an unconscious desire: "Perhaps there *was* an un-conscious will behind it" (W 41). Lawrence also illustrated his theory of "blood consciousness" by exposing the lack of framework through which to express his radical ontological theory. The thinking body can only emerge in discourse as a paradoxical assertion. Birkin, for instance, finds he has suddenly drunk a full glass of champagne before him and wonders, "Did I do it by accident, or did I do it out of a subconscious purpose?," only to decide that he had done it "accidentally on purpose" (W 24).

Lawrence's Literary Theory: The Value of Coal and the Cost of the Diamond

In his famous letter to Edward Garnett, Lawrence appropriated the sci-entific concept of allotropy to describe the constituent elements of hu-man nature. He advised his readers not to look in his work "for the old stable ego of the character," but for:

> another ego, according to whose action the individual is unrecognis-able, and passes through, as it were, allotropic states which it needs a deeper sense than any we've been used to exercise, to discover are states of the same single radically-unchanged element. (Like as diamond and coal are the same pure single element of carbon.

> The ordinary novel would trace the history of the diamond—but I say "diamond, what! This is carbon." And my diamond might be coal or soot, and my theme is carbon.) (2*LD* 183)

From the outset, Lawrence indicates here that allotropy is indispensable to understanding his ontological theory and approach to creating literary art.[89] Derived from the Greek ἄλλος (allos), meaning "other," and τρόπος (tropos), meaning "manner, form," allotropy is the property of certain chemical elements to exist in two or more different forms, so that, for example, depending on the architectonics of carbon, we may have coal or diamond. What therefore distinguishes coal from diamond, in terms of their respective chemical construction, is the arrangement of a common element at their core: carbon. This scientific concept of allotropy is Lawrence's central literary metaphor in giving expression to a literary theory and an ontological outlook whereby both the conscious and the unconscious are two different manifestations of an essentially identical property: intelligence. Thomas Gibbons observed that the source of Lawrence's "allotrope" is a passage from *Human Personality and Its Survival of Bodily Death* by F.W.H. Myers,[90] co-founder of the Society for Psychical Research in Cambridge and, as we have seen in Chapter 1, a leading figure in the theorization of unconscious consciousness. At this point we should be reminded that the late 19th century saw the emergence of psychology books that had clear affinities with the disciplines of physiology, philosophy and psychiatry. Psychologists like William James, Pierre Janet and Alfred Binet dealt with the topic of "multiple or secondary personality." Myers's magnum opus, *Human Personality and Its Survival of Bodily Death*, addresses a wide range of topics on psychic manifestations. This two-volume work explores psychic states like sleep, hypnotism, trance, genius and possession and finally asserts that they are interrelated. As Gibbons wrote, the similarities between the passage from Lawrence and Myers's account are striking:

> I do not wish to assert that *all* unfamiliar psychical states are necessarily evolutive or dissolutive in any assignable manner. I should prefer to suppose that there are states which may better be styled *allotropic*;—modifications of the arrangements of nervous elements on which our conscious identity depends, but with no more conspicuous *superiority* of the one state over the other than (for instance) charcoal possesses over graphite or graphite over charcoal. But there may also be states in which the (metaphorical) carbon becomes *diamond*;—with so much at least of *advance* on previous states as is involved in the substitution of the crystalline for the amorphous structure.[91]

Myers considers phenomena like messages and words uttered without conscious intention, which he ascribed to unconscious manifestations that reveal the existence of a subliminal self: "this subliminal self represents, more fully than the supraliminal self, our central and abiding being."[92] The fusion of science with the literary certainly appealed to Lawrence. As Roger Luckhurts argues, it must have been his opposition to Freudianism and Ouspenskian mysticism that drew Lawrence closer to Myers's work, since it "shared his disgust of mechanical or reductionist accounts for more dynamic, inherently metaphorical language."[93] According to Gibbons, Myers considers the secondary personalities as "manifestations or 'allotropic states' of a unitary *un*consciousness or subliminal self."[94] Gibbons concludes that Myers's subliminal self is what Lawrence refers to as "another ego according to whose action the individual is unrecognisable."[95]

Myers used the concept of allotropy in conjunction with the famous case of Mary Reynolds, first reported in 1816; it was widely discussed in the medical and popular press throughout the 19th century.[96] As Boris Sidis wrote, it was "a case which has been copied from book to book and which has circulated in literature for over a century."[97] It was identified at the time as "the only case of complete double consciousness on record,"[98] and interested Myers because it was "remarkable in respect of the change of character involved."[99] The image of diamond versus coal was used to mirror the stark difference between the two states of consciousness. The metaphor of allotropy is reflected in the development of a dissociated state into a third one, encompassing the two previously opposed and differentiated states. As Myers noted: "Observe, also, in Mary Reynolds's case the tendency of the two states gradually to *coalesce* apparently in a third phase likely to be preferable to either of the two already known."[100] For Myers,

> The deliverance from gloomy preoccupations—the childish insouciance of the secondary state—again illustrates the difference between these *allotropic* changes or reconstructions of personality and that mere predominance of a morbid factor which marked the cases of *idée fixe* and hysteria.[101]

Allotropy exemplifies a dissociation in which the unconscious is not characterized by morbid elements, but characterized as a return to a "childish nuisance" and a "deliverance from gloomy preoccupations." Myers alternatively named this allotropic change a "reconstruction of personality," stressing its positive associations. The metaphor of allotropy is then identified with the potential of the unconscious to act as a regenerative force, and it is proposed by Myers as an alternative model to the conclusions reached from "cases of *idée fixe* and hysteria," which involve the "mere predominance of a morbid factor."

Like Myers's, Lawrence's language is heavily figurative, calling for the need to take a closer look at the passage under discussion. Allotropy draws attention to a radically unchanged element in human nature, which can evince itself in two different forms. In Lawrence's account, these two forms appear on the surface as opposites. For Lawrence, coal represents the unconscious. In his essay "Nottingham and the Mining Country," for instance, he asserts that in darkness one may discover his or her "real being," which resembles "the gloss of coal": "if I think of my childhood, it is always as if there was a lustrous sort of inner darkness, like the gloss of coal, in which we moved and had our real being."[102] The unconscious—like the coal in the industrial world of modernism—is the driving principle, the fuel that enlivens humans and energizes human contact and behaviour. The authentic self, our "real being," moves within the unconscious, the "inner darkness," which is figuratively brought forth through the metaphor of the coal. We may capture a glimpse of the meaning of "real being" in Lawrence's thought in his description of what the colliers brought back with them upon their ascent to the surface: "When the men came up into the light," Lawrence continued, "they blinked. They had, in a measure, to change their flow. Nevertheless they brought with them above-ground the curious dark intimacy of the mine, the naked sort of contact."[103] They brought to the surface a robust agent that connected them in a sacred communion. This is what Lawrence called "instinct of community" or "societal instinct."[104] Light (conscious) and darkness (unconscious) are sharply contrasted, just like the diamond (bright, consciousness) and the coal (dark, unconscious). By applying the concept of allotropy to the human condition, Lawrence (and Myers) draws attention to a radically unchanged element of human nature that can manifest itself in two different forms, which may appear on the surface as opposites. In the context of Lawrence's psychobiology, the unconscious, like the conscious sphere, is capable of performing rational cognitive processes.

The son of a miner, born in Eastwood, an English mining village, Lawrence had quite unexpectedly idealized the profession's intense physical labour. This is because, for Lawrence, the technological advances that propelled industrialization had damaging consequences for human relations and the process of human cognition and understanding: they undermined what he called "the societal instinct" at the same time that the mechanical principles underlying the workings of machinery were being increasingly applied to the workings of human cognition. This "societal instinct," along with the somatic and spontaneous mode of cognition, was built upon the workers' physical labour and contact with each other. But the introduction of machines into their world opened up a gap between the workers and their object of work. Consequently,

Lawrence witnessed the ways many of his acquaintances had to adjust to the principles of industrialism. He witnessed the change of mentality following the early stages of the industrial system, and he described it with poignancy in many of his essays:

> In my generation, the boys I went to school with, colliers now, have all been beaten down, what with the din-din-dinning of Board Schools, books, cinemas, clergymen, the whole national and human consciousness hammering on the fact of material prosperity above all things.[105]

It was the destruction of the "instinct of community" that Lawrence despised in the industrial society he lived in.[106] He believed in the possibility of work to offer, through physical proximity, a sense of community in which people would be in touch with their spontaneous soul rather than the automatons to which industrialism had reduced them. He had the vision of a society where no one is superior or inferior to a fellow human being, but simply feels a "recognition of *present otherness*."[107] The industrial system, however, eroded this connectedness: "Comparison enters only when one of us departs from his own integral being, and enters the material mechanical world. Then equality and inequity starts at once."[108]

He criticized many novelists for their stress on consciousness, or the "history of the diamond," as he called it in his letter to Edward Garnett. In the same spirit, he advised Kyle Crichton that the treatment of the unconscious is vital in a literary work. Finding how to present this human aspect in fiction is what Lawrence strove to achieve. He considered this to be the author's duty:

> you've got to use the artist's faculty of making the sub-conscious conscious [...] look *under* his blankness [...] look for his hidden wistfulness, his absolutely shut-off passion [...] and give the story in terms of these, not of his mechanical upper self.
>
> (5LD 294)

To focus only on the conscious aspect of the characters results simply in a "good *record*, and excellent for conveying fact" (5LD 294). Lawrence endorsed in the same letter the need for the unconscious (coal, darkness) to become the raw material the artist should bring into consciousness (light, diamond), just like the colliers brought back with them from the depths of the mines an "otherworldness," a darkness and physicality charged with powerful bonds and feelings: "What was there in the mines that held the boy's feelings? The darkness, the mystery, the otherworldness, the peculiar camaraderie, the sort of naked intimacy: men

as gods in the underworld, or as elementals. Create *that* in a picture"
(5LD 294). An author is like a collier, descending into the depth of the
human constitution in order to bring the elements s/he mined to light.
While characterizing Crichton's story as a "steel" or "record," Lawrence
explained the role the unconscious dimension should take in a story in
order to redefine and reform consciousness:

> Give the mystery, the cruelty, the deathliness of steel, as against the
> comparative softness, silkiness, naturalness of coal. Throw in that
> Alice as a symbol of the human ego striving in its vanity, superficial:
> but the man's soul really magnetised by steel, by coal, as two oppos-
> ing master–elements: carbon versus iron, c and f.
>
> (5LD 294)

Lawrence characterized Crichton's tendency to embrace "steel" as a primarily American trait, the quintessence of what he despised in modern
culture: "You've got to allow yourself to be, in some measure, the mystic
that your real self is, under all the American efficiency and smartness of
the ego" (5LD 294).

In his review of Trigant Burrow's *The Social Basis of Consciousness*,
Lawrence wrote that "what must be broken is the egocentric absolute
of the individual," heralding a society where "the me-and-you tension
and contest, the inevitable contest of two individualities" is "brought
into connexion." The industrialist society gave rise to egocentric
self-interestedness, and "so long as men are inwardly dominated [...]
nothing is possible but insanity more or less pronounced." In a final
twist of thought, Lawrence called upon his readers to "shatter the mirror" of self-absorbed paralysis "and fall again into true relatedness."[109]
To use R.E. Pritchard's words, in Lawrence's works the "'impersonal'
activity of male communion has become subordinated in the sense of
ease in a larger inclusive body." Especially in his more mature writings, Pritchard continues, Lawrence expressed a "yearning for a resurrection in a fantasied community of 'togetherness,'" for a return to
his childhood, when "miners were not brutalised by the industry, but
in their dark underworld knew 'a sort of intimate community' developing their intuitive consciousness."[110] Lawrence believed in physical
proximity and comradeship, bonding people in a sense of community
in which they are literally in touch, united in a "naked intimacy." The
industrial system eroded this harmonious connectedness: "Comparison
enters only when one of us departs from his own integral being, and
enters the material-mechanical world. Then equality and inequity starts
at once."[111]

Lawrence stressed the importance of the "societal instinct" as an inherently somatic experience. It is what he called the experience of the
"blood" which involves the sensory and intuitive elements of human

nature. In his essay "Introduction to These Paintings," Lawrence described the electric immediacy of this phenomenon:

> *A deep instinct of kinship joins men together, and the kinship of flesh-and-blood keeps the warm flow of intuitional awareness streaming between human beings.* Our true awareness of one another is intuitional, not mental. Attraction between people is really instinctive and intuitional, not an affair of judgement [...] We have become ideal beings, creatures that exist in idea, to one another, rather than flesh-and-blood kin. And *with the collapse of the feeling of physical, flesh-and-blood kinship, and the substitution of our ideal*, social or political oneness, *came the failing of our intuitive awareness*, and the great unease, the *nervousness* of mankind. We are *afraid* of the instincts. We are *afraid* of the intuition within us. We suppress the instincts, and we cut off our intuitional awareness from one another and from the world.[112]

The atrophy of the "flesh-and-blood" kinship was a symptom of the industrialist spirit, causing what Lawrence called "nervousness" in people. The medicinal virtues for the cure of the material, mechanical world, a world that turns humans into machines, lie in the re-establishment of the connection between humans and their cognitive/social unconscious through physical interaction. In the transition from Crich's to Gerald's generation, we see the transformation of the mines from a setting in which people were communicating instinctively and physically into a mechanized setting. Crich represents the pre-mechanization era of the mines, an era that Lawrence idealized in "Nottingham and the Mining Countryside." In this essay, Lawrence presented the mines as a working space in which the colliers could communicate physically: "Under the butty system, the miners worked underground as a sort of intimate community, they knew each other practically naked, and with curious close intimacy."[113] What enabled this somatic communication was "the darkness and the underground remoteness of the pit 'stall,' and the continual presence of danger."[114] This setting brought unconscious drives to the forefront. It "made the physical, instinctive and intuitional contact between men very highly developed, a contact almost as close as touch, very real and very powerful. This physical awareness and intimate *togetherness* was at its strongest down pit."[115] As noted earlier, Lawrence's diamond is coal (i.e. "I say 'diamond, what! This is carbon'"), but this should be understood within the framework of a dialectics whereby the refusal to acknowledge the presence of carbon within the diamond evacuates the chemical substance of its real being, rendering it a worthless casket, just like a conscious self that suppresses the instinctual, the physical and the unconscious, loses its real being, becoming a mechanical, industrialized artefact.

Lawrence's Literary Theory into Practice

Women in Love voices the need for these central issues to find the most apt linguistic expression: "This struggle for verbal consciousness should not be left out in art [...] *It is the passionate struggle into conscious being*" (*W* 486). An integral part of the community, Thomas Crich wanted his mines to be "primarily great fields to produce bread and plenty for all the hundreds of human beings gathered about them [...] He wanted his industry to be run on love. Oh, he wanted love to be the directing power even of the mines" (*W* 224, 225). The "patriarch," as he is called, represents the "unifying idea of mankind" that bonded people through the cultivation of their communal instinct (*W* 221). However, the momentum of industrial reality seemed unstoppable. Mines were being transformed at a fast pace. The "sword of mechanical necessity" was drawn, with Crich finding retreat in charity work (*W* 225). The new grim reality is summarized in Lawrence's essay "Nottingham and the Mining Countryside": "condemning of the workers to ugliness, ugliness, ugliness: meanness and formless and ugly surroundings, ugly ideals, ugly religion, ugly hope, ugly love, ugly clothes, ugly furniture, ugly houses, ugly relationship between workers and employers."[116] Gerald represents the new spirit of the modern era, he is the "Industrial Magnate" (*W* 211). Upon succeeding his father, he abolished the old system and employed many of the latest scientific advancements. Under his management, "electricity was carried into every mine. New machinery was brought from America, such as the miners had never seen before" (*W* 230). These new machines, the "great iron men," blurred the distinction between the human and the machine. The colliers were no longer in charge of the mines. Instead, "educated and expert men were in control everywhere, the miners were reduced to mere mechanical instruments" (*W* 230). Not only did industrialization mean more work and less pay, but it also meant that their work became "terrible and heart-breaking in its mechanicalness [...] the hope seemed to perish as they became more and more mechanised" (*W* 230).

Lawrence portrayed the transition from "the butty system" of Crich's epoch to Gerald's mechanical era in terms of the increasing numbing of the unconscious and instinctual somatic drives. It is, in other words, the transition from a cognitive to a mechanical materiality. For Lawrence, the only way out of the deadening spirit of industrialism was the revival of the cognitive body that constitutes the antithesis of mechanization. Gerald's treatment of people as a kind of machinery that can be disposed of once used (*W* 231) brings him close to Lawrence's definition of the neurasthenic, a person dissociated from the "flesh-and-blood" kinship: "such a strange pressure was upon him, as if the very middle of him were a vacuum, and outside were an awful tension" (*W* 233). In contrast to his father, who achieved a balance between the bodily and the mental, Gerald is in agony, suffering an existential crisis:

> he had suddenly stood up in terror, not knowing what he was. And he went to the mirror and looked long and closely at his own face, at his own eyes, seeking for something. He was afraid, in mortal dry fear, but he knew not what of.
>
> (*W* 232)

Gerald's refusal to embrace his "real being," to walk like the colliers in the mines of the pristine unconscious inflicted upon him a sense of "emptiness" (*W* 266). Gerald's reference to his eyes as two "blue false bubbles" in which he could only see "the darkness in them, as if they were only bubbles of darkness" (*W* 232), plunges the reader in the world of *Fantasia*. There, Lawrence referred to the eyes as one of the great gateways of the psyche. They are the window of the soul from which it "goes in and out of the body, as a bird flying forth and coming home" (*PFU* 101). According to Charles Ross, Lawrence rewrote scene after scene in *Women in Love* in order to accentuate Gerald's "ice-destructive" consciousness as a "nonhuman aspect of the terrible, static ice-built mountain-top" of the will, reductive to phenomena, symbolic of "the resonance of this vocabulary for conveying the sterile abuse of the will [...] characteristic of modern society."[117] "The Industrial Magnate" represents the mental life, the idea of the machine, and personifies "not only British industrialism but the whole deathly vector of northern Europe."[118] As Mark Kinkead-Weekes asserted, "Lawrence put into Gerald all his fascination with power [...] the power of mind over matter, the power of technology which revolutionized the coal industry in his lifetime."[119] Gerald finds pleasure in industrial production and development; he is the one who installed electrical plants to the mines, and as Birkin makes clear at the end of "Class-Room" (*W* 35), electricity is synonymous with the "deliberate, mental consciousness" (*PFU* 29). Gerald is the embodiment of "the God of the machine," whose religion is "the pure instrumentality of mankind" (*W* 223). As David Trotter has noted, "Gerald [...] can be associated with early twentieth-century campaigns for 'national efficiency'; physical health; scientific and technological training; military and naval preparedness; industrial modernization; a government of national unity."[120]

Conversely, Birkin represents the principle of fluid organic life and regeneration. In an attempt to immerse himself in physical experience, he resorts to a nearby forest, where he strips off his clothes and moves naked among the flowers and fir-trees. He takes satisfaction there from the sting of the fir-boughs on his skin, from the smooth hardness of the birch-trunks, and from the "lovely, subtle, responsive vegetation," which literally enters into his blood, into his "living self" (*W* 107). His worldview idealizes experience rather than intellect, the latter bearing little homage to one's "spontaneous-creative fullness of being" (*PFU* 43). To gain knowledge of Ursula's "other self," Birkin has to go under the skin (*W* 188). He asserts, "I don't *want* to see you. I've seen plenty of women, I'm sick and weary of seeing them. I want a woman I don't see" (*W* 147). The same deprecation of surface appearances is found in *Fantasia of the Unconscious*: "sight is the least sensual of all the senses. And we strain ourselves to see, see, see—everything, everything through the eye, in one mode of objective curiosity" (*PFU* 102–3). It is the same wish that leads him to confess to Ursula that "I want to find you, where you don't know your existence, the you that your common self denies utterly" (*W* 147). Birkin expresses the view that real connection can be achieved only through physical communion. He is the primary representative of the unconscious and the instinctual, the "coal" that Lawrence intended to embed in his work. He is the advocate of "the great dark knowledge you can't have in your head—the dark involuntary being" (*W* 43).

However, much like Gerald, he fails to reach equilibrium, since he is unable to communicate with others on the level he wishes. The one sees himself mirrored in the other and the two seem to merge in a peculiar oneness, their "two bodies clinched into oneness" (*W* 270). Despite the different form of consciousness that each represents, in reality they represent two forms of the same mode of being. Gerald admits that "Only Birkin kept the fear definitely off him," but he denies, in a symbolic gesture, Birkin's offer of a "blood-brotherhood" (*W* 232). More than disguised homoeroticism,[121] Birkin's proposal functions as an opportunity for Gerald to embrace "the instinct of community." Gerald's reply, "'We'll leave it till I understand it better,'" is a testament to his dissociation from the physical, but he does not reject it outright (*W* 207). He defers definite answer until he understands the meaning of this kind of bondage. In the intensely physical scene of the "Gladiatorial," Birkin's proposal for a "blood-brotherhood" is one way of expressing his desire to establish a naked intimacy with him, in which sexual desire is elevated to noble ideals of male devotion and loyalty. However, Gerald proves unable to understand this, because his mind is fixated on the tendency to trust the mental and the mechanical: "His mind was very active. But it was like a bubble floating in the darkness. At any moment it might burst and leave him in chaos" (*W* 232). Although robust in outward appearance and very often cruel in his behaviour, Gerald is as soft and fragile within as a "bubble." The frail and hollow "haven" he created can only tentatively shut out the instinctual and the natural, the darkness of soot and coal.

The "Gladiatorial" embodies the very essence of the allotropic technique. Gerald's tendency to intellectualize compulsively every aspect of life is paradigmatic of the conscious reasoning symbolized by the diamond in Lawrence's allotropic analogy. Birkin, however, is energized by his physical (un)consciousness (coal). Despite their differences, both characters suffer from internal conflict. Gerald was "deeply bondaged in fascinated attraction [...] he was mistrustful, resenting the bondage, hating the attraction" (W 207). At once fascinated by and resentful of their bondage, Gerald is caught at the crossroads of contradictory feelings. His relationship with Birkin is presented as an inevitably physical communion that cannot be consciously controlled. It is a physical reality that his conscious mind, governed by the spirit and philosophy of industrialism, is unable to control. As the primary representative of the tendency to over-intellectualize every aspect of life and rely solely on mental reasoning, he is unable to "understand," as he says, their bond (W 207). Birkin experiences similar feelings of attraction-repulsion towards Gerald. Their first interaction, for instance, is described in the following terms:

> There was a pause of strange enmity between the two men, that was very near to love. It was always the same between them; always their talk brought them into a deadly nearness of contact, a strange, perilous intimacy which was either hate or love, or both [....] they kept it at the level of trivial occurrence. Yet the heart of each burned from the other. They burned each other inwardly. This they would never admit.
>
> (W 33)

From the very beginning, their hostility is juxtaposed to an inner organic unity as "the heart of each burned from the other." This sense of external difference, underpinned by an organic unity on a deeper level, points towards the formation of an allotropic relationship. The complementarity of the two male protagonists is initially conveyed on the physical level. The organic, bodily consciousness that Birkin advocates is physically materialized through Gerald's stout physique, a point constantly stressed in the novel. Lawrence began the "Gladiatorial" by stressing the physical opposition of the two protagonists, initiating in this way the framing of the two on the allotropic diamond-coal opposition. His description of Gerald's body as a "concrete and noticeable, a piece of pure final substance" (W 269) is energized through Birkin's "white and thin" body (W 269). Following the allotropic pattern, Lawrence stressed the fact that the two men were, appearance-wise, "very dissimilar" (W 269). Birkin is "tall and narrow, his bones were very thin," while Gerald is "much heavier and more plastic. His bones were strong and round" (W 269). The "Gladiatorial" corresponds to a physical rite allowing them to communicate through their somatic faculties and gain carnal knowledge of each other. It is through a "physical understanding" that they are able to grasp their singularity and "break into a oneness" (W 270).

The bodily language used by each mirrors the different ontology each represents: Gerald is "frictional" and "mechanical," whereas Birkin "abstract as to be almost intangible" (*W* 269). Lawrence used an ambiguous lexical register to describe Birkin's movements: "He impinged invisibly upon the other man, scarcely seeming to touch him, like a garment [...] like some hard wind" (*W* 269–70). The paradoxical "impinged invisibly" identifies the forceful physical collision as imperceptible and is followed by a stress on physical contact ("like a garment"). The choice of the word "wind" suggests a physical type of communication that affects one's inner being, penetrating one's carnal shell to reach deep inside. Lawrence's use of the wind metaphor conveys the infusion of Birkin's "physical intelligence" into Gerald as a means of communion and connection (*W* 269). His mode of being penetrates, as if in a sexual congress, Gerald's monolithic intellectualism, "piercing in a tense fine grip that seemed to penetrate into the very quick of Gerald's being" (*W* 270). Despite his resistance, Gerald felt mesmerized by Birkin's approach: to him, Birkin possessed some "great subtle energy, that would press upon the other man with an uncanny force, weigh him like a spell put upon him" (*W* 270). Birkin has to break through Gerald's conscious shell to make him embrace his physical unconscious and recognize its nature. To this end, he moves like a "fine net, a prison, through the muscles into the very depths of Gerald's physical being" (*W* 270). Lawrence noted that the two merge into a single being as "Birkin's whole physical intelligence interpenetrated into Gerald's body" (*W* 270). At this point, Lawrence indicates how it is Birkin's "physical intelligence" that is striving to achieve unity with Gerald. Here, we have the coexistence of two different forms of reasoning, namely, the mental, represented by Gerald, and the bodily, represented by Birkin. What fascinated Lawrence in the concept of allotropy is that a single substance, carbon, forms such distinct bodies like diamond and coal. In a similar manner, reasoning process may take two distinct forms, the one somatic and unconscious, and the other mental and conscious. Birkin has to break through Gerald's conscious shell to make him embrace his physical unconscious and recognize its androgynous nature.

They finally manage to reach the desired state when they are "intent and mindless" (*W* 270). The antithetical meaning used to describe their union enabled Lawrence to capture a state in which another form of cognition takes place, as distinct from the mental one. Through the use of the adjective "intent," Lawrence gives expression to the different processes used in unconscious thinking. In this state, reasoning is disentangled from its mental framework, and attentiveness takes its place in order that physical thinking may occur. By merging into oneness through a physical communion, they embody the allotropic subjectivity that unites them. As Birkin put it, it is "a final, almost extra-human relationship with him—a relationship in the ultimates of me and him"

(W 363). Integral to the "white knot of flesh" that the two protagonists form is the idea of a physical and psychical union (W 270). Although surviving only momentarily, this is the kind of diamond of which Lawrence had spoken, one in which we may recognize the carbon at its core as its constituent component. The formation of this subjectivity can only find expression in the realm of the unconscious after removing the garments of opposition: "It was in the other world of the subconsciousness that the interplay took place, the interchange of spiritual and physical richness, the relieving of physical and spiritual poverty" (W 493). What might seem contradictory (the physical-mental intelligence) is actually the expression of one "element": cognition. The process of knowing through the body involves knowing through antitheses (e.g. coal/ diamond), and moving beyond them to develop new cognitive processes. For him, materiality encompasses the highest form of reasoning, it is "the fountain-head" of thinking itself, "incorruptible and unsearchable" (W 479). Even if the world came to an end, it would be from this "fountain-head" that "new forms of consciousness" and "new units of being" would emerge (W 479). The "Gladiatorial" is an externalized psychomachia wherein the constituent elements of human nature merge into oneness at the same time that they are striving to break free.

In a final call for unity, Birkin proclaims, "'We are mentally, spiritually intimate, therefore we should be more or less physically intimate too—it is more whole'" (W 272). Being "awake and potent in that other basic mind, the deepest physical mind," Birkin is able to recognize the importance of his union with Gerald (W 318). This, however, is a logic that Gerald ultimately rejects. He refuses the union that would involve each "given to each other, organically," and is thereby condemned to "a sort of fatal halfness" (W 207). A psychological impasse follows: "He felt that his *mind* needed acute stimulation, before he could be physically roused" (W 233). Gerald experiences a death of the body; he becomes a mental machine-like being driven purely by mental reason. His physical intelligence freezes in a state that triggers a process of disintegration that will finally lead to his death in the Alps. It should nevertheless be noted that despite his denial, Gerald is unable to disentangle himself from Birkin, who seems to be the only one able to take his feeling of vacuity away. Birkin kindled the embers of coal within him, but Gerald remained unable to free himself from his obstinate intellectualism. Their interaction is described in religious terms. It is compared to a "church service," a communion fusing two beings into one that "seemed to contain the quintessence of faith" (W 232). The quintessence of this holy faith involves the inability to grasp conceptually and intellectually the signified. In the critically contested chapter "Excurse" that Lawrence rewrote to show a "mystically-physically satisfying" experience between Birkin and Ursula,[122] the narrator comments, it is a "sensual reality that can never be transmuted into mind content," an unspeakable communication in touch, dark, subtle [...] the reality of that which can never be known, vital, sensual reality that can never be transmuted into mind content, but remains outside, living body of darkness and silence and subtlety, the mystic body of reality.

(W 320)

A stubborn intellectualist who embodies the spirit of mechanical industrialization and rationalization, Gerald is unable to introduce his experience with Birkin into the symbolic order of understanding. He does not efface it but denies it.

Early on in his career, Lawrence had in mind the art he was aspiring to achieve, which was given full expression in *Women in Love*. In the *Study of Thomas Hardy*, he looked ahead to an art "which knows the struggle between two conflicting laws and knows the final reconciliation, where both are equal, two-in-one, complete."[123] He also referred to the inability of consciousness to experience anything with the sense of a living communion:

Man is himself the vivid body of life, rolling glimmering against the void. In his fullest living he does not know what he does, his mind, his consciousness, unacquaint, hovers behind, full of extraneous gleams and glances, and altogether devoid of knowledge.[124]

Intellect is presented here as a feeble repetition of previous occurrences. Its only ability is to reflect the already given; its reasoning is only able to understand in terms of mutually exclusive opposites. Studying the cognitive capabilities of the unconscious in Lawrence's theory, we realize that even though the opposites "are, in a way, contradictions each of the other,"[125] they nevertheless remain connected on a deeper level.

Notes

1 David Ellis, "Lawrence and the Biological Psyche," in *D. H. Lawrence: Centenary Essays*, ed. by Mara Kalnins (Bristol: Bristol Classical Press, 1986), 91.
2 Michael Black, *D. H. Lawrence: The Early Fiction: A Commentary* (London: Macmillan, 1986), 27.
3 Robert E. Montgomery, *The Visionary D. H. Lawrence: Beyond Philosophy and Art* (Cambridge: Cambridge University Press, 2009), 15.
4 Nancy Katherine Hayles, "The Ambivalent Approach: D.H. Lawrence and the New Physics," *Mosaic* 15: 3 (1982): 108 and "Evasion: The Field of the Unconscious in D. H. Lawrence," in *The Cosmic Web: Scientific Field Models and Literary Strategies in the Twentieth Century* (Ithaca, NY: Cornell University Press, 1984), 110.
5 Michael Wutz, "The Thermodynamics of Gender: Lawrence, Science and Sexism," *Mosaic* 28: 2 (1995): 83–108.
6 Nicholas Crawford, "Altar of Paradox: Women in Love and the Mystery of Dualism," in *Like a Black and White Kaleidoscope Tossed at Random:*

Essays on D.H. Lawrence's Women in Love, ed. by Phillipe Romanski and Jean-Paul Richardie (Rouen: University of Rouen Press, 2001), 46.

7 Jeff Wallace, *D. H. Lawrence, Science and the Posthuman* (Basingstoke: Palgrave Macmillan, 2005) and "51/ 49: democracy, abstraction and the machine in Lawrence, Deleuze and their readings of Whitman," in *New D. H. Lawrence*, ed. by Howard J. Booth (Manchester: Manchester University Press, 2009), 98–116.

8 Jennifer Spitzer, "On Not Reading Freud: Amateurism, Expertise, and the 'Pristine Unconscious' in D.H. Lawrence," *MODERNISM/modernity* 21: 1 (2014): 102–3.

9 Michael Bell, "Freud and Lawrence: Thoughts on War and Instinct," *Études Lawrenciennes* [Online] 46 (2015).

10 Thomas Scott Lambert, *Practical Anatomy, Physiology, and Pathology* (Portland: Sanborn, Carter & Co., 1852), 28.

11 Oliver Wendell Holmes, "Mechanism of Vital Actions," *North American Review* 85 (1857): 53.

12 William A. Alcott, *The Structure, Uses and Abuses of the Human Hand* (Boston, MA: Massachusetts Sabbath School Society, 1856), 116.

13 John H. Griscom, *Animal Mechanism and Physiology: Being a Plain and Familiar Exposition of the Structure and Functions of the Human System* (New York: Harper & Brothers, 1848), ix, 174, 15.

14 Lambert, *Practical Anatomy*, 31.

15 Charles Caldwell, *Thoughts on Physical Education* (Boston, MA: Marsh, Capen & Lyon, 1834), 4, 22.

16 Worthington Hooker, *First Book in Physiology for the Use of Schools and Families* (New York: Farmer, Brace & Co., 1855), 190.

17 Lambert, *Practical Anatomy*, 46.

18 William A. Alcott, "Physical Education," *Moral Reformer* I (1835): 21 and *The Laws of Health* (Boston, MA: John Jewett and Company, 1857).

19 See, for instance, Anson Rabinbach, *The Human Motor: Energy, Fatigue, and the Origins of Modernity* (New York: Basic Books, 1990) and James C. Whorton, *Crusaders for Fitness: The History of American Health Reformers* (Princeton, NJ: Princeton University Press, 1982).

20 Stephen Nissenbaum, *Sex, Diet, and Debility in Jacksonian America: Sylvester Graham and Health Reform* (Westport, CT: Greenwood Press, 1980).

21 Martha H. Verbrugge, *Able-Bodied Womanhood: Personal Health and Social Change in Nineteenth-Century Boston* (New York: Oxford University Press, 1988), 48.

22 Joan Burbick, *Healing the Republic: The Language of Health and the Culture of Nationalism in Nineteenth-Century America* (New York: Cambridge University Press, 1994), 5.

23 Stephen Rice, *Minding the Machine Languages of Class in Early Industrial America* (Berkeley and Los Angeles: University of California Press, 2004), 99.

24 Edward Thompson, "Time, Work Discipline and Industrial Capitalism," *Past and Present* 38 (1969): 56–97.

25 Anson Rabinbach, "The European Science of Work: The Economy of the Body at the End of the Nineteenth Century," in *Work in France: Representations, Meaning, Organization, and Practice*, ed. by Stephen Laurence Kaplan and Cynthia J. Koepp (Ithaca, NY: Cornell University Press, 1986), 47.

26 Jean Marie Lahy, *Le système taylor et la physiologie du travail professionnel* (Paris: Masson, 1916), 122.

27 Ibid., 156–7.

28 Stanley Joel Reisser, *Medicine and the Reign of Technology* (Cambridge: Cambridge University Press, 1981), 99–102; H. A. Snellen, *E. J. Marey and Cardiology: Physiologist and Pioneer of Technology* (Rotterdam: Kooyker Scientific Publications, 1980), 16; and Edgar Holden, *The Sphygmograph and the Physiology of the Circulation* (New York, William Wood, 1871).
29 René Quinton, "E.J. Marey," *Revue des idées*, 7 (1904): 484.
30 Etienne-Jules Marey, *Animal Mechanism: A Treatise on Terrestrial and Aerial Locomotion* (New York, 1874), 59.
31 Etienne-Jules Marey, *Du mouvement dans les fonctions de la vie: Leçons faites au Collège de France* (Paris: Germer Baillière, 1868), 69–70.
32 Marey, *Animal Mechanism*, 69.
33 Rabinbach, "The European Science," 507.
34 Angelo Mosso, *Fatigue*, trans. by Margaret Drummond and W.B. Drummond (London: Swan Sonnenschein, 1906), 82–8.
35 Jules Amar, *The Human Motor: The Scientific Foundations of Labour and Industry* (London: Routledge, 1920).
36 Charles Labriffe, *L' apprentissage dans l' industrie textile* (Paris: Editions de l"industrie textile, 1945).
37 Ibid., 104–10.
38 Catharine E. Beecher, *Letters to the People on Health and Happiness* (New York: Harper & Brothers, 1855), 88.
39 Francis William Bird, *Physiological Reform: An Address, Delivered before the American Physiological Society at Their First Annual Meeting, June 1, 1837* (Boston, MA: Marsh, Capen & Lyon, 1837), 14–5.
40 See Indrek Männiste, ed., *D.H. Lawrence, Technology, and Modernity* (London and New York: Bloomsbury, 2019).
41 Spitzer, "On Not Reading Freud," 97.
42 Don Marquis, *New York Tribune*, 25 September 1921, 6.
43 On the dust-jacket of *Fantasia of the Unconscious* (New York, 1923), n.d.
44 T.S. Eliot, *After Strange Gods: A Primer of Modern Heresy* (London: Faber and Faber, 1934), 60.
45 Fiona Becket, "Lawrence and Psychoanalysis," in *The Cambridge Companion to D.H. Lawrence* (Cambridge: Cambridge University Press, 2001), 218.
46 D.H. Lawrence, *Studies in Classic American Literature*, ed. by Ezra Greenspan, Lindeth Vasey and John Worthen (Cambridge: Cambridge University Press, 2003), 192.
47 Lawrence, *Studies*, 192.
48 D. H. Lawrence, *Phoenix II: Uncollected, Unpublished, and Other Prose Works by D. H. Lawrence*, ed. by Warren Roberts and Harry T. Moore (London: William Heinemann, 1968), 493.
49 John Turner also points out the similarity between James and Lawrence's understanding of emotion as one still held by 21st-century neurologists, such as Antonio Damasio. See *D.H. Lawrence and Psychoanalysis* (New York: Routledge, 2020), 158.
50 D. H. Lawrence, *Phoenix: The Posthumous Papers of D. H. Lawrence*, ed. by Edward D. McDonald (New York: Penguin, 1978), 637.
51 Ibid., 620.
52 Becket, "Lawrence and Psychoanalysis," 219–20.
53 For a historical investigation of the impact of psychoanalysis (including the analysts Otto Gross and Trigant Burrow) on the thinking and writing of D.H. Lawrence, see Turner, *D.H. Lawrence and Psychoanalysis*.
54 David Ellis and Howard Mills, *D.H. Lawrence's Non-fiction: Art, Thought and Genre* (Cambridge: Cambridge University Press, 1988), 182.

55 Frederick J. Hoffman, *Freudianism and the Literary Mind* (Baton Rouge: Louisiana State University Press, 1957), 71.

56 John Turner observes Lawrence's characterization of life as "incalculable" and James's stress of the importance of the "incalculable" in the living process. See *D.H. Lawrence and Psychoanalysis*, 180–1.

57 William James, *Writings 1878–1899*, ed. by Gerald E. Myers (New York: Literary Classics of the United States, 1992), 502.

58 Gerald E. Myers, "Introduction: The Intellectual Context," in William James, *The Principles of Psychology* Cambridge, MA: Harvard University Press, 1981), xvi.

59 George M. Johnson, *Dynamic Psychology in Modernist British Fiction* (Basingstoke: Palgrave Macmillan, 2006), 150–7.

60 Lawrence, *Studies*, 109.

61 Jessie Chambers, *D.H. Lawrence: A Personal Record* (Cambridge: Cambridge University Press, 1935), 112, 86.

62 Daniel J. Schneider, *D.H. Lawrence, the Artist as Psychologist* (Kansas: University Press of Kansas, 1984), 25–7.

63 John Adams, *The Herbartian Psychology Applied to Education* (Boston, MA: DC Heath & Co., 1898), 255.

64 Spitzer, "On not Reading Freud," 100.

65 Lawrence, *The Symbolic Meaning*, 135.

66 Spitzer, "On not Reading Freud," 100–1.

67 Sigmund Freud, "Extracts from the Fleiss Papers: Draft B, the Aetiology of Neurosis," in *The Standard Edition of the Complete Works of Sigmund Freud*, 8 vols, ed. by James Strachey (London: Hogarth Press, 1966) vol. 1, 180.

68 Ibid., 179.

69 Ibid., 268.

70 For the inhibition to action, in melancholy, as an antithesis to labour, see Wolf Lepenies, *Melancholy and Society*, trans. by Jeremy Gaines and Doris Jones (Cambridge, MA: Harvard University Press, 1992), 207–13.

71 Adrien Proust and Gilbert Ballet, *Treatment of Neurasthenia*, trans. by Peter Campbell Smith (London: Kimpton, 1902), 102.

72 George Miller Beard, *A Practical Treatise on Nervous Exhaustion* (New York: W. Wood & Co., 1880), vi.

73 Robert A. Nye, *Crime, Madness, and Politics in Modern France: The Medical Concept of National Decline* (Princeton, NJ: Princeton University Press, 1984), 148.

74 Max Simon Nordau, *Degeneration* (Lincoln: University of Nebraska Press, 1968), 15.

75 Jean Martin Charcot, "Préface," in Levillain, Fernand, *La Neurasthénie, maladie de Beard* (Paris: A. Maloine, 1891), x.

76 Nye, *Crime*, 125, 128.

77 Jenny Bourne Taylor and Sally Shuttleworth, *Embodies Selves: An Anthology of Psychological Texts 1830–1890* (Oxford: Clarendon Press, 1998).

78 George Miller Beard, *American Nervousness: Its Causes and Consequences* (New York: G. Putnam's Sons, 1881), 10.

79 Albert Deschamps, *Les maladies de l' énergie: les asthénies générales, épuisements, insuffisances, inhibitions, clinique, thérapeutique* (Paris: Félix Alcan, 1908), 46.

80 Ibid., 37.

81 Clifford Allbutt, "Neurasthenia," in *A System of Medecine*, ed. by Clifford Allbutt and Humphry Davy Rolleston (London: Macmillan, 1910), 733.

82 Ibid., 734.

83 Becket, "Lawrence and Psychanalysis," 220.
84 Alfred Booth Kuttner, "'Sons and Lovers': A Freudian Appreciation," *Psychoanalytic Review* 3: 3 (1916): 295–317. See also Frederick J. Hoffman, "Lawrence's Quarrel with Freud," in *The Achievement of D. H. Lawrence*, ed. by Frederick J. Hoffman and Harry T. Moore (Norman: University of Oklahoma Press, 1953).
85 Turner, *D.H. Lawrence and Psychoanalysis*, 160.
86 D.H. Lawrence, "Why the Novel Matters," in *Study of Thomas Hardy and other Essays*, ed. by Bruce Steele (Cambridge: Cambridge University Press, 1985), 193.
87 D.H. Lawrence, *Sons and Lovers*, ed. by David Trotter (Oxford: Oxford University Press, 1995), 410.
88 D.H. Lawrence, *Lady Chatterley's Lover* (New York: Grove Press, 1993), 107.
89 On the "other ego" and the allotropic, a further useful background discussion is Mark Kinkead-Weekes, *DHL: Triumph to Exile* (Cambridge: Cambridge University Press, 1996), 125, which includes reference to C. Ravilious, "Lawrence's 'Chladni Figures,'" *Notes and Queries*, 20: 9 (1973): 331–2. For a stylistic analysis of Lawrence's allotropy, see Garrett Stewart's, "Lawrence, 'Being' and the Allotropic Style," *Novel*, 9 (1976): 217–42.
90 Tom Gibbons, "'Allotropic states' and 'fiddle-bow': D. H. Lawrence's Occult Sources," *Notes and Queries*, 35: 3 (1988): 338–41.
91 F.W.H. Myers, *Human Personality and Its Survival of Bodily Death*, 2 vols (New York: Longmans, Green & Co. 1903), vol. 1, 85. The same metaphor is also employed on page 198.
92 Ibid., vol. 2, 81.
93 Roger Luckhurst, *The Invention of Telepathy* (Oxford: Oxford University Press, 2002), 260.
94 Gibbons, "'Allotropic states' and 'fiddle–bow',", 340.
95 Ibid.
96 John Kearsley Mitchell, *Medical Repository* 3 (1816): 185–6.
97 Boris Sidis, *Multiple Personality: An Experimental Investigation into the Nature of Human Individuality* (New York: D. Appleton and Company, 1905), 85.
98 Ibid., 86.
99 Myers, *Human Personality*, vol. 1, 62.
100 Ibid.
101 Ibid.
102 D.H. Lawrence, *Late Essays and Articles*, ed. by James T. Boulton (Cambridge: Cambridge University Press, 2004), 290.
103 Ibid., 289–90.
104 Ibid., 293.
105 Ibid., 119.
106 Ibid., 293.
107 D.H. Lawrence, *Reflections on the Death of a Porcupine and other Essays*, ed. by Michael Herbert (Cambridge: Cambridge University Press, 1988), 80.
108 Lawrence, *Phoenix*, 699.
109 Ibid., 379, 382.
110 R. E. Pritchard, *D. H. Lawrence: Body of Darkness* (London: Hutchinson, 1971), 181.
111 Lawrence, *Phoenix*, 715–6.
112 Ibid., 556.
113 Ibid., 135.

114 Ibid.
115 Ibid., 135–6
116 Ibid., 138.
117 Charles L. Ross, *Women in Love: A Novel of Mythic Realism* (Boston, MA: Twayne, 1991), 110.
118 See David Bradshaw's "Introduction," in *Women in Love* by D.H. Lawrence (Oxford: Oxford University Press, 1998), xxi.
119 Kinkead-Weekes, *D. H. Lawrence: Triumph to Exile*, 337.
120 David Trotter, *The English Novel in History 1895–1920* (London: Routledge, 1993), 126.
121 See, for example, Michael Squires, "Dickens, Lawrence, and the English Novel," in *The Challenge of D.H. Lawrence*, ed. by Michael Squires and Keith Cushman (Madison: University of Wisconsin Press, 1990), 42–59; C.L. Ross, "Homoerotic Feeling in Women in Love: Lawrence's 'Struggle for Verbal Consciousness,' in the Manuscripts," in *D. H. Lawrence, the Man who Lived: Papers Delivered at the D.H. Lawrence Conference at Southern Illinois University, Carbondale April 1979*, ed. by Robert B. Partlow, Jr. and Harry T. Moore (Carbondale: Southern Illinois University Press, 1980), 168–82; Jeffrey Meyers, *D.H. Lawrence: A Biography* (New York: Knopf, Random House, 2002); and George Donaldson, "'Men in Love'? D.H. Lawrence, Rupert Birkin and Gerald Crich," in *D. H. Lawrence: Centenary Essays*, ed. by Mara Kalnins, (Bristol: Bristol Classical Press, 1986), 41–67. Squires places Birkin in a novelistic tradition of seducers and suggests that in earlier works his dalliance would have been with a woman (54). For Meyers, the "Prologue" clarifies such aspects of the novel as Birkin's intimacy with Crich, and his repressed homosexual desires (143). Meyers reads Birkin's homoerotic attractions in the "Prologue" as overt "homosexual affairs with working men" (143) and thinks that "the homosexuality in 'Gladiatorial' is overt" (148). The "Prologue," however, states clearly that Birkin's "reserve, which was as strong as a chain of iron in him, kept him from any demonstration" (502). For Ross, a study of the manuscripts clarifies Lawrence's artistic intentions in cancelling the "Prologue" and leaving the *Blutbrüderschaft* theme submerged until chapter 16, "Man to Man" (181).
122 Pierre Vitoux, "The Chapter 'Excurse' in Women in Love; Its Genesis and the Critical Problem," *Texas Studies in Literature and Language* 17: 4 (1976): 821.
123 Lawrence, *Study*, 128.
124 Ibid., 41.
125 Ibid., 125.

4   Virginia Woolf's Stream of (Un)Consciousness

The Ontology of Unconscious Androgyny

Virginia Woolf has long since been recognized as one of the most important writers who employed the literary technique of the stream of consciousness in their writings. Yet, despite the fact that it is a well-trodden aspect of Woolf's art, it remains relatively understudied when it comes to its connections to the unconscious. A study of these connections has significant consequences for our understanding of her philosophical and ideological outlook, particularly in relation to gender identity. This chapter is divided into three sections. The first one concentrates on the historical and philosophical background of the stream of consciousness, paying particular attention to the writings of Herbart, Lewis, Sinclair, Richardson and James. The aim here is to address a significant gap in extant studies: the function of the unconscious in the stream of consciousness. The second section looks into the ways in which Woolf built on these theories in order to develop her own understanding of how the cognitive properties of the unconscious forge the paths of the stream of consciousness and affect the processes of creating and receiving literary art. The last section explores the ways in which her theory of the stream led her to technical developments and shaped her feminist project.

The Historical Background of the Stream

The term "stream of consciousness" was coined by Alexander Bain in 1855 in *The Senses and the Intellect*.[1] In the posthumous fifth volume of his major undertaking, *Problems of Life and Mind* (1879), George Henry Lewes (1817–1878) was the first to write a detailed discussion of the "stream of consciousness" in English.[2] Lewes, nevertheless, acknowledged his debt for the concept of the stream to Gustav Theodor Fechner (1801–1887), the famous psychophysicist at the University of Leipzig.[3] In his *Elements of Psychophysics* (1860), Fechner frequently used the metaphor of a mental wave (*Welle*) to describe the thinking processes, drawing attention to the role played by the unconscious:

> If it [a stimulation] is below the level, or if it has no escort of excitations above the level, it is then said to be "not accompanied by

consciousness"; this means that in and for itself the movement has had neither the interest which connects it with feeling, nor the significance which connects it with Thought.

Lewes described the unconscious process that singles out what is significant and interesting, and he asserted the existence of a selective mechanism performing cognitive processes for the benefit of the individual. He provided as an example the somnambulist, "who moves securely through a crowded room, sees the objects and persons (since he avoids them) but is not conscious of them."[4] Lewes represented mental activity as a curve that "rises into the stage of consciousness, which having attained its maximum sinks into subconsciousness and without changing its course falls to the level of unconsciousness, perhaps again to rise with like gradation."[5]

In *Problems of Life and Mind*, Lewes looked under the waves and found that "systemic sensation, emotion, or ideal preoccupation" comprise an unconscious cognitive domain, which is "silently operating, determining the direction of the general current, and obscurely preparing the impulses which burst forth into action."[6] The fluctuating "Moods" are another result of the unconscious processes at work under the wave, which Lewes called "residual feelings of systemic stimulation." He related them to bodily processes and asserted that sensibility originates in physical processes and can be traced in the development from protoplasm to organs. According to Lewes, sensibility forms a part of *sentience*, which includes the unconscious.[7] As in the case of James's formulation of the unconscious, we see a close alliance between physiology and psychology, an alliance that characterizes these early explorations of the unconscious mind.

Although J. Gill Holland's statement that it was the German philosopher and psychologist Johann Friedrich Herbart (1776–1841) who coined the term is inaccurate, it is nevertheless indicative of the importance of Herbart's analysis for contemporary thinkers.[8] Herbart did not father the term "stream of consciousness," but he coined the intimately related term "threshold of consciousness," which exerted a major influence, as we will see below in more detail, on William James's own theory of the stream of consciousness. He came up with the term through his analysis of the circumstances under which representations enter consciousness. In his own words, it relates to the "boundary which a thought seems to cross when it passes from a totally inhibited state to a degree of actual representation as the *threshold of consciousness*."[9] The reason why certain representations sink under this threshold is that they are conflicting, and therefore need to sink away from consciousness until they are able to coexist and reach equilibrium. Herbart elaborated on the mathematical laws governing these relations and provided a theory of an auspicious unconscious working to maintain stability. The unconscious becomes in

Herbart's thought a selective mechanism, allowing only a small number of representations to reach consciousness. It is governed by laws that involve the calculation of equilibrium and the motion of representations needed to reach this equilibrium, which as Herbart admitted are "very complicated."[10] According to George M. Johnson, it is "the Herbartian conception of repression [...] that Woolf works with, rather than the Freudian," as it had circulated in Britain via G.F. Stout's essays in which he compared Herbart with other English psychologists (1888–1889).[11]

As noted above, another important theorist of the "stream of consciousness" is Fechner, who deepened Herbart's idea of the unconscious and its relation to consciousness. In the context of 19th-century German psychology, the unconscious was conceived as a "mental state in which representations (the contents of consciousness) exist effectively without the subject being able to apprehend them immediately."[12] Following this conceptualization, Fechner proposed a system of unconscious phenomena in which "the unconscious is a state of consciousness resulting from the isolation of representational activity from the rest of psychic life." Rather than an opposition between the conscious and the unconscious mental phenomena, Fechner understands the latter as "unattended mental states that behave autonomously while remaining able to act on consciousness." For Fechner, the existence of unconscious phenomena is revealed through the "influence that they have on the unfolding of conscious life"—it is through unconscious associative processes that perception is shaped and coloured.[13] Fechner's theory focusses on the ways in which unconscious cognition shapes conscious thought with the corollary of this assumption being that "there is fundamentally no difference of nature between the conscious and the unconscious" since "every cognitive function can be performed unconsciously."[14] Fechner also coined the concept of the "wave" that can be studied spatially and temporally to analyse psychophysical activity. Using this theoretical representation, Fechner distinguished between the upper and lower waves. Borrowing the concept of the threshold from Herbart, Fechner created a typology that describes the movement of the upper and lower wave in relation to the threshold in order to explain the origin of the various states of consciousness.[15] His contribution also extends to empirical observations that pertain to psychical phenomena and representational life occurring during sleep. These investigations were, in Romand's words, "the first systematic attempts to prove empirically the existence of unconscious mental phenomena."[16] Fechner's premises, Romand continues, "should be interpreted as being an early model of cognitive unconscious or unconscious cognition."[17]

The first literary writer to use the term "stream of consciousness" was Matthew Arnold in *Culture and Anarchy* (1869).[18] But it was not until May Sinclair's review of the first three novels of Dorothy Richardson's *Pilgrimage* series that the term was used as a technique in a literary-critical context.[19] However, as Suzanne Raitt points out, Sinclair might not have borrowed the term directly from James since the phrase was widely used in the early 20th century with many of the works Sinclair references in *Mary Olivier* and *A Defence of Idealism* employing the term.[20] A long-time member of the Society for Psychical Research, Sinclair was introduced to Herbart by Dorothea Bealea, an early mentor at Cheltenham Ladies College.[21] Sinclair, in agreement with James, found the creative force of individual consciousness to lie in its unity:

> say that consciousness is nothing but a stream, and that though it appears to have islands in it, the islands are really only part of the stream; still the stream would not be a stream if it had not a certain unity.[22]

The islands in this passage provide the very unity that is represented by the "substantive parts" in James's metaphor of perching. In her attempt to establish the unity of consciousness, Sinclair, like Herbart, examined the role of the unconscious. She integrated into her discussion Pierre Janet's theory that the dissociation of an idea from the stream of consciousness is the cause of mental illness and concluded that the stream is the outcome of unconscious processes reworking the material before bringing it up to consciousness:

> if we are to keep the image of consciousness as a "stream" we had better say that [they] sink to the bottom and stay there until some eddy in the deep stirs them up again. You can reverse the image [...] and think of consciousness as some city of the sea, raised on land partly submerged, partly reclaimed from the sea; a sea that threatens perpetually to overflow the thresholds of its palaces.[23]

Sinclair argues that the stream of consciousness metaphor created many problems because it didn't sufficiently represent the complexities involved in the formation of a unified self. The metaphor used to describe consciousness should incorporate what lies under the stream, although, evidently, Sinclair adopted the term despite her scepticism. Dorothy Richardson objected to Sinclair's use of the stream of consciousness metaphor to describe her work because she felt that the term does not suggest depth sufficiently. She promoted instead the notions of "a pool, a sea, an ocean" and "a fountain."[24] These metaphors were deemed more accurate because they reflected "greater depth [...] and when you give yourself up to one current you are suddenly possessed by another."[25] The "fountain," as we have seen in Chapter 2, was the main metaphor used by D.H. Lawrence to describe the unconscious, pointing at the possibility that Richardson is paying homage to his work. Richardson also suggested the image of a tree as an alternative metaphor, whose "central core, *luminous* point, [...] though more or less continuously expanding from birth to maturity, remains stable, one with itself throughout life."[26] The conscious mind is entwined with the unconscious. The two can hardly be conceived as separate: they are "one," with the unconscious being the "central core," the "luminous point" of the tree. It should also be noted that the adjective "luminous" also appears in Virginia Woolf's essay "Modernist Fiction" as the "luminous halo," an aspect to which we will return below.[27] What is important to note for our current purposes is that both Sinclair and Richardson felt that the stream metaphor was better discarded, since it did not readily convey how consciousness is shaped by the depths of the stream.

The primacy of the unconscious in shaping thought was also expressed by Wyndham Lewis in *Time and Western Man* (1927). His assessment of the "theory of Sensa" in Alexander Bain, Bertrand Russell and William James involves a treatment of the unconscious processing of our environment. "The sensa-world," according to Lewis, is the "world of the Unconscious," of things that "we do not explicitly notice, which we *repress* and push down and away, out of sight, and which throng our sense-field." Together, they form what Lewis refers to as "the stream of sensations that pour in." Lewis's water metaphor is not accidental. It bears homage to James's formulation of the stream of consciousness, which, for Lewis, should be more accurately termed "the stream of unconsciousness": "*the stream of unconsciousness* would be a better way of putting James' *stream of consciousness*." This is because, according to Lewis, "we are not conscious of this inrush, but only of its accommodation to the waiting forms of cognition, the 'physical objects' that it feeds." In the "*stream of the Unconscious*," Lewis continues, "we are once more invited to plunge."[28]

Acknowledging his debt to Fechner for the metaphor of the wave and the "threshold,"[29] James asserted that what appears to consciousness depends on the height of the threshold: "When it falls, as in states of great lucidity, we grow conscious of things of which we should be unconscious at other times; when it rises, as in drowsiness, consciousness sinks in amount."[30] The unconscious is depicted as the cognizing mechanism and the more it emerges in consciousness the more clarity and awareness it provides. The threshold represents an obstruction to our thinking capacity, which "may, in our brains, grow alternately greater or less."[31] Therefore, the reason why we only gain some moments of lucidity is because "the threshold throughout nature in general is very high." James related the "subliminal self"—to use Myer's definition— and the revelation it ensues, to an "influx" that "well describes this impression of new insight, or new willingness, sweeping over us like a tide."[32] In line with his belief in the physical origin of thought, James treated sensory perception as an indication of a "greater life" that remains largely hidden from us:

it seems to the subjects themselves of the experience as if a power from without, quite different from the ordinary action of the senses or of the sense-led mind, came into their life, as if the latter suddenly opened into that greater life in which it has its source.[33]

The unconscious, as the "mother-sea" of thought, stirs up waves and wakes consciousness into existence. Expanding on Fechner's wave metaphor, James compared the brain to a dam or threshold whose height varies, so that when it is elevated, consciousness is widened:

> We need only suppose the continuity of our consciousness with a mother–sea, to allow for exceptional waves occasionally pouring over the dam. Of course the causes of these odd lowerings of the brain's threshold still remain a mystery on any terms.[34]

In "The Consciousness of Self" James identified the stream as "the Self," and focussed on the section of the stream that is "identified in an altogether peculiar degree, and is felt by all men as a sort of innermost centre within the circle, of sanctuary within the citadel, constituted by the subjective life as a whole" (*PP* 285). In this passage, James described the portion of the stream of consciousness that lies under the stream which is removed from the watching consciousness. He noted that we should call it an "unconscious consciousness," and due to its pivotal role in thought, he identified it as the "central nucleus of the Self" (*PP* 286). This word-choice is echoed in Lawrence's description of the unconscious as the core of being: "The inherent unconscious, or soul, is the first nucleus subdivided, and from its own subdivisions produced, from its own still-creative constellated nuclei, the organs, glands, nerve-centers of the human organism" (*PFU* 33). James related the awareness of its existence to an awareness that is "*felt*; just as the body is felt." The "unconscious consciousness" is also "something with which we also have direct sensible acquaintance, and which is as fully present at any moment of consciousness" (*PP* 286). It is therefore the part of the stream which ensures the sense of continuity in consciousness. As James noted, consciousness itself is formed by waves that keep "pouring over the dam."[35] It is the unconscious that creates the sense of a continuous stream: "such consciousness as this, whatever it be for the onlooking psychologist, is for itself unbroken. It *feels* unbroken" (*PP* 231). As we saw in Chapter 2, James argued that these important relations, transitions or "flights" connect experience and provide a sense of continuity.

As indicated above, James distinguished between consciousness and the "self of selves." He placed the latter at the core of thought, clarifying at the same time the specific nature of the stream of consciousness. The stream of thought is the process responsible for the types of experience we undergo, it chooses from the outside world what will form a sense of "self" and discards the rest as "not-Self." These spontaneous acts evade any sense of conscious control: we are not aware of the *"things experienced* at the moment; this knowing is not immediately *known"* (*PP* 290). James asserted that we only become aware of our experiences "in subsequent reflection," concluding that:

> Instead, then, of the stream of thought being one of *con*-sciousness, "thinking its own existence along with whatever else it thinks," [...] it might better be called a stream of *Scious*ness pure and simple, thinking objects of some of which it makes what it calls a "Me" [...] The sciousness in question would be the *Thinker*, and the existence of this thinker would be given to us rather as a logical postulate than as that direct inner perception of spiritual activity which we naturally believe ourselves to have.
>
> (*PP* 291)

Since we are incapable of immediate knowledge, James was led to assume the existence of an independent thinker within the self-same subject. The need to make this distinction is caused by the realization that the stream of consciousness metaphor does not readily suggest the fact that there is no direct sense of self or control of the thinking process. This unconscious mechanism, taking the form of a separate self, is what James defined as "sciousness." Like Sinclair and Richardson, he stressed the fact that the stream of consciousness metaphor could be misleading as it may suggest an element of control over thought, or the impression that one can be directly aware of the thinking process as it occurs. "Sciousness," on the other hand, conveys the existence of an autonomous *"Thinker,"* as it reveals the independence of this "logical" mechanism and denies any implications of conscious thinking. The reason is the primary component of this thinking mechanism: "Each 'section' of the stream would then be a bit of sciousness or knowledge of this sort" (*PP* 291).

Expanding on the ways that the unconscious provides continuity and direction to the stream of thought, James distinguished between words and their meaning. He asserted that meaning is not inherent in words, and that it is not accessible to direct examination. Rather, it can only be felt or intuited. Since words are not the vehicle, or medium of expression, James attempted to locate their difference:

> What makes that meaning different in one phrase from what it is in the other? "Who?" "When?" "Where?" Is the difference of felt meaning in these interrogatives nothing more than their differences of sound? And is it not (just like the difference of sound itself) known and understood in an affection of consciousness correlative to it, though so impalpable to direct examination?
>
> (*PP* 244)

Meanings of words are, according to James, mental accompaniments of the words, notable as feelings of direction which lead our thinking towards other words, images or actions. He therefore related the meaning of words to the transitive rather than the substantive parts of thought:

> *The sense of our meaning is an entirely peculiar element of thought.* It is one of those evanescent and "transitive" facts of mind which introspection cannot turn round upon, and isolate and hold up for examination [...] In the somewhat clumsy terminology I have used, it pertains to the "fringe" of the subjective state, and is a "feeling of tendency," whose neural counterpart is undoubtedly a lot of dawning and dying processes too faint and complex to be traced.
>
> (*PP* 446)

Meanings are located at the fringe of awareness and are thus only dimly intuited, minimally describable as "bare images of logical movement" (*PP* 244).[36] When we think we are caught in the sweep of our consciousness and are fully conscious of words. We are nevertheless less vividly aware of the fringe of words or the felt direction of thinking. This is what gives continuity to thought—the racing ahead without pausing until it reaches a terminal point—which is like algebra in that we do not interpret words one after another but understand them collectively when a sentence is completed. In other words, it is this unconscious structure or "sciousness" that provides continuity to thought.

Summing up his basic convictions on the stream, James emphasized that "tendencies" are "among the *objects* of the stream, which is thus aware then from within, and must be described as in very large measure constituted of *feeling of tendency*, often so vague that we are unable to name them at all" (*PP* 246). Subliminal processes actively forge the paths and directions or "streams" that conscious thought follows. The use of various terms by James to describe the role of the unconscious or semi-conscious in thought has also been pointed out by Joseph Hart: "*Felt meaning, lingering consciousness, feelings of tendency, the fringes, overtones* of consciousness are all phrases pointing toward what clinicians now call the preconscious or unconscious."[37] He stated his objective, which was to illuminate the dim regions of our thought: "It is in short, the re-instatement of the vague to its proper place in our mental life which I am so anxious to press on the attention" (*PP* 246). He also related the stream to the unconscious and accused psychologists of having overlooked its pivotal importance:

> It is just this free water of consciousness that psychologists resolutely overlook. Every definite image in the mind is steeped and dyed in the free water that flows round it. With it goes the sense of its relations, near and remote, the dying echo of whence it came to us, the

dawning sense of whither it is to lead. The significance, the value, of the image is all in this halo or penumbra that surrounds and escorts it,—or rather that is fused into one with it and has become bone of its bone and flesh of its flesh; leaving it, it is true, an image of the same thing it was before, but making it an image of that thing newly taken and freshly understood.

(*PP* 246)

In this passage, James summarized the ways that the stream shapes thought. It provides the sense of direction and continuity, "the dying echo of whence it came to us, the dawning sense of whither it is to lead" (*PP* 246). For James, whatever is of value and importance to thought lies in processes that are impossible to grasp consciously while they occur.

The Cognitive Streams of Unconsciousness in Woolf's Diaries, Letters and Essays

Just like Lawrence, Woolf questioned the scientific validity of psycho-analysis: "these Germans think it proves something—besides their own gull-like imbecility" (*3LV* 134–5). As Jouve asserted, "her own writing seems to bear no trace of what might be called an influence. Searching the letters and journals for signs of admiration or informed knowledge, one encounters instead ironic or dismissive asides."[38] Woolf's reaction to psychoanalysis is recounted in James Strachey's letter to Alix Strachey after a dinner with the Woolfs: "Virginia made a more than usually ferocious onslaught upon psychoanalysis and psychoanalysts, more par-ticularly the latter."[39] By the late 20s, Woolf was the only member of the Bloomsbury group who refused the idea of being analysed.[40] According to Alix Strachey, she was concerned that psychoanalysis could be det-rimental to her creativity.[41] The satirical portrayal of psychiatrists in her fiction (like Holmes and Bradshaw in *Mrs Dalloway*) has also been related to her unpleasant experiences at the hands of Dr Savage and his colleague Sir William Gull.[42] In her review "Freudian Fiction," Woolf attacked J.D. Beresford's *An Imperfect Mother,* drawing a clear line be-tween the positivistic nature of psychoanalysis and the artistic insight into the human psyche:

> The triumphs of science are beautifully positive. But for novelists the matter is much more complex [...] Yes, says the scientific side of the brain, that [...] explains a great deal. No, says the artistic side of the brain, that is dull and has no human significance.

(*3E* 196–7)

Woolf was particularly interested in the workings of the unconscious. She expressed her interest in the unconscious at least as early as in 1905.

In an examination of her early diaries, for instance, Lounsberry points out that "Her 1905 ghostly, haunted Cornwall diary and the 1906 to 1908 Great Britain travel diary that follows it display her growing trust in her own unconscious as both reservoir and compositor."[43] In these diaries, "her growing embrace of the night-conscious—the unconscious" takes up properties that she would elaborate later on in her non-fictional writings, "the first diary [has] signs of unwilled, spontaneous invention and, in 1907, of her 'scene-making' gift."[44] Woolf regarded the unconscious as one of modernism's most compelling subjects:

> For the moderns "that," the point of interest, lies very likely in the dark places of psychology. At once, therefore, the accent falls a little differently; the emphasis is upon something hitherto ignored; at once a different outline of form becomes necessary.[45]

She understood the unconscious in the context of contemporary non-Freudian psychological theories. For Woolf, this preoccupation created a need for technical developments in literature that would adequately address this "hitherto ignored" concept.[46]

Woolf expressed the need for formal innovations in fiction in her famous essay "Mr. Bennett and Mrs. Brown." In a controversial statement, Woolf asserted that "on or about December, 1910, human character changed," and conveyed the need for fiction to change in order to accommodate itself to a modern selfhood (3E 421).[47] Her pursuit for an adequate way to represent "Mrs Brown" is established as counter to the attempts of Arnold Bennett and other realists who tried to uncover the mystery of subjectivity by focussing on the public self of the characters (1E 319–37). Woolf, like Lawrence, stressed the need to establish a new modern consciousness that represents effectively a more elusive and less consciously known sense of self. Her aim was to allow access to the unconscious self beneath the restricted contents that lie on the surface of consciousness. Woolf's statement in *A Writer's Diary* that Lawrence "and I have too much in common—the same pressure to be ourselves," is particularly pertinent here.[48] They shared a belief that the vital aspects of the self lie in a realm to which a writer must try to gain access if s/he wants to describe the full spectrum of the psyche.

The serious attention that Woolf gave to Lawrence's work is well known. Within one year of his death in 1930, she read *Sons and Lovers*, *The Man Who Died*, and her friend Aldous Huxley's edition of Lawrence's letters.[49] There are references to him in her diaries and she wrote two essays that include discussions of Lawrence: "Notes on D. H. Lawrence" and "The Leaning Tower."[50] In "Notes on D. H. Lawrence," Woolf showed awareness of his psychology books and specifically of the terminology used in them. She also praised his fiction as "fuller of life than one could have thought real life could be."[51] Just like Lawrence,

Woolf related the body to the unconscious and embraced its role as the origin of inspiration. In her essay "On Being Ill," she criticized the tendency in literature to ignore the role of the body, or even worse to treat it as a "sheet of plain glass" (*5E* 195). Instead, she stressed that "the very opposite is true. All day, all night the body intervenes; blunts or sharpens, colours or discolours" (*5E* 195). Through the use of active verbs to describe the operations of the body, Woolf suggests the existence of an autonomous mechanism always shaping our life in ways that we are unable to perceive and control. Echoing Lawrence's theoretical writings on the bodily unconscious, she expressed the need for a new philosophy: "To look these things squarely in the face would need the courage of a lion tamer; a robust philosophy; a reason rooted in the bowels of the earth" (*5E* 195–6). She proposed a return to the body and its passions for the regeneration of literature:

> Yet it is not only a new language that we need, more primitive, more sensual, more obscene, but a new hierarchy of the passions; love must be deposed in favor of a temperature of 104; jealousy give place to the pangs of sciatica; sleeplessness play the part of villain, and the hero become a white liquid with a sweet taste.
>
> (*5E* 196)

The drama of the body held a tangible and truer representation of life. In illness, when the senses and the body dominate and "the lights of health go down," Woolf described the "astonishing" spiritual changes that take place (*5E* 195). She cherished these states since they provide insights impossible to attain in full consciousness. Illness became for her a chance to bring unconscious thoughts to the surface and, in Woolf's words, those "Undiscovered countries that are then disclosed" (*5E* 195). She encapsulated this experience in a telling and resonant phrase—"Left to ourselves we speculate thus carnally"—revealing our unconscious mode of thinking that is intensified in illness (*5E* 201).

In the same essay, Woolf commented on the nature of words in this state of unconsciousness drawing a distinction that is highly reminiscent of James's own distinction between the sound of words and their meaning. This distinction is vital as it assumes the relation of the unconscious to the meaning of words that provide continuity to the stream of consciousness and allow thinking to move forward. James found the intuitive meaning of words to be inextricably linked to the transitive parts that enable thought despite the fact that we cannot be fully aware of the cognitive process that takes place at the time of the utterance. Woolf expanded on the quality that words take in unconsciousness:

> In illness words seem to possess a mystic quality. We grasp what is beyond their surface meaning, gather instinctively this, that, and the

other—a sound, a colour, here a stress, there a pause which the poet, knowing words to be meagre in comparison with ideas, has strewn about his page to evoke, when collected, a state of mind which neither words can express nor the reason explain [...] In health meaning has encroached upon sound. Our intelligence domineers over our senses. But in illness, with the police off duty, we creep beneath some obscure poems by Mallarme or Donne, some phrase in Latin or Greek, and the words give out their scent and distil their flavour, and then, if at last we grasp the meaning, it is all the richer for having come to us sensually first, by way of the palate and the nostrils, like some queer odour.

(5E 201–2)

Woolf shifts our attention from physical illness to the illness of the sign; she criticizes the linguistic medium as being limited to a "surface meaning." She further advocates the revelation of an inner truth in the world that can only be known instinctively. In illness, the body allows sense to domineer and words to become disentangled from their sound and reach closer to ideas. When unconscious, one can reach out sensually to the world allowing a different mode of perception that cannot be easily attained when we think with our conscious mind. As Woolf noted, inducing this state is very difficult, and even if one succeeds it doesn't last for long. It requires greater effort than in illness, when the body naturally overshadows the mental processes. Woolf celebrated this state because it unveils facets of experience otherwise hidden, creating a meaningful dialogue between self and world. The body enables an immediacy that contributes to the conveyance of meaning sensually, in a manner that "neither words can express nor the reason explain" (5E 202). The unconscious enlivens the sheer qualitative immediacy of felt experience. Grasping "obscure poems" or "some phrase in Latin or Greek" also requires an unconscious comprehension that takes the form of a sensual reading response (5E 202). Her diaries include numerous references to the revelatory powers of unconscious cognitive processes: "I believe these illnesses are in my case—how shall I express it? — partly mystical" (3D 287). Her challenge as a writer was to represent adequately the multiplicity of her bodily sensations: "what a little I can get down with my pen of what is so vivid to my eyes, & not only to my eyes: also to some nervous fibre or fan like membrane in my spine" (3D 191). The corporeal process of writing entailed meticulous attention to the manifestations of her body as it becomes evident from recordings of various bodily symptoms produced by her books (4D 143). Her diaries stress the active role of the body that in some cases interrupts or aids writing; "interventions" that Woolf favoured as she refused to use the typewriter (3LV 507).

In her essays, Woolf spelled out her understanding of the thinking processes, while her word-choices and theory of the "life of the mind" bespeak a substantial Jamesian influence. In her discussion of Hardy's fiction, Woolf noted:

> As we read *Jude the Obscure* we are not rushed to a finish; we brood and ponder and drift away from the text in plethoric trains of thought which build up round the characters an atmosphere of question and suggestion of which they are themselves, as often as not, unconscious.[52]

Commenting on the reading process, Woolf asserted that thinking takes place, for the most part, in the unconscious, which she related to the "trains of thought." Recalling James's discussion of the "train of thought," Woolf stressed the pivotal role that the unconscious plays in thinking. In her essay "On Not Knowing Greek," Woolf noted that Aeschylus managed to offer "in some mysterious way a general force, a symbolic power" to his dramas by

> Connecting them [words] in a rapid flight of the mind we know instantly and instinctively what they mean, but could not decant that meaning afresh into any other words. There is an ambiguity which is the mark of the highest poetry; we cannot know exactly what it means [...] The meaning is just on the far side of language. It is the meaning which in moments of astonishing excitement and stress we perceive in our minds without words; it is the meaning that Dostoevsky [...] leads us to by some astonishing run up the scale of emotions and points at but cannot indicate.[53]

Here, Woolf used another Jamesian metaphor: the "flight of the mind" that describes the unconscious mental processes. She also related it to an instant and instinctive mode of comprehending that surrounds words with a sense of ambiguity that takes them to the limits of language. She considered the attempt to express the ineffable as the attribute of great literature. Woolf commented that the Greek classics embarked "to be writers to the extreme; to attain that unconsciousness which means that the consciousness is stimulated to the highest extent."[54] Consciousness is the tip of the iceberg, a small portion of the unconscious, emerging above the threshold. This view undermines the commonly held belief that reasoning lies in consciousness.

Commenting on Dostoevsky's "The Eternal Husband," Woolf once again adopted the terminology employed by James. She elaborated upon the relation between conscious and unconscious processes, suggesting a continuity of the two systems that together form an information processing system, a stream of consciousness forged in the recesses of the unconscious mind:

Velchaninov, as he broods over the bloodstained razor, passes over his involved and crowded train of thought, without a single hitch, just, in fact, as we ourselves are conscious of thinking when some startling fact has dropped into the pool of our consciousness [...] From the crowd of objects pressing upon our attention we select now this one, now that one, weaving them inconsequently into our thought [...] and the whole process seems both inevitable and perfectly lucid. But if we try to construct our mental processes later, we find that the links between one thought and another are submerged. The chain is sunk out of sight and only the leading points emerge to mark the course. Alone among writers Dostoevsky has the power of reconstructing those most swift and complicated states of mind, of rethinking the whole train of thought in all its speed, now as it flashes into light, now as it lapses into darkness; for he is able to follow not only the vivid streak of achieved thought, but to suggest the dim and populous underworld of the mind's consciousness where desires and impulses are moving blindly beneath the sod. Just as we awaken ourselves from a trance of this kind by striking a chair or a table to assure ourselves of an external reality, so Dostoevsky suddenly makes us behold, for an instant, the face of his hero, or some object in the room. This is the exact opposite of the method adopted, perforce, by most of our novelists. They reproduce all the external appearances—tricks of manner, landscape, dress, and the effect of the hero upon his friends but very rarely, and only for an instant, penetrate to the tumult of thought which rages within his own mind [...] Intuition is the term which we should apply to Dostoevsky's genius at its best.

(2E 85–6)

In this passage, Woolf's detailed analysis of mental processes proposed that the impression of discontinuity in thought is caused by the sudden emergence of the unconscious in consciousness. Just like James, she supported the view that thought is in fact continuous, but "the links between one thought and another are submerged." What we may consciously feel as discontinuity is therefore an illusion. The unconscious is not simply a passive recipient of external impressions, but a cognitive agent that actively shapes thought. Woolf described the "involved and crowded train of thought" as a "trance" that takes the form of involuntary thinking.[55] Woolf provided another example of the way in which the unconscious directs thought. She described the way "we select now this one, now that one" as inevitable and lucid. Our perception and attention to a certain object is therefore defined by our unconscious in ways that we are unable to control. Woolf explored the workings of this mechanism. After presenting Dostoyevsky as a master in grasping "these most swift and complicated states of mind," she expressed her intention to render in her writings "the dim and populous underworld of the mind's consciousness." Woolf admitted that the only guide to this underworld was "intuition" which was also, for her, a mark of literary genius.

Woolf admired Proust as a psychological writer because he created characters "made of a different substance. Thoughts, dreams, knowledge are part of them" (5E 67). In a remark very telling of her own fiction, and particularly of the characters that emerge from *The Waves*, Woolf commented on Proust's characters: "It is from these depths that his characters rise, like waves forming, then break and sink again into the moving sea of thought and comment and analysis which gave them birth" (5E 67). Using again the water metaphor to describe the unconscious, Woolf envisaged fictional characters as waves rising from the unconscious reservoir of perception. Exemplifying again her conviction that the unconscious has the power to "make patterns; by its power to bring relations in things," she stressed its formative role: "The mind cannot be content with holding sensation after sensation passively to itself; something must be done with them; their abundance must be shaped" (5E 65, 67).

Woolf's endorsement of the techniques which Thomas De Quincey used to liberate the reader's unconscious is also of pertinent importance,[56] as it bespeaks her own approach towards literary writing:

> If we try to analyse our sensations we shall find that we are worked upon as if by music—the senses are stirred rather than the brain [...] Our minds, thus widened and lulled to a width of apprehension, stand open to receive one by one in slow and stately procession the ideas which De Quincey wishes us to receive [...] The emotion is never stated; it is suggested and brought slowly by repeated images before us until it stays, in all its complexity, complete.[57]

In this passage, Woolf stressed the importance of sensual perception in enabling unconscious cognition. By emphasizing the imagist dimension of language, the writer succeeds in extending our cognitive capacities and creating a "width of apprehension." Woolf embraced De Quincey's techniques of evoking emotion in the reader, through the use of "repeated images before us until it stays." She realized that her wish to freeze consciousness and liberate the reader's unconscious could be achieved by stirring the emotions establishing therefore a communion between the two egos.

Woolf's discussions of these literary authors are indicative of her belief in the contribution of unconscious cognition in the process of reading. In "How Should One Read a Book?" she highlighted the unconscious comprehension in reading as a distinct stage, prior to conscious understanding:

The first process, to receive impressions with the utmost understanding, is only half the process of reading; it must be completed,
if we are to get the whole pleasure from a book, by another. We
must pass judgment upon these multitudinous impressions; we must
make of these fleeting shapes one that is hard and lasting. But not
directly. Wait for the dust of reading to settle; for the conflict and
the questioning to die down; walk, talk, pull the dead petals from
a rose, or fall asleep. Then suddenly without our willing it, for it is
thus that Nature undertakes these transitions, the book will return,
but differently. It will float to the top of the mind as a whole.[58]

In this passage, Woolf understands the unconscious as a mechanism
that has the ability to "pass judgement" and form conclusions out of
"multitudinous impressions." She proposed an unconscious immersion
into the book followed by a time lapse after which assumptions emerge
"without our willing it," and "float to the top of the mind." Woolf
used James's metaphor of the transitive states and of consciousness
as a stream through her repeated figuration of the unconscious as a
submerged world. She located the cognitive process of reading in the
unconscious, while consciousness is depicted as passively waiting for
the judgements to float up to the top of the mind. Accordingly, Woolf
envisioned the existence of two distinct mental processes: the unconscious performs judgements and consciousness takes up the role of articulation. And in her diary she described the ideal reading process
as turning into an unconscious reading engine: "What a joy what a
sense as of a Rolls Royce engine once more purring its 70 miles an
hour in my brain" (4D 142). She also related reading to a feeling of
flying: "When one reads the mind is like an aeroplane propeller invisibly quick and unconscious," (5D 151) and "heaven must be one
continuous unexhausted reading. Its a disembodied trance-like intense
rapture" (4D 142).

The involvement of unconsciousness propelled Woolf's "flood of cre-
ativeness." When she was planning *The Pargiters*, she was "in sublime
reading fettle [...] at the height of my powers in that line [...] all books
become fluid & swell the stream" (4D 142). Woolf suggested the way
that reading is assimilated in this "sublime" process, reworked in a way
that defies clear distinctions, and finally, pushed "the stream" to the surface of the mind. In *A Room of One's Own*, Woolf commented, "it is in
our idleness, in our dreams, that the submerged truth sometimes comes
to the top" (RO 40). In "Craftsmanship," she expressed the need for an
unconscious assimilation of words in order to move below their surface
meaning: "In reading we have to allow the sunken meanings to remain
sunken, suggested, not stated; lapsing and flowing into each other like
reeds on the bed of a river."[59] And in "The Cherry Orchard" Woolf singled out the emotions as a way to grasp the workings of this submerged

world: "we seemed to have sunk below the surface of things and to be feeling our way among submerged but recognisable emotions" (3E 248).

For Woolf reading comprehension should be interchangeable with the creative process. The "quickest way to understand [...] what a novelist is doing is not to read," she asserted, "but to write"; and "the time to read poetry" is "when we are almost able to write it" (5E 574, 577). Accordingly, Woolf's ideas on the creative process reflect the ways in which readers should approach and receive her writings. "The Leaning Tower" includes Woolf's analysis of the mental processes that take place during the creative process. Literary inspiration, according to Woolf, does not emanate from any conscious mental effort. Rather, it emerges when the "upper mind drowses":

> Unconsciousness, which means presumably that the under-mind works at top speed while the upper-mind drowses, is a state we all know. We all have experience of the work done by unconsciousness in our own daily lives. You have had a crowded day, let us suppose, sightseeing in London. Could you say what you had seen and done when you came back? Was it not all a blur, a confusion? But after what seemed a rest a chance to turn aside and look something different, the sights and sounds and sayings that had been of most interest to you swam to the surface, apparently of their own accord; and remained in memory; what was unimportant sank into forgetfulness. So it is with the writer. After a hard day's work, trudging round, seeing all he can, feeling all he can, taking in the book of his mind innumerable notes, the writer becomes—if he can—unconscious. In fact, his under mind works at top speed while his upper mind drowses. Then, after a pause the veil lifts; and there is the thing—the thing he wants to write about—simplified, composed. Do we strain Wordsworth's famous saying about emotion recollected in tranquillity when we infer that by tranquillity he meant that the writer needs to become unconscious before he can create?[60]

Woolf began by drawing a distinction between two cognitive systems: "the under-mind" and the "upper-mind." Her belief in the existence of an under and an upper mind places her within the context of psychologists who postulated the existence of a threshold that erects a division in the mind between conscious and unconscious cognitive processes. Woolf privileged the latter as it singles out significant perceptions, draws conclusions and then allows them to swim to the surface, "apparently of their own accord." Within this framework, "Unconsciousness [...] is necessary if writers are to get beneath the surface, and to write something that people remember when they are alone."[61] What a writer needs is to spend some time in tranquillity and have a time lapse during which the "under mind works at top speed" and then successfully overcomes the restrictions of consciousness.

The articulation of these unconscious processes onto the page also implicates the upper mind. Referring to the male writers of the 1930s, Woolf noted that if they aspire to produce lasting literary works they have to find how to lower the threshold and allow unconscious inspiration to enter consciousness:

> During all the most impressionable years of their lives they were stung into consciousness—into self-consciousness, into class-consciousness, into the consciousness of things changing [...] The inner mind was paralysed because the surface mind was always hard at work. [...] they have lacked the creative power of the poet and the novelist, the power—does it come from a fusion of the two minds, the upper and the under?—that creates characters that live, poems that we all remember.[62]

In "Professions for Women," Woolf again asserted that the ideal condition for writing is "a state of perpetual lethargy." To achieve this unconsciousness the writer needs a sense of regularity, to live with the illusion that nothing changes in order to enable the "sudden discoveries of that very shy and illusive spirit, the imagination." Confiding her own writing habits, she admitted that she usually remains in a state of trance for hours without dipping into the inkpot. In her attempt to convey the feeling of this mental state the only image that she finds apt is the "image of a fisherman lying sunk in dreams on the verge of a deep lake with a rod held out over the water." The trope of the water as the unconscious shows that for Woolf—and indeed for James—the stream of sciousness becomes the driving force of thought. The independence of sciousness is again shown in the image of the fisherman who skilfully sets up the night conditions and patiently waits to hook what lies beneath the surface of the water. In this submerged world the imagination starts to "sweep unchecked round every rock and cranny of the world that lies submerged in the depths of our unconscious being." The moment of sudden revelation is evocatively described as the capture of an elusive entity:

> The line raced through the girl's fingers. Her imagination had rushed away. It had sought the pools, the depths, the dark places where the largest fish slumber. And then there was a smash. There was an explosion. There was foam and confusion. The imagination had dashed itself against something hard. The girl was roused from her dream.[63]

Woolf also hinted at the importance of letters in revealing the unconscious recesses of her writing. In her request to Ethel Smyth to quote letters in her book, Woolf wrote that "they often shed a whole cuttle fish bag of suggestion" (5LV 354). Her letters bespeak the difficulty she faced in her attempt to represent reality and tinge the affects of the reader:[64] "how can one weight and sharpen dialogue till each sentence tears its way like a harpoon and grapples with the shingles at the bottom of the reader's soul?" (*3LV* 36). This struggle is expressed in her diary as the need to form a new "being" or existence: "I have to some extent forced myself to break every mould & find a fresh form of being, that is of expression, for everything I feel & think" (*4D* 233). This new mode of being aims to incorporate the workings of the under-mind that Woolf considered vital to the creative process: "I dont think you can get your words to come till youre almost unconscious; and unconsciousness only comes when youve been beaten and broken and gone through every sort of grinding mill" (*5LV* 408). In line with James, Woolf asserted the impossibility to fully capture the unconscious processes and affirmed the need of suggestiveness in writing: "I shall see a light in the depths of the sea, and stealthily approach—for one's sentences are only an approximation, a net one flings over some sea pearl which may vanish; and if one brings it up it wont be anything like what it was when I saw it, under the sea" (*4LV* 223).

The diaries and letters disclose another strategy used by Woolf to reach unconsciousness, that of speedy writing. Woolf noted that she wrote her diary at a "rapid haphazard gallop," "rather faster than the fastest typewriting," and "if I stopped & took thought, it would never be written at all" (*1D* 233–4). Her advice to Clive Bell's letter-writing demonstrates that her own letters, just like her diaries, were written at a frantic speed: "you think more pains are needed than I do," and urged him to "put your style at the gallop" (*1LV* 362). "I dont think I've ever taken more time than it takes to form a word in writing to you," she confessed to Ethel Smyth (*6LV* 439). The minimal control that she aimed to have over her letter-writing is evident in her letter to Gerald Brenan, where she described it as "a mere tossing of omelettes [...] if they break and squash, can't be helped" (*3LV* 80). Woolf's tendency to regard any influence from the conscious mind as detrimental brings her letter and diary writing close to automatic writing. She confessed to Ethel Smyth that she could not rewrite a letter because it would be "stale" (*6LV* 78). Her letter to Pernel Strachey also bespeaks this belief: "I can only write, letters that is, if I don't read them: once think and I destroy" (*3LV* 63). However, Woolf's redrafting of her published work is well known. This "strain" was removed in her diaries and letters that offered her a "relief" at being able "to write a free sentence here" (*5D* 190). Her confession to John Lehmann that her aim in *The Waves* had been "to eliminate [...] myself" reveals a wish to develop in her novel-writing a similar technique to the one employed in her diaries and letters (*4LV* 381).

Woolf's most quoted essay, "Modern Fiction," demonstrates how her conception of the workings of the mind cut right through the heart of the novel's form:

Examine for a moment an ordinary mind on an ordinary day. The mind receives a myriad impressions—trivial, fantastic, evanescent, or engraved with the sharpness of steel. From all sides they come, an incessant shower of innumerable atoms; and as they fall, as they shape themselves into the life of Monday or Tuesday, the accent falls differently from of old; the moment of importance came not here but there [...] Life is not a series of gig lamps symmetrically arranged; life is a luminous halo, a semi–transparent envelope surrounding us from the beginning of consciousness to the end. Is it not the task of the novelist to convey this varying, this unknown and uncircumscribed spirit, whatever aberration or complexity it may display, with as little mixture of the alien and external as possible? [...] Let us record the atoms as they fall upon the mind in the order in which they fall, let us trace the pattern, however disconnected and incoherent in appearance, which each sight or incident scores upon the consciousness. Let us not take it for granted that life exists more fully in what is commonly thought big than in what is commonly thought small [...] Mr. Joyce is spiritual; he is concerned at all costs to reveal the flickerings of that innermost flame which flashes its messages through the brain [...] The scene in the cemetery, for instance, with its brilliancy, its sordidity, its incoherence, its sudden lightning flashes of significance, does undoubtedly come so close to the quick of the mind that, on a first reading at any rate, it is difficult not to acclaim a masterpiece [...] Any method is right, every method is right, that expresses what we wish to express, if we are writers; that brings us closer to the novelist's intention if we are readers. This method has the merit of bringing us closer to what we were prepared to call life itself; did not the reading of Ulysses suggest how much of life is excluded or ignored [...] He has to have the courage to say that what interests him is no longer "this" but "that": out of "that" alone must he construct his work. For the moderns "that," the point of interest, lies very likely in the dark places of psychology.[65]

Woolf asserted that the novelists' duty is to trace the ways that the "unknown or uncircumscribed spirit" shapes life. This spirit singles out from the "incessant shower of innumerable atoms" that fall on the mind moments of importance that serve its aesthetic or practical interests. Woolf's reference to an unconscious mechanism that decides whether the "moment of importance came not here but there" recalls James's analysis of the teleological nature of the unconscious. The notion of an unconscious shaping of objective reality is also evident in her belief in organic perception. The eye does not simply record objects but instead assumes a selective and structuring function that arranges and interiorizes reality. The phrase "life is a luminous halo, a semi-transparent envelope" echoes James's word-choices in "The Stream of Thought." "Halo" was also used repeatedly by James and, in some cases, alternatively with his concept of the "fringe" that surrounds consciousness (*PP* 246, 247, 251, 255, 260, 266, 271, 452). Her assertion that life lies in the "luminous halo" is suggestive of her belief that subjectivity itself is formed subliminally, in the halo of consciousness that surrounds and shapes it. Woolf stressed the need to explore this "unknown and uncircumscribed spirit, whatever aberration or complexity it may display" and study "the pattern" and its end-product that is thought. She provides as an example the writings of Joyce and his attempts "at all costs to reveal the flickerings of that innermost flame which flashes its messages through the brain." Joyce conveys life by recreating the very process of thought, that is, the impressions that fall on the mind along with the "lightning flashes of significance" brought forth by the unconscious. This method allows the reader to "feel" thought as it develops and instantly appreciate a quality that defies any conscious detailed analysis. Coming "so close to the quick of the mind" means that "on a first reading at any rate, it is difficult not to acclaim a masterpiece." Her "point of interest" lies in depicting how our multitudinous experience is shaped into thought and in exploring what "lies very likely in the dark places of psychology."

At the early stages of *The Waves*, Woolf declared her intention to present "the idea of some continuous stream." (3D 139) In order to achieve this continuity, Woolf avoided chapter divisions and chose "rhythm" instead for the structuring of the novel (3D 139).[66] Her intention to grasp and render in writing the unconscious mental life was a particularly strenuous one.[67] Woolf's letters testify to the pivotal role of the unconscious in this novel. Her conception of the conscious and unconscious as two distinct cognitive systems is exemplified in her insistence that the conscious mind should "lie asleep like a tideless sea" for the waves to form in the unconscious (3D 249). Thinking is imagined as a process whereby the currents lying under the stream emerge in consciousness as waves. Woolf suggested that a period of solitude is required for the thinking processes to take place, the ideal time for her is the "fertile hour after tea for hatching, planning" (4LV 222). To surmount all obstacles regarding the composition of *The Waves*, she would have to "take her writing board and let herself down like a diver very cautiously into the last sentence" (4LV 233). She sees "a light in the depths of the sea and stealthily approaches" for sentences are an approximation, a "net one flings over some sea pearls which may vanish" (4LV 223). Woolf's appreciation for the "pearls" lying in the unconscious prepares her to face the dangers of distortion lurking behind any attempt to translate unconscious thought into consciousness. The immersion in the unconscious gave her the feeling of "a fish in a stream; deflected; held in place; but cannot describe the stream."[68]

Woolf's comment upon the completion of the novel that she successfully "netted that fin in the waste of waters"[69] is indicative of the persistence of a Jamesian context in the conception of the unconscious. The water metaphor used both for the title of the work and for the creative process itself recalls the Jamesian description of the unconscious mental life as a stream. The metaphor of sea, water and waves to describe cognition is also dominant in *To the Lighthouse*. The novel is populated with references to the unconscious as a "current that flows" and the insights it provides as "dark weeds which grow at the bottom" that suddenly emerge in consciousness and "pound us with their waves" (W 116–7). The unconscious is not related simply to "passions" but also to "something deeper [...] and more subterranean" (W 117). Bernard is struggling throughout the novel with ways to grasp the nature of the stream, "the world that lies submerged in the depths of our unconscious being."[70] The unconscious is here related, as in D.H. Lawrence, to the fountain, the source of the stream of thought. Bernard describes it as an independent thinking mechanism lying in the subterranean parts of his being: "it is alive too and deep, this stream" (W 213). His conception of these cognitive operations provides us with a picture of thought formed outside of the conscious realm, at "the fringe of intelligence" (W 208) with only part of it successfully emerging in consciousness.

The Waves of Sciousness and Their Androgynous Currents

Woolf's conception of the cognitive unconscious has implications for her feminist project. It allowed her to see beyond sexual differentiation and form a rather radical theory of androgyny. The challenge she posed to the conscious/ unconscious dualism by investing the unconscious with reason is mirrored in her challenge to the male/female dualism. Her response to the essentialist position—that formulated psychological conclusions based on sexual differentiation—is another attempt to deconstruct dualities that obstruct free thinking. Woolf attempted to counter the essentialist discourse which assumed that women's social existence can be derived from their physiology.[71] Androgyny has become one of the main debates surrounding feminist criticism on Woolf. Some critics have described androgyny in Woolf's works as a balance between intuition and reason,[72] subjectivity and objectivity,[73] anima and animus,[74] manic-depression and sanity[75] and heterosexuality and homosexuality.[76] Others see androgyny as Woolf's way of reaching a mystical moment "of the oneness of mankind."[77] Archetype criticism has mainly used the concept of androgyny as Woolf's means of reconciling opposites.[78] Recent feminist critics have argued that androgyny seeks to eliminate female and male characteristics by fusing them together.[79] Mary Jacobus reads androgyny through psychoanalysis and deconstruction, and argues that it represents a "play of difference."[80]

Woolf's preoccupation with androgyny grew out of a fascination with the concept in 19th- and early 20th-century science. Authors like

Richard von Krafft-Ebing, Edward Carpenter, Havelock Ellis and Otto Weininger formulated theories about a third sex that embodied both masculine and feminine characteristics.[81] Carpenter identified androgyny as a psychic condition and related it to the artistic tendencies that characterize a third sex. His works were widely circulated both in Britain and America provoking "creative interpretation and appropriation."[82] Weininger, in his best-seller *Sex and Character*, asserted that each cell possesses varying amounts of Arrhenoplasm (male plasm) and Thelyplasm (female plasm), refusing to accept the existence of beings such as "man" and "woman." As Barbara Fassler noted, both Ellis and Carpenter were read by the Bloomsbury group and most members shared "the common belief that to be artistic one must have the unique combination of masculine and feminine elements found in hermaphrodites and homosexuals."[83] Woolf was aware of these sexual theories through her involvement with groups that repeatedly brought these ideas under scrutiny.[84] Despite the fact that these theorists helped Woolf think outside of the strict boundaries that distinguished between male and female, they still, with varying degrees, drew along the lines of biological essentialist binary thought.

Drawing conclusions about the mind based on the sexual organs was a common platform for many theorists of the time. The main exponents of this position that tended to support psychological differences based on the physiological form were, among others, Freud and C.G. Jung. Freud was thought to be a notorious supporter of the essentialist position which assumed that certain characteristics are fundamentally connected to one sex rather than to the other. Although a series of later Freud interpreters have complicated such readings of his work,[85] it is not difficult to see how one could arrive at this position, particularly in the light of passages from Freud's work where he claims, for instance, that

> psychoanalysis cannot elucidate the intrinsic nature of what in conventional or biological phraseology is termed "masculine" and "feminine": it simply takes over the two concepts and makes them the foundation of its work. When we attempt to reduce them further, we find masculinity vanishing into activity and femininity into passivity.[86]

Despite sharing the assumption of many biologists that the infant is bisexual,[87] he regarded sex differences as indisputable and natural. He also suggested that women were more prone to emotional excesses like masochism, hysteria and narcissism.[88] His aphorisms that "biology is destiny"[89] only furthered his prejudices and sexist assumptions; while his support of "the biological fact that of the duality of the sexes"[90] led him to maintain social constructs summed up in his account that: "Maleness combines (the factors of) subject, activity and possession of the penis, femaleness takes over (those of) object and passivity."[91] C.G. Jung also based his whole psychology on what he assumed to be an indisputable premise, namely, the existence of two opposed psychological models: the feminine and the masculine. The two primary archetypes of the unconscious mind—the anima and the animus—correspond to the female personality in the male unconscious and the masculine personality in the female unconscious respectively.[92]

Here I argue that Woolf's preoccupation with androgyny is an example of her attempts to deconstruct dualities. Her purpose was to offer a framework that would allow the cognitive potentials of the unconscious to be embraced and thus free the mind from dichotomies propounded as natural. The unconscious emerges as a force that can expand the cognitive potential of people by relieving them from restrictions of sexual differentiation. As in D.H. Lawrence, sex consciousness is identified with the ego while the unconscious becomes a way of re-establishing identity. She exposed the ego and its defining characteristic—gender—as socially constructed, a matter of imitation rather than an inherent set of attributes.[93] Her call for a liberation from gender was also connected to her wish to eliminate the extent to which ideas about gender influence the process of creating literary art. It is therefore no surprise to find that she created an abstract and impersonal voice, distinguished from "the damned egotistical self" (2D 13). Her desire to escape the "thick little ego" and form a voice that speaks as "we" or "one" could only be accomplished by overcoming the essentialist identity.[94] Her conceptualization of androgyny aimed to offer men and women the chance to write without consciousness of their sex—the result of which would ideally result in uninhibited creativity. In the "Foreword" to Vanessa Bell's 1930 exhibition catalogue, Woolf writes: "One says, 'Anyhow Mrs Bell is a woman'; and then half way round the room one says, 'But she may be a man.'"[95] For Woolf, the androgynous mind, that is inherent in artistic creation, has the capacity to overcome sex consciousness. Art and its relation to the unconscious emerge as a powerful means of re-establishing subjectivity and identity.

In *A Room of One's Own* Woolf underlined the role of the unconscious in artistic creation. The writer should "let the line of thought dip deep into the stream" so as to allow a bigger portion of the unconscious to come to the surface (RO 101). Woolf perceived the androgynous state of mind as a precondition for the unconscious cognitive process to take place: "The writer [...] must lie back and let his mind celebrate its nuptials in darkness" (RO 97). The unconscious is portrayed as "another self" that thinks separately, it is a process that must not be interrupted, controlled or altered by the conscious mind (O 294). In Woolf's words, "He must not look or question what is being done" (RO 97). She conceived the two thinking processes as really distinct and struggled with how to lower the threshold of consciousness in order to enrich her creative horizon. The same strain is evident in her diaries, where she asserted that a similar state of mind is required by the reader: "The whole of the mind must lie wide open if we are to get the sense that the writer is communicating his experience with perfect fullness."[96] For her, one needs to get in touch with his/her androgynous nature in order to produce truly original and lasting works of art.[97] In the same essay, for instance, she praises Mary Carmichael for her writing because she has

> mastered the first great lesson: she wrote as a woman, but as a woman who has forgotten that she is a woman, so that her pages [are] full of that curious sexual quality which comes only when sex is unconscious of itself.[98]

The same disposition is apparent in a letter to Ethel Smyth: "I believe unconsciousness, and complete anonymity to be the only conditions in which I can write. Not to be aware of oneself" (*5LV* 289). To be unconscious of oneself, to be completely anonymous, for Woolf, involves sex unconsciousness.

Even when "The imagination falters under the enormous strain" and "The insight is confused," Woolf denied that sex differences influence how one deals with mental strain: "how could all this be affected by the sex of the novelist" (*RO* 68). Woolf provided a personal experience of this state of mind: while being in a reverie, her imagination invested the surroundings with a "rhythmical order" allowing her to see through sex distinctions and perceive the young man and girl simply as "two people getting into a cab." She realized that thinking "of one sex as distinct from the other is an effort. It interferes with the unity of the mind." During this incident, she felt that "unity had been restored" and regarded it as the ideal state of mind for artistic creation (*RO* 90). Summing up the consequences of this event for human subjectivity, Woolf related it to "androgyny":

> in each of us two powers preside, one male, one female; and in man's brain the man predominates over the woman, and in the woman's brain the woman predominates over the man. The normal and comfortable state of being is that when the two live in harmony together, spiritually co-operating. If one is a man, still the woman part of his brain must have effect; and a woman also must have intercourse with the man in her. Coleridge perhaps meant this when he said that a great mind is androgynous. It is when this fusion takes place that the mind is fully fertilized and uses all its faculties.

> (*RO* 91–2)

Woolf envisioned the "man-womanly" and "woman-manly" mind that would eliminate the "stridently sex-conscious" society (*RO* 92). The androgynous quality of unconsciousness allowed the free play of imagination: "some collaboration has to take place in the mind between the woman and the man before the art of creation can be accomplished" (*RO* 97). She asserted that this way of "seeing" could last for more than a temporary reverie and deemed it possible that "one could continue without effort because nothing is required to be held back" (*RO* 91). According to Woolf, this unconscious state can be adopted permanently as it is the natural way of seeing the world.

It has become a common practice in Woolfian criticism to treat the unconscious as another word for femininity. Following Kristeva, many critics have connected Woolf's narrative forms and style to the rhythms of the body and the unconscious.[99] Taking a biographical approach, John R. Maze uses Freudian symbols to reveal Woolf's repressed sexual desires for her mother and her brother Thoby.[100] Susan Stanford Friedman looks into the textual unconscious that is found in the background of Woolf's final texts and drafts.[101] For Michèle Barrett, Woolf's problem of femininity is rooted at an unconscious level rather than in social convention.[102] In exploring Woolf's reaction to the Victorians, Gillian Beer sees Woolf as appreciating Ruskin's androgyny: "Fortunately, in the whimsical good sense of the unconscious, fathers can be mothers, and so in looking back through our mothers, as she says women must do, Ruskin may be among them."[103] Beer relates the unconscious to androgyny but her focus lies in Woolf's historically located subjectivity. In a lesbian approach to Woolf's work Jane Marcus claims that "Woolf's feeling for sexual difference privileges the female."[104] Melba Cuddy-Keane argues that Woolf's attitude towards bisexuality expresses her "openness to both conscious and unconscious processes"[105] Cuddy-Keane draws this conclusion from the following extract: "when it comes to saying that a poet should be bi-sexual, and that I think is what he was about to say, even I, who have had no scientific training whatsoever, draw the line and tell that voice to be silent."[106] Treating Woolf's objection to bisexuality as an indirect affirmation, Keane represents a common tendency to relate the unconscious with femininity which is precisely what the author tried to avoid.

Yet, Woolf's denial of "bisexuality" does not represent a peculiar way of expressing her view, as Keane argues, or an inadvertent reassertion of the gendered distinction she is trying to overcome, as per Daniel Harris's argument.[107] Instead, it reveals her anxiety to dissociate androgyny from physical sexuality and represent the idea of the androgynous writing mind. Woolf rejected bisexuality because it maintains sex distinctions and perpetuates the failure to convey a sex-transcendent androgyny. She proposed a theory of the mind dissociated from the realm of physical sexuality. The androgynous vision is inextricably related to the unconscious and the act of creation as "it transmits emotion without impediment; it is naturally creative, incandescent and undivided" (*RO* 92).

Expanding on the androgynous quality of the unconscious, Woolf clarified that it should not be treated as an idealized female attribute. In so doing, she diverged from traditional feminist writings. She treated the creativity of the unconscious as a universal quality of the mind that is not gender specific or related to "a mind that has any special sympathy with women; a mind that takes up their cause." For Woolf, these are habits of the single-sexed mind (*RO* 92). She asserted that "All who have brought about a state of sex-consciousness are to blame" (*RO* 96), attacked "the Suffrage campaign,"[108] and called for a society that does not distinguish between sexes but allows instead for a communion between androgynous individuals. Implied in her theory of the androgynous mind is that the elimination of sexual difference and the envisioning of androgynous individuals instantly cancels the notion of sexual preference and opens up the possibility of sexual intercourse with individuals regardless of their gender.[109] Literary productivity, for Woolf, can only ensue after a forgetfulness of sex. Relieved from essentialist dualities that generate the construct of sex, the mind can free the individual and be productive.

The Waves enacts the interplay of creativity and androgyny. The intricate connection between androgyny and creativity is exemplified through Bernard's multiplicity. "For this is not one life," Bernard notes, "nor do I always know if I am man or woman" (*W* 234). Woolf's comment "But I did mean that in some vague way we are the same person, and not separate people. The six characters were meant to be one" reinforces the idea of Bernard as an androgynous writer (*4LV* 397). As Bernard asserts: "I am not one and single, but complex and many" (*W* 61). That half of the characters are men (Neville, Louis, Percival) and half women (Susan, Jinny, Rhoda) bears further testimony to Bernard's androgyny. The merging of one character's speech into the other's "when these soliloquies [are] shared" (*W* 30), along with the stylistic and linguistic similarity of the dialogues, creates the impression of a single, androgynous speaking voice.[110] The shift to Bernard's soliloquy at the end of the novel confirms his multiple subjectivity by replacing polyphony with monophony. Bernard emerges as the master puppeteer and the originator of all the dialogues that develop between the rest of the characters. As he concludes: "We are not single, we are one" (*W* 53). This final act of "sum[ming] up" the lives of the six characters makes Bernard the author of an autobiography, indicating how androgyny is implicated with creativity. In Neville's words, "We are all phrases in Bernard's story, things he writes down in his notebook under A or under B" (*W* 55).

The effect of the unconscious quality of the stream is achieved by the rhythmical pattern that structures the novel. The merging of the speeches and the absence of any chapter divisions gives a sense of fluidity and allows the reader to submerge under the "continuous stream" (*3D* 139). Woolf stated her intention in the later stages of composition: she was "writing *The Waves* to a rhythm not to a plot" (*3D* 316). Rhythm became the structural pattern of the work that lulls the reader into the stream of unconsciousness. The link between the wave metaphor and the rhythmical pattern of the unconscious is apparent in Woolf's letter to Vita Sackville-West: "This is very profound what rhythm is and goes far deeper than words. A sight, an emotion, created this wave in the mind" (3LV 247). Woolf describes the creative process that takes place before words come into existence. In order to grasp the meaning of the work, the reader has to abandon the control of the upper mind and follow the rhythmical pattern. We are taken back to the process of creation when words are still unformulated and meaning emerges out of rhythm rather than the semantic content of the words.

Bernard relates his multiplicity to the rhythmical stream of unconsciousness: "The sound of the chorus came across the water" (W 232). However, he chooses to distance himself from this polyphony. As he notes, "I felt leap up that old impulse, which has moved me all my life" (W 232). Refusing to listen to the wave rhythm that has "moved" him all along Bernard will have to reassert himself on a different basis whereby consciousness will dominate his cognitive processes. Bernard conceives of the waves as a menacing force:

> I could not help letting fall the things that had made me a minute ago eager [...] into the water [...] I could not recover myself from that endless throwing away, dissipation, flooding forth [...] over the roughened water to become waves in the sea—I could not recover myself from that dissipation. So we parted
>
> (W 232, 233)

Characters, which represent aspects of his psyche, are identified as waves that move Bernard in every direction, disrupting his wish for strict sequence and linearity. His decision to separate himself from the stream has important implications for his creativity. Conceiving of the stream as a kind of death brings about his death as an author. In his own words, "Was this, then, this streaming away mixed with Susan, Jinny, Neville, Rhoda, Louis, a sort of death?" (W 233). The impersonality and loss of conscious control over one's mental operations seemed to Bernard as "a sort of death." He perceives the wave of sciousness as a threat to his identity; a kind of living death. The wave of the unconscious, of androgyny, threatens to choke his familiar ego-consciousness.

Bernard's attachment to what lies above the stream is threatening to creativity and is enacted as a struggle with the linguistic medium. Even though he is disillusioned by the power of stories to adequately represent reality, he creates them compulsively, using mathematically "consecutive sentences" (W 210) comprised of "ready-made phrases" (W 38) he has recorded in his diary. He is implicated in a vicious cycle, failing to realize that creativity cannot thrive through a fixation on the symbolic, by "carry[ing] a notebook—a fat book with many pages, methodically lettered," in which he "shall enter [his] phrases" (*W* 27). His increasing linguistic scepticism is obvious in the gradual disintegration of language. Terms such as "love," the "moon" and "death" seem insufficient (*W* 246), and so he longs for "broken words, inarticulate words" (*W* 199) only to dismiss them as too "consecutive" (*W* 210). He wishes to move to a presymbolic mode of expression, to an extrasemantic field of intonation and rhythm. In his final protest against the artificiality of language he asserts: "I need a little language such as lovers use, words of one syllable such as children speak when they [...] pick up some scrap of bright wool, a feather, or a shred of chintz" (*W* 246). Bernard's focus on the "scrap[s]" and "shred[s]" that comprise language's fragmentary nature serve as a counterpoint to the unity and continuity offered by the stream of consciousness. The cycle of fragmentation is finally completed by silence, as Bernard declares his final resort: "How much better is silence" (*W* 246). He distinguishes his unconscious self as a separate being, as a "man who has been so mysteriously and with sudden accretions of being built up" (*W* 236, 237). The realization that the death of his other self was also the cause of a spiritual death makes him lament: "Now there is nothing. No fin breaks the waste of this immeasurable sea" (*W* 237). The image of the fin, just like in Woolf's diaries and letters, represents moments of epiphany whereby contents of the unconscious suddenly emerge in consciousness. As in James, the water metaphor represents the unconscious as the source of inspiration and creativity. Bernard's attempt to "subjugate" the unconscious led to his overreliance on sequence and linearity (*W* 120).

In contrast to Bernard, Woolf's Orlando is in touch with her unconscious mode of thinking and so manages to dismantle sex distinctions. Her main tool for the presentation of this worldview is the stress on the mental aspect of androgyny that exposes the performative role of gender. In the company of the gypsies who give little thought to sex, Orlando is able to live life in fullness by remaining unconscious of her gender: "It is a strange fact, but a true one, that up to this moment she had scarcely given her sex a thought" (*O* 147). Having embodied both sexes, Orlando is able to live a multiplicity of experience and identities despite the societal restrictions and difficulties she has to face upon her return to England. The fluidity of Orlando's gender indicates that her identification as a female would be a mere classification; it would not offer the reader any new insight into the nature of the hero/ine that he/she has been "following" for half of the novel. The biographer therefore asserts: "Whether, then, Orlando was most man or woman, it is difficult to say and cannot now be decided" (*O* 182). Orlando opens up to the world only after having moved beyond the confines of the sexes, "she had, it seems, no difficulty in sustaining the different parts, for her sex changed far more frequently than those who have worn only one set of clothing can conceive [...] the pleasures of life were increased and its experiences multiplied" (*O* 211). Having eliminated sex consciousness, Orlando "enjoyed the love of both sexes equally" (*O* 211). By choosing lovers irrespective of their sex, Orlando embodies Woolf's theory of androgyny that involves an inability to distinguish between the sexes.

Orlando's fantastical traits do not merely involve his/her four-century life span or the sudden sex change, but also involve the potential it offers readers to imagine how subjectivity would be reconfigured without gender distinctions. Orlando wishes to embody this multiplicity by wearing the Turkish trousers that are "worn indifferently by either sex" (*O* 134). Instead of a detailed description that one would expect after a change of sex we are only provided with a short reference that "he was a woman" (*O* 132). Woolf chose to stress the unchangeability of the mental state after Orlando's change of sex: "in every other respect, Orlando remained precisely as he had been. The change of sex [...] did nothing whatever to alter their identity" (*O* 133) and exposed self-definition, based on sex, as paradoxical: "he was a woman." Gender distinctions are not only disrupted but also parodied by the biographer: "in future we must, for convention's sake, say 'her' for 'his,' and 'she' for 'he'" (*O* 133). The biographer's need to remind him/herself about the necessary change of pronoun only stresses its insignificance and exposes the artificiality of language that is based on sex difference without corresponding to any real distinction.

Woolf emphasized the experience of an androgynous state of mind; "she seemed to vacillate; she was man; she was woman [...] It was the most bewildering and whirligig state of mind to be in" (*O* 152). As we have seen, in *A Room* she had explored the ability of the androgynous mind to open up to the unconscious. *Orlando* offers a significant insight into the possibilities emerging from this awakening. The cognitive potential is described as a sudden revelation that takes hold of him/her: "in the ardour of this discovery, and in the pursuit of all those treasures which were now revealed, she was so rapt and enchanted" (*O* 155). Woolf deconstructs gender distinctions by asserting that the effect of Orlando's female awakening was "to quicken and deepen those feelings which she had had as a man" (*O* 154). Having embodied both sexes, Orlando is able to see through the social forces shaping each gender. Orlando's anthropology is described as a revelation, as a force that undermines arbitrary sex distinctions and widens his/her cognitive horizon: "For now a thousand hints and mysteries became plain to her that were dark. Now, the obscurity, which divides the sexes and lets linger innumerable impurities in its gloom, was removed" (*O* 154).

Woolf exposed the fixation on gender identities as a conscious acting out. In this, she is echoed in Judith Butler who, following Foucault's *The History of Sexuality*, criticizes the cultural tendency to treat sexuality as a fundamental part of identity. Butler tries to undermine sexually defined identities by revealing that rather than a natural trait they consti-tute, in fact, a social construct. Butler's main thesis, in *Gender Trouble*, is that gender is performative. No identity exists behind the acts that supposedly "express" gender; it is these very acts that create the illusion of a stable gender identity.[111] Since gender is merely an effect of cultur-ally defined acts, it follows that there exists no universal idea of gen-der. Butler argues that the performative nature of the gender "woman" or "man" renders them open to "resignification."[112] The opportunity for subversive action lies therefore in performativity, in gender trouble, that unsettles the categories of gender through performance.[113] Despite the obvious affinities between Woolf and Butler's treatment of gender, there is a main difference in their conceptualizations of the unconscious. Butler bases her argument on the existence of an all-encompassing dis-cursive power shaping us at an unconscious level.[114] Woolf traced the potential for liberation in the unconscious, which maintains its reason-ing capacities and keeps the core of the self intact. The performative role of gender is repeatedly stressed in the novel. Gender-specific clothes, for example, are characterized as a "device" (*O* 211). Being a man or a woman is presented as role-playing while clothes become costumes help-ing each gender play its part.[115] Even Orlando is forced to comply with social conventions, which have left their mark: "having now worn skirts for a considerable time, a certain change was visible in Orlando" (*O* 180). Orlando's posture, as is evident in the portraits, changes accord-ing to the role they are embodying. As the biographer is keen to clarify, "Had they worn the same clothes, it is possible that their outlook might have been the same" (*O* 180). Woolf becomes a forerunner of the propo-nents of dramaturgical aspects of social behaviour that involve a delib-erate attempt to construct an impression through social performance.[116] *Orlando* could be seen as a satire of gender roles that hinder interaction by creating artificial barriers between people. While commenting on Or-lando's interaction with the Archduke, the narrator brings up the idea of gender as a game requiring "great vigour": "they acted the parts of man and woman for ten times with great vigour and then fell into natu-ral discourse" (*O* 171). Gender in this context is exposed as extraneous to a substantial model of identity, as a performative accomplishment shaping the lives of actors and audience alike. By choosing the Archduke to converse with Orlando, Woolf encourages the reader to face the im-possibility of forming a fixed idea of the gender dynamics involved in the interaction. Like Orlando, the Archduke—despite the fact that he did not go through an actual sex change—is characterized by gender fluidity and is in the habit of dressing in clothes of a different gender. The confusion in defining which of the two "acted the parts of man and [which the] woman" or if they actually alternated between the two roles entails the possibility of gender elimination through a different sort of repeating. By stressing the arbitrary nature of these acts, Woolf enacts a subversive repetition as a way to undo gender.

For Woolf, the only way of moving beyond this impasse is through our unconscious intelligence which constitutes our "Key self" and is extraneous to the sex binary. In *Orlando*, Woolf distinguished between what she calls "the Captain self" and "the Key self" (O 296). The former represents "the conscious self, which is the uppermost" (O 295). It is the "compact of all the selves we have it in us to be" (O 296). If we try to combine the various discourses and trace their origin, we realize that they are "commanded and locked up by the Captain self" (O 296). The conscious sphere is presided over by the unconscious, "the Key self, which amalgamates and controls them all" (O 296). Orlando's various selves—represented over by the disconnected discourses, each named and inserted parenthetically within the text—are "conscious of disseverment" (O 299) until they are united by "the Captain self" that provides coherence. Woolf's conception of the conscious and unconscious processes as a stream re-emerges through the use of the word "Captain" signifying the conglomeration of the conscious selves. "The Captain self," located above the stream, suggests an absolute ability to command and stir the thinking process. Nevertheless, this dominion is questioned since the real power resides in the water or stream that can, if awakened, take control and define the route and destination of the cognitive journey. Woolf indicates this hierarchy by tracing "the Captain self" in its turn to "the Key self," leading us under the stream, to a non-linguistic realm where Orlando "fell silent" (O 300). Woolf's description of this state gives a sense of the indispensable part of unconsciousness in the attempt to achieve a complete self:

> The whole of her darkened and settled, as when some foil whose addition makes the round and solidity of a surface is added to it, and the shallow becomes deep and the near distant; and all is contained as water is contained by the sides of a well. So she was now darkened, stilled, and become, with the addition of this Orlando, what is called, rightly or wrongly, a single self, a real self [...] Her mind had become a fluid that flowed round things and enclosed them completely.
>
> (O 299, 300)

The depiction of the unconscious as "some foil" that provides "solidity" and acts as "the sides of a well" to contain all the selves further relates it to "the Key self," the core of subjectivity from which all the selves spring. The water metaphor is used again to describe the depths and fluidity of the unconscious, exhibiting the highest cognitive capacity as it "flowed round things and enclosed them completely."

Woolf's literary project counters the sort of identity politics that groups people according to a sexual identity. Her conception of the unconscious and androgyny allowed her to move a step further and unfix sex-identities that create and sustain rigid categories. She moved beyond the system of compulsory heterosexuality, questioning its status as a natural inclination. Her work challenges the grouping together of body functions, conducts, sensations and pleasures that enabled the establishment to present this fictitious unity as a causal principle. In *Orlando*, the socially established, ritualized nature of gender is uncovered along with its performative character that has the strategic aim of maintaining gender within the binary frame.

Notes

1 Alexander Bain, *The Senses and the Intellect* (London: John W Parker and Son., 1855), 359.
2 J. Gill Holland, "George Henry Lewes and 'Stream of Consciousness': The First Use of the Term in English," *South Atlantic Review*, 51: 1 (1986): 31–9.
3 Ibid., 31.
4 Ibid., 36.
5 Ibid., 33.
6 Ibid., 37.
7 Ibid., 34.
8 Ibid., 38.
9 Ibid., 470.
10 Ibid., 472.
11 George M. Johnson, "'The Spirit of the Age': Virginia Woolf's Response to Second Wave Psychology," *Twentieth Century Literature*, 40: 2 (1994): 147.
12 Ibid., 563.
13 Ibid., 567.
14 Ibid., 568.
15 Ibid., 567.
16 Ibid., 568.
17 Ibid., 563.
18 Matthew Arnold, *Culture and Anarchy* (London: Thomas Nelson and Sons, 1869), 11, 15, 295, 308, 333, 337, 362.
19 In France, the innovator of this technique was Édouard Dujardin, who nevertheless termed it "interior monologue" and employed it in his 1887 novel *Les lauriers sont coupés*.
20 Suzanne Raitt, *May Sinclair: A Modern Victorian* (Oxford: Clarendon Press, 2000), 219.
21 George M. Johnson, "May Sinclair: From Psychological Analyst to Anachronistic Modernist," *Journal of Evolutionary Psychology*, 25 (2004): 179.
22 May Sinclair, *A Defense of Idealism: Some Questions and Conclusions* (New York: Macmillan, 1922), 38.
23 Ibid., 258.
24 Vincent Brome, "A Last Meeting with Dorothy Richardson," *London Magazine*, VI (June 1959): 29.
25 Ibid.

26 Stanley Kunitz, *Authors Today and Yesterday* (New York: H. W. Wilson, 1993), 562.

27 Virginia Woolf, *The Common Reader: First Series*, ed. by Andrew McNeillie (London: Hogarth, 1984), 150.

28 Wyndham Lewis, *Time and Western Man*, ed. by Paul Edwards (Santa Rosa, CA: Black Sparrow Press, 1993), 388–9.

29 On the affinities between James and Fechner see Stephanie L. Hawkins, "William James, Gustav Fechner, and Early Psychophysics," *Frontiers in Physiology*, 2:68 (2011).

30 William James, *Essays in Religion and Morality* (Cambridge, MA: Harvard University Press, 1982), 90.

31 Ibid., 90.

32 William James, *Human Immortality. Two Supposed Objections to the Doctrine* (Boston, MA and New York: Riverside Press, 1898), 27.

33 Ibid.

34 Ibid.

35 Ibid.

36 James's fringe experience is included among unconscious cognitive factors by Bruce Mangan, who revises the notion of the cognitive unconscious to adapt it to James's fringe. See "The Conscious 'Fringe': Bringing William James Up to Date," in *Essential Sources in the Scientific Study of Consciousness*, ed. by Bernard J. Baars et al. (Cambridge, MA: MIT Press, 2003), 741–60.

37 Joseph Hart, *Modern Eclectic Therapy* (New York: Springer, 1983), 31.

38 Nicole Ward Jouve, "Virginia Woolf and Psychoanalysis," in *The Cambridge Companion to Virginia Woolf*, ed. by Sue Roe and Susan Sellers (Cambridge: Cambridge University Press, 2000), 245.

39 James Strachey, *Bloomsbury/Freud: The Letters of James and Alix Strachey, 1924–1925* (New York: Basic Books, 1985), 264.

40 Ibid., 309.

41 Elizabeth Abel, *Virginia Woolf and the Fictions of Psychoanalysis* (Chicago, IL: University of Chicago Press, 1993), 14, 138.

42 See Jane Marcus, *Virginia Woolf and the Languages of Patriarchy* (Bloomington and Indianapolis: Indiana University Press, 1987) and Elaine Showalter, *The Female Malady: Women, Madness, and English Culture, 1830–1980* (New York: Penguin Books, 1987).

43 Barbara Lounsberry, "Embracing the Unconscious," in *Becoming Virginia Woolf: Her Early Diaries and the Diaries She Read* (Gainesville: University Press of Florida, 2015), 81.

44 Ibid.

45 Woolf, *Common Reader*, 152.

46 Gian Balsamo, "William James's Stream of Consciousness and the River of the Unconscious in Joyce and Proust," in *Understanding James, Understanding Modernism*, ed. by D.H. Evans (London: Bloomsbury, 2015), 215–34.

47 On the significance of 1910 see Peter Stansky, *On or about December 1910: Early Bloomsbury and Its Intimate World* (Cambridge, MA: Harvard University Press, 1996). Her example of this change in human character was the "character of one's cook." Whereas the "Victorian cook lived like a leviathan in the lower depths," modern cooks were forever coming out of the kitchen to borrow the *Daily Herald* and ask "advice about a hat." Woolf was alluding to social and political changes that overtook England soon after the death of Edward VII, symbolized by the changing

patterns of class and gender relations implicit in the transformation of the Victorian cook.

48 Virginia Woolf, *A Writer's Diary: Being Extracts from the Diary of Virginia Woolf*, ed. by Leonard Woolf (New York: Harcourt Inc., 1954), 182.

49 Carol Siegel, *Lawrence among the Women* (Charlottesville: University Press of Virginia, 1991), 91.

50 Virginia Woolf, "Notes on D. H. Lawrence," in *The Moment and Other Essays*, ed. by Leonard Woolf (London: Hogarth Press, 1947), 79–80 and Virginia Woolf, "The Leaning Tower," in *Collected Essays* (London: The Hogarth Press, 1966), vol. 2, 162–76.

51 Virginia Woolf, *The Moment and Other Essays*, ed. by Leonard Woolf (London: Hogarth Press, 1947), 80.

52 Woolf, *Common Reader: First Series*, 157.

53 Ibid., 30–1.

54 Ibid., 37.

55 In her praise of *Trivia* by Persal Smith Woolf endorses her intention to depict in her work the sudden emergence of the unconscious in consciousness: "it is his purpose to catch and enclose certain moments which break off from the mass, in which without bidding things come together in a combination of inexplicable significance, to arrest those thoughts which suddenly, to the thinker at least, are almost menacing with meaning. Such moments of vision are of an unaccountable nature; leave them alone and they persist for years; try to explain them and they disappear; write them down and they die beneath the pen" (4E 250–1).

56 On Thomas De Quincey's notion of the unconscious in the light of modern cognitive science and 19th-century science, see Markus Iseli, *Thomas De Quincey and the Cognitive Unconscious* (Basingstoke: Palgrave Macmillan, 2015). The book challenges Freudian theories as the default methodology in order to understand De Quincey's oeuvre.

57 Virginia Woolf, *The Common Reader: Second Series*, ed. by Andrew McNeillie (London: The Hogarth Press, 1959), 133–4.

58 Ibid., 266–7.

59 Virginia Woolf, *Selected Essays*, ed. by David Bradshaw (Oxford: Oxford University Press, 2009), 87.

60 Woolf, *Collected Essays*, vol. 2, 166.

61 Ibid., 178.

62 Ibid., 176–7.

63 Woolf, *Selected Essays*, 143.

64 For instance, "I was telling myself the story of our visit to the Hardys & I began to compose it [...] But the actual event was different" (3D 102).

65 Woolf, *Common Reader*, 149–52.

66 See, for instance, Eric Warner, *Virginia Woolf: The Waves* (Cambridge: Cambridge University Press, 1987), 106; Patricia Ondek Laurence, *The Reading of Silence: Virginia Woolf in the English Tradition* (Stanford, CA: Stanford University Press, 1991), 186; Lyndsey Stonebridge, *The Destructive Element: British Psychoanalysis and Modernism* (Basingstoke: Macmillan, 1998), 79–107.

67 "How am I to begin it? And what is it to be? I feel no great impulse; no fever; only a great pressure of difficulty. Why write it then? Why write at all? [...] A mind thinking. They might be islands of light—islands in the stream that I am trying to convey" (3D 229).

68 Virginia Woolf, *Moments of Being: Unpublished Autobiographical Writings*, ed. by Jeanne Schulkind (New York: Harcourt Brace Jovanovich, 1985), 80.

69 Woolf, *A Writer's*, 165.
70 Woolf, *Selected Essays*, 143.
71 Robert A. Schmidt and Barbara L. Voss, *Archaeologies of sexuality* (London: Routledge, 2000), 3–4.
72 See, for instance, Nancy Topping Bazin, *Virginia Woolf and the Androgynous Vision* (New Brunswick, NJ: Rutgers University Press, 1973), and James Hafley, *The Glass Roof: Virginia Woolf as Novelist* (New York: Russell and Russell, 1963).
73 See, for instance, Herbert Marder, *The Measure of Life: Virginia Woolf's Last Years* (London: Cornell University Press, 2000), 122–4, and Ralph Freedman, "Awareness and Fact: The Lyrical Vision of Virginia Woolf," in *The Lyrical Novel* (Princeton, NJ: Princeton University Press, 1963), 198.
74 See, for instance, Annis Pratt, "Sexual Imagery in *To the Lighthouse*: A New Feminist Approach," *Contemporary Literature*, 18 (1972): 431.
75 See, for instance, Elaine Showalter, *A Literature of Their Own* (London: Virago, 1978), and Bazin, *Virginia Woolf and the Androgynous Vision*. Showalter conceives androgyny as Woolf's expression of anger. Bazin argues that, through androgyny, Woolf achieved psychological balance. Using a psychoanalytic and Jungian approach Bazin concludes that the binaries found in her fiction are a result of her manic-depression.
76 See, for instance, Carolyn G. Heilbrun, *Toward a Recognition of Androgyny* (New York: Alfred A. Knopf, 1973), 116–72. Heilbrun offers a general study of androgyny in myth, history and literature. She also relates the homosexuality of the Bloomsbury group to an androgynous sensibility.
77 See, for instance, Mary Graham Lund, "The Androgynous Moment: Woolf and Eliot," *Renascence*, 12 (1960): 76.
78 See, for instance, Herbert Marder, *Feminism and Art: A Study of Virginia Woolf* (Chicago, IL: University of Chicago Press, 1968).
79 See, for instance, Makiko Minow-Pinkney, *Virginia Woolf and the Problem of the Subject* (Brighton: Harvester, 1987); Mark Hussey, *Virginia Woolf and War: Fiction, Reality and Myth* (Syracuse: Syracuse University Press, 1991), 3–6; Kari Weil, *Androgyny and the Denial of Difference* (Charlottesville and London: University Press of Virginia, 1992); and Lisa Rado, *The Modern Androgyne Imagination: A Failed Sublime* (Charlottesville and London: University Press of Virginia, 2000).
80 Mary Jacobus, "The Difference of View," in *Women Writing and Writing about Women*, ed. by Mary Jacobus (New York: Barnes and Noble/Harper Row, 1979), 10–21.
81 Richard von Krafft-Ebing, *Psychopathia Sexualis*, trans. by Charles Gilbert Chaddock, 7th edn (Philadelphia: F. A. Davis, 1908); Edward Carpenter, *The Intermediate Sex: A Study of Some Transitional Types of Men and Women* (London: S. Sonnenschein, 1909); Havelock Ellis, *Studies in the Psychology of Sex*, 7 vols (Philadelphia, PA: F. A. Davis, 1915); and Otto Weininger, *Sex and Character* (London: William Heinemann, 1906).
82 Judy Greenway, "It's What You Do with It That Counts: Interpretations of Otto Weininger," in *Sexology in Culture: Labelling Bodies and Desires*, ed. by Lucy Bland and Laura Doan (Cambridge, MA: Polity, 1998), 36.
83 Barbara Fassler, "Theories of Homosexuality as Sources of Bloomsbury's Androgyny," *Signs*, 5: 2 (1979): 250.
84 Virginia Woolf, "Old Bloomsbury," *Moments of Being*, 172 and Quentin Bell, *Virginia Woolf: A Biography*, 2 vols (New York: Harcourt Brace Jovanovich, 1972), vol. 1, 128.

85 See Rachel Bowlby, *Still Crazy After All These Years: Women, Writing and Psychoanalysis* (New York: Routledge, 2003); Elizabeth Cowie, *Representing the Woman: Cinema and Psychoanalysis* (Basingstoke: Macmillan, 1997); and Jacqueline Rose, *Sexuality in the Field of Vision* (London: Verso, 1986).

86 Sigmund Freud, "The Psychogenesis of a Case of Homosexuality in a Woman," in *The Pelican Freud Library*, 15 vols (Harmondsworth: Penguin, 1973–1986), vol. 9, 399–400.

87 Ibid., "Three Essays on the Theory of Sexuality," vol. 7, n. 2, 54–5. Here Freud attributes the theory of bisexuality to Wilhelm Fliess.

88 See Kate Millett, *Sexual Politics* (London: Hart–Davis, 1971), 179, 196, 205. Millett opposes Freud's essentialist views and criticized his failure to separate "two radically different phenomena, female biology and female status" (190).

89 Diane F. Halpern, *Sex Differences in Cognitive Abilities* (New York: Taylor & Francis, 2000), 281.

90 Sigmund Freud, *The Standard Edition of the Complete Psychological Works of Sigmund Freud*, 24 vols (London: Hogarth Press, 1953–1974), vol. 22, 188.

91 Ibid., vol. 19, 173–9.

92 Jeffrey C. Miller, *The Transcendent Function: Jung's Model of Psychological Growth through Dialogue with the Unconscious* (Albany: State University of New York Press, 2004), 63–71.

93 Woolf sounds like a forerunner of 20th-century gender theory that examines the extent to which gender roles are defined by biology and shaped by cultural forces. Michael Foucault, for example, in *History of Sexuality* 3 vols. (London: Penguin, 1976–1984), argues that sexual categories are produced by modern power in order to structure the world in certain ways. Judith Butler's *Gender Trouble* (London: Routledge, 1990) argues against a biologically determined gender identity and asserts that society inscribes our identities on our bodies. Influenced by Foucault's ideas about the construction of self-identity, she develops a performative theory of gender which argues that our sex is not something fixed but fluid and open. Susan Bordo, also influenced by Foucault, focusses on the discourses through which society produces, understands, defines and interprets the female body. In *Unbearable Weight* (London: University of California Press, 1993) she stressed the ways in which the body is a "text of culture." According to Bordo, cultural notions of gender differences are inscribed on the body, as it shapes itself to fit conventions of proper appearance.

94 Clive Bell, *Proust* (New York: Harcourt Brace Jovanovich, 1929), 85.

95 Virginia Woolf, "Foreword," Exhibition Catalogue, 1930 in Jane Goldman, *The Feminine Aesthetics of Virginia Woolf* (Cambridge: Cambridge University Press, 1998), 158.

96 Ibid.

97 Ibid., 95.

98 Ibid., 121.

99 See, for instance, Margaret Homans, *Bearing the Word: Language and Female Experience in Nineteenth-Century Women's Writing* (Chicago, IL: University of Chicago Press, 1986); Makiko Minow-Pinkney, *Virginia Woolf and the Problem of the Subject* (Brighton: Harvester, 1987); Patricia Waugh, *Feminine Fictions: Revisiting the Postmodern* (London: Routledge, 1989); Sue Roe, *Writing and Gender: Virginia Woolf's Writing Practice* (Hemel Hempstead: Harvester Wheatsheaf, 1990); Patricia Ondek

Lawrence, *The Reading of Silence: Virginia Woolf in the English Tradition* (Stanford, CA: Stanford University Press, 1991); and Clare Hanson, *Virginia Woolf* (Basingstoke: Macmillan, 1994).

100 John R. Maze, *Virginia Woolf: Feminism, Creativity, and the Unconscious* (Westport, CT and London: Greenwood Press, 1997).

101 Susan Stanford Friedman, "The Return of the Repressed in Women's Narrative," *The Journal of Narrative Technique* 19 (1989): 141–56.

102 Michèle Barrett, *Imagination in Theory: Culture, Writing, Words, and Things* (New York Square: New York University Press, 1999), 41.

103 Gillian Beer, *Arguing with the Past: Essays in Narrative from Woolf to Sidney* (London: Routledge, 1989), 147.

104 Jane Marcus, "Sapphistry: Narration as Lesbian Seduction in *A Room of One's Own*," in *Virginia Woolf and the Languages of Patriarchy* (Bloomington: Indiana University Press, 1987), 170.

105 Melba Cuddy-Keane, *Virginia Woolf, the Intellectual, and the Public Sphere* (Cambridge: Cambridge University Press, 2003), 132.

106 Virginia Woolf, *The Hogarth Letters* (Athens: University of Georgia Press, 1986), 232.

107 Daniel Harris, "Androgyny: The Sexist Myth in Disguise," *Women's Studies*, 2 (1974): 172.

108 Ibid., 92.

109 The criticism of the gender binary that tries to draw a gender boundary and discourage gender fluidity has also been voiced, among others, by Foucault. For Foucault, the association of a biological sex with a specific gender—and with a presumably natural attraction to the opposing sex/ gender—was an unnatural union of cultural constructs for reproductive interests. See, for instance, Judith Butler, "Variations on Sex and Gender: Beauvoir, Witting, and Foucault," in *Feminism as Critique*, ed. by Seyla Benhabib and Drucila Cornell (London: Basil Blackwell, 1987); and Michel Foucault, *The History of Sexuality: An Introduction*, trans. by Robert Hurley (New York: Random House, 1980), 154.

110 Many critics have misrepresented the logic behind Woolf's stylistic uniformity. David Daiches, for example, complains of the book's "rigid" prose (107) and James Naremore characterizes the form of the book as inflexible and "rather stifling" (189). In David Daiches, *Virginia Woolf* (Norfolk, CT: New Directions, 1942), and James Naremore, *The World Without a Self: Virginia Woolf and the Novel* (New Haven, CT: Yale University Press, 1973).

111 Judith Butler, "Subjects of Sex/ Gender/ Desire," in *Gender Trouble: Feminism and the Subversion of Identity* (London: Routledge, 2006), 1–46.

112 Ibid., 188.

113 Ibid., 46.

114 Judith Butler, *Bodies that Matter: On the Discursive Limits of "sex"* (New York; London: Routledge, 1993), 12–13.

115 The relation between the theatrical and the social role is intricate. See for the boundaries of the comparison: Bruce Wilshire, *Role-Playing and Identity: The Limits of Theatre as Metaphor* (Boston, MA: Routledge and Kegan Paul, 1981).

116 See, for instance, Erving Goffmann, *The Presentation of Self in Everyday Life* (London: Allen Lane, 1969) and Eric Berne, *Games People Play: The Psychology of Human Relationships* (London: A. Deutsch, 1966).

5   Feeling Unconscious Thoughts in T.S. Eliot

This chapter is divided into three main sections: the first provides an account of Eliot's theory of the unconscious; the second explores the ways in which it informed his literary theory; and the third investigates how the results of the previous two sections converge to deepen our understanding of his literary practice. In terms of his philosophical outlook, I argue that Eliot developed Bradley's notion of "immediate experience," formulated what he referred to as "amended behaviorism" via his study of the physiological processes that underpin our unconscious forms of cognition, and discerned a tripartite unconscious structure, *viz.*, the historical, collective and metaphysical, all of which are linked to his notion of "immediate experience." Equipped with this intellectual framework, the chapter turns to the ways in which "immediate experience" informed Eliot's literary theory, paying particular attention to his discussion of the connections between tradition, the unconscious and individual talent, as well as to his theory of the objective correlative. Following this account, the chapter proceeds to show, via an analysis of *The Four Quartets*, how Eliot's (and the reader's) liberation from time and language is accomplished through a language that consumes itself, the end product of which is a conceptually incomprehensible notion of spatio-temporality that can nevertheless be communicated to and make sense at an unconscious level. It is within this alien to consciousness spatio-temporality that the intended sense of Eliot's purified language is communicated. Reading Eliot's *Quartets* becomes a form of a prayer that gives rise to a mystical, inarticulate, immediate cognitive experience that liberates us from the finiteness of logocentric thinking and experiencing, of consciousness itself.

Eliot among the Philosophers and Scientists

Immediate Experience and the Unconscious

While an undergraduate at Harvard (1906–1909), Eliot studied comparative literature, philosophy and psychology. After graduating in 1910, he left America to spend a year at the Sorbonne in a Paris exploding with new ideas in philosophy and the social sciences. This year was formative in Eliot's intellectual odyssey, partly because it boosted his interest in philosophy. Years later, he looked back: "At the Sorbonne, [...] the sociologists, Durkheim, Lévy-Bruhl, held new doctrines; Janet was the great psychologist; [...] and over all swung the spider-like figure of Bergson."[1] These figures had a significant impact on Eliot's thought as they shaped his psychological theory and approach to creating literary art.

Having attended Bergson's lectures, Eliot became fascinated by the Frenchman's vitalism, a post-Darwinian attempt to overcome dualism by dissolving the barriers between mind and world. The course in 1911–1912, "Descartes, Spinoza, and Leibniz," dealt with three iconic figures of the European Enlightenment and their role in the triumph of rationalism in Western thought.[2] A decade after this course, Eliot, in his Clark Lectures at Cambridge, quoted a passage from *Meditations*, maintaining that "This extraordinary crude and stupid piece of reasoning is the sort of thing which gave rise to the whole of the pseudo-science of epistemology which has haunted the nightmares of the last three hundred years."[3] Another course from the Harvard years was the capstone seminar in logic led by Josiah Royce in 1913–1914.[4] Offered regularly over many years, Royce's seminar had by 1913 achieved legendary status at Harvard. Royce, who became Eliot's mentor and supervised his doctoral dissertation, based the course on his belief in an underlying unity connecting the arts and sciences. In collaboration with students, he explored different methodologies from the new science that would enable a transcendence of various dualisms in philosophy. The seminar consisted of a spirited discussion of papers read by visiting scholars and seminar participants.[5] Royce's metaphysics was a synthesis of European idealism and American pragmatism as outlined earlier by his senior colleague William James. His major contribution to the effort to overcome dualism was the establishment of a connection between hermeneutics and reality, between the work of communities of interpreters and the progressive realization of the world in which we live. As Charles Blakewell wrote on Royce's work: "He has succeeded in cutting under the old Cartesian dualism of mind and matter [...] the interpreter is at once on the object as well as the subject side of the subject-object relation."[6] Hence, Eliot was exposed, from an early stage, to spirited attempts at overcoming dualism.

Royce figures as a soldier in *The Revolt Against Dualism* (1930) by A.O. Lovejoy, who studied philosophy at Harvard under William James and Josiah Royce. In his landmark study, Lovejoy explored this turn in intellectual history. Descartes, Locke and Newton, he argued, had dominated Western thought for three centuries, their bedrock assumption being that the pre-condition for understanding the world was the strict separation of subject and object. Early 20th-century philosophers attempted to move beyond the epistemological dualism of subject and object, as well as from the parallel psychophysical dualism of mind and matter.[7] The theory that subject and object are connected in an integral way and that mind and body are aspects of a single world turned the Cartesian ontological outlook on its head. Lovejoy's argument was resumed by such intellectual historians as Thomas Kuhn and Gerald Holton.[8]

Eliot, too, embarked on a revision of the subject-object question and the mind-matter problem in an attempt to discredit the dualism that imposes divisions on the world. In 1914–1915, Eliot studied Aristotle and F.H. Bradley at Merton College, Oxford, with Harold Joachim, Bradley's friend and disciple. This was a capstone experience for Eliot. He wrote his doctoral thesis on Bradley, showing his agreement with the basic premises of Bradley's philosophy, even while being explicit about various points of disagreement.[9] Eliot criticized Bradley, first, for not explaining whether immediate experience is prior to conscious experience temporally or merely logically, and second, for not being radical enough in examining the self and not-self into which immediate experience resolves itself. Third, he found that Bradley was not comprehensive enough in his examination of the non-self side of experience and, fourth, that he underestimated the difficulty of re-absorbing finite centres into a greater whole.[10]

Eliot ended the first chapter of his dissertation with a summary of Bradley's stages of cognition, a theory of which Eliot approved in part. Bradley distinguished between three cognitive stages: "immediate experience," "intellectual experience" and "transcendent experience."[11] This is how he described the acquisition of knowledge via immediate experience:

> We in short have experience in which there is no distinction between my awareness and that of which it is aware. There is an immediate feeling, a knowing and being in one, with which knowledge begins; and, though this [...] is transcended, it nevertheless remains throughout as the present foundation of my known world.[12]

Knowledge does not begin with thought but with feeling. It is a sensuous knowing prior to the development both of consciousness and of temporal and logical categories. In Bradley's philosophy, reality is an all-inclusive "experience" where dualities are transcended; subjects and objects are parts of something larger than either one. Eliot summarized the nature of the second stage by contrasting it to immediate experience: "By the failure of any experience to be merely immediate, by its lack of harmony and cohesion, we find ourselves a conscious soul in a world of objects" (*KE* 31). Eliot identified consciousness with fragmentation and a world of subject-object distinction, contrasting it to immediate experience, characterized by direct apprehension whose workings take place at an unconscious level. Eliot criticized Bradley for leaving unanswered the question of as to whether "there is a stage at which experience is merely immediate," *viz.*, it is not communicated to consciousness in any form. In fact, he went on to note that "there is indeed no such stage [of immediate experience]" (*KE* 16). This critique is intimately connected to his attempts to overcome dualism because, as he goes on to assert, even though we cannot know immediate experience, "we can yet arrive at it by inference, and even conclude that it is the starting point of our knowing, since it is only in immediate experience that knowledge and its object are one" (*KE* 19). In immediate experience, there is no distinction between subject and object; any reference to the "I" is a construction that occurs after fragmentation and reflection, an abstraction. In our attempts to think about experience, we are forced into an inevitable split that makes immediate experience impossible. According to Eliot, immediate experience does not survive in its pure form in the conscious subject, that is, in the second stage. Rather, we can only find its residue in consciousness, its source remaining in the unconscious and inarticulable:

> When we turn to inspect a lower stage of mind, child or animal, or our own when it is least active, we do not find one or another of these elements into which we analyse the developed consciousness, but we find them all at a lower stage. We do not find feeling without thought, or presentation without reflection: we find both feeling and thought, presentation, reintegration and abstraction, all at a lower stage.
>
> (*KE* 17)

Eliot asserts here that when consciousness is barely active, the subject undergoes an immediate experience wherein feeling and thought are fused into an undifferentiated unity. In drawing an analogy between this lower state of mind and the cognitive psychology of a child or an animal, he is suggesting that consciousness is least active when the conceptual and discursive apparatus of the mind lay dormant or inactive. Conceptual analysis and discursive reasoning, however, cause a fissure between feeling and thought, thereby leading to the conclusion that an adult has to withdraw from consciousness and language in order to attain immediate experience. Thus, Eliot insists, "Experience, we may assert, both begins and ends in something which is not conscious." Eliot's "not conscious" is to be distinguished from the traditional notion of "unconsciousness," which is for the most part viewed as a repository of reactionary and repressed drives that affect our thinking and behaviour:

> And that this "not conscious" is not what we call "unconscious" should be sufficiently obvious. For what we term unconscious is simply an element in experience which arises in contrast to other elements in experience. It refers to certain supposed mental entities which guide or influence our conscious action.
>
> (*KE* 28)

Eliot's "not conscious," by contrast, is a non-symbolic, non-discursive cognitive phenomenon that harbours a perfect symphony between feeling and thought, the echoes of which often rise to the conscious mind. The task of the conscious mind is to decipher the contents of these echoes. Eliot concluded that immediate experience can therefore be located only in the unconscious, where dualities have not yet taken place. Although immediate experience is a state that cannot occur fully in conscious life, it nevertheless erupts into consciousness: "although immediate experience is the foundation and the goal of our knowing, yet no experience is only immediate" (*KE* 28). The third stage of knowing in Bradleyan philosophy occurs by reclaiming the felt residue of immediate experience and arriving at unity. Bradley described the movement towards the Absolute of the third stage: "From such an experience of unity below relations we can rise to the idea of a superior unity above them."[13] Immediate experience is, therefore, prior to relations, while transcendent experience occurs after relations. Transcendent experience involves, consequently, a return to the wholeness and unity of immediate experience, to which neither the unconscious nor consciousness can arrive.

These three cognitive stages had considerable bearing on Eliot's poetic writing. A testimony to this is his 1926 Clark Lectures at Cambridge University, published under the title *Varieties of Metaphysical Poetry*. Eliot defined the "philosophic poet" in Bradleyan terms as one who "enlarges immediate experience" by "drawing within the orbit of feeling and sense what had existed only in thought."[14] Eliot adopted Bradley's term of "felt thought": "Tennyson and Browning are poets, and they think; but they do not feel their thought as immediately as the odour of a rose."[15] This is the cognitive experience a poet should aspire to communicate:

> [A]n enlargement of immediate experience [...] is a general function of poetry [...] [T]he characteristic of the poetry I am trying to define is that it elevates sense for a moment to regions ordinarily attainable only by abstract thought, [...] [it] clothes the abstract, for a moment, with all the painful delight of flesh.[16]

Immediate experience is non-conceptual and non-discursive, but its residues find their way into consciousness, where they are now fragmented. The goal of poetry should be to find the expressive means to reproduce immediate experience, where feeling and thought are now fused into an undifferentiated unity that reflects the contents of that immediate experience, *viz.*, the fusion of subject and object, feeling and thought. In order to fully appreciate Eliot's psychological theory and to understand how it informed his poetics, it is instructive to turn to contemporary non-Bradleyan cognitive theories, which also had a significant influence on his thought and literary output.

Eliot's Physiological Unconscious and
"Amended Behaviourism"

When Eliot visited France in 1910–1911, he was already aware of the work of Pierre Janet, whom he later recalled as "the great psychologist."[17] While at Harvard, Eliot read Janet's *Neuroses et idées fixes* (1898) and *Obsessions et psychasthénie* (1903),[18] and referred in his dissertation to Janet's observations of hysterical patients (*KE* 115). In 1918, he mentioned that he had been following the developments of the clinics of Theodule Ribot and Janet (*SE* 49). As Jain notes, "not only did Eliot take quite extensive notes from the work of Janet and of psychologists influenced by Janet, but their analysis and observations heightened his perception of mental processes."[19] Scientific psychology revealed to Eliot another facet of the unconscious, namely, the unconscious as a *physiological* phenomenon. While Eliot was at Harvard, many psychological experiments confirmed that mental processes depend upon various states of the body. Such evidence gave renewed vigour to a reconsideration of the old mind-body problem. The psychologists and philosophers whom Eliot mentioned in his seminar with Royce, in his dissertation, and in book reviews—William James, Samuel Alexander, Theodor Lipps, G.F. Stout, E.B. Titchener, James Ward (*KE* 57–83)[20] and Wilhelm Wundt[21]—were preoccupied with solving the mind-body problem, which shaped the debate over the proper subject matter of psychology. In this intellectual and scientific framework, Eliot postulated the existence of a physiological unconscious on which mental processes depend:

> Undoubtedly our mental life is directed by many influences of which we are not conscious, and undoubtedly there is no clear line to be drawn between that of which we are conscious and that which as "feeling" melts imperceptibly into a physiological background.
>
> (*KE* 28–9)

Given Eliot's insistence on a physiological unconscious as the source of a kind of knowledge towards which the conscious mind should aspire to return, it is no surprise that he spoke with a degree of admiration of Lawrence's own theory of the unconscious:

> Against the living death of modern material civilisation he spoke again and again. And even if these dead could speak, what he said is unanswerable. As a criticism of the modern world, *Fantasia of the Unconscious* is a book to keep at hand and re-read.[22]

Eliot's theory of the physiological unconscious has affinities with the James-Lange theory of emotion as well, which attributed psychological and emotional changes to physiological processes. While at Royce's seminar, Costello witnessed Eliot contending that psychological events are dependent on the physical things "to which they refer." Royce prodded Eliot, asking him about the ways in which his contention compares to the "James-Lange theory" and "Behaviorism." Eliot's response was that he was proposing an "amended behaviorism," explaining that "in James' theory you have an illusion to explain. For me the emotion is real but there is a point of view from which it is reducible. Psychology reduces to physiology" (*KE* 175).[23] Eliot seems to have been receptive to the claims made by James and Lange. That said, he did not embrace their theories uncritically. For Eliot, the James-Lange theory does not adequately explain illusion or hallucination, other than to say that "the child 'thinks it sees' a bear" (*KE* 115). According to James and Lange, the world consists of real, material objects and the subject that perceives these objects. On this premise, one cannot perceive an object that does not exist in reality. The child cannot therefore be said to perceive the bear. There is an inherent division in the James-Lange theory between the perceived and the perceiver, the object and the subject, the internal and the external. In contrast to this realist thesis, idealism holds that the world and the mind are fundamentally united and continuous; an object is not a separate agent from the mind that perceives and experiences it. Embracing this idealist position, Eliot contended that from the child's point of view, the bear is actually and in reality there. The child perceives the bear, but since the bear cannot be perceived from other points of view, it cannot be termed "real." Following Bradley, Eliot supported "the unity and continuity of feeling and objectivity," the intrinsic connection of an emotion and the physical object that arouses that emotion. He was also in agreement with James's and Lange's theory that the mental event does not occur without the involvement of physiological processes (*KE* 115). However, rejected "any priority of image over emotion, or vice versa." Instead, the two events, the physiological process triggered by the perceived object and the emotional response associated with it are "inextricably related" and simultaneous (*KE* 116).[24] Our mental processes are therefore either a result of real stimuli or figments erected before us by our physiology as if they were real (*KE* 112). Eliot adopted the position of the James-Lange theory, but used idealism to criticize its position on hallucination, favouring the continuity between the mental and the physical sphere.

Eliot characterized his philosophy as "amended" behaviourism, since he still considered the emotional and logical components as material: "physiological activity or logical activity, both independent of and more fundamental than what we call the activity of the mind" (*KE* 153). Logic is located not in the mental sphere to which it is commonly attributed, but in physiological activity. He regarded the mind as an end product of this process. He agreed with the physiological explanation of emotion, but he identified a gap in this theory, since it does not explain the cause for the physiological changes which enable us to feel an emotion: "our emotions may be reducible to subject-matter for physiology. But physiology gives no cause for emotions: it gives causes for operations upon which, for us, emotions supervene."[25] In other words, although physiology explains how, for example, the emotion of fear supervenes as we run away from the bear, it does not explain what caused the physiological changes that produced the emotion of fear, since both the cause (bear, object) and the effect (fear, emotion) come to us immediately as a unified experience. According to the idealist, all mental contents are real to the subject that experiences them. Identifying the physiological alterations that give rise to these contents does not render any less real the presence of the subject's emotional experience. As Eliot observes of a book by A.J. Balfour, "no scientist can claim, as the author makes science claim, that 'all premises, all conclusions, and all logical links by which they are connected must be regarded as natural products.'" The aim scientific positivism is to eliminate all other points of view in favour of its own. However, it is only in metaphysics that one can arrive at a conclusion where varied perspectives are transcended, not by substitution, but via synthesis. And it is only logical analysis that can concoct the varied perspectives into an integrated whole that transcends its parts. This is the truth that metaphysics offers. Thus, Eliot answers that "our apprehension of the truth can surely have no cause other than the truth itself."[26] Behaviourism's approach does not represent Eliot's philosophy either; it is "unbalanced" because it eliminates other points of view and proclaims its view as the only valid one. Such a "purely 'scientific' philosophy ends by denying what we know to be true" (*SE* 403). Adopting the approach of scientific positivism, behaviourists substitute moral values and emotions for reflex and conditioning, stimulus and response, thereby engaging in a process of elimination.

Immediate Experience: Primitive, Historical and Collective

Eliot also conceived of the unconscious as "collective" and "historical." These main properties of the unconscious were suggested to Eliot by the anthropological studies of Émile Durkheim and Lucien Lévy-Bruhl, which Eliot characterized as sociology and social psychology.[27] Another major source for Eliot was James Frazer's study of comparative mythology. Immediate experience which, as we have seen, is characterized by an integration of various points of view, represents the "collective" aspect of an unconscious preceding the personal. Being immune to change, it is also "historical," providing a unified view of our experience.

Eliot's paper on comparative religious studies for Royce's seminar was based on Durkheim's *Les Règles de la méthode sociologique* and "Représentations individuelles et représentations collectives."[28] In a book review, Eliot encouraged his readers to peruse the final chapter of Durkheim's *The Elementary Forms of the Religious Life* because it provides a concise summary of Durkheim's thought.[29] According to Durkheim, "collective representations" form the organizational categories that the mind uses in order to taxonomize the influx of experiences. In this way, they shape our reality, "their stability and impersonality are such that they have often passed as being absolutely universal and immutable."[30] Not a product of the conscious mind, these categories are formed unconsciously by the society that shapes our experience. Durkheim recognized the affinity between the concept of totality and the philosophic idea of the Absolute. Stressing the social dimension of the concept, he asserted that "the concept of totality is only the abstract form of the concept of society: it is the whole which includes all things, the supreme class which embraces all other classes."[31] In its ubiquitous and inclusive nature, the collective conscience is analogous to the unity of the Absolute. As Durkheim defined it:

> The collective conscience is the highest form of the psychic life, since it is the consciousness of consciousnesses. Being placed outside of and above individual and local contingencies, it sees things only in their permanent and essential aspects, which it crystallizes into communicable ideas. At the same time that it sees from above, it sees farther; at every moment of time, it embraces all known reality; that is why it alone can furnish the mind with the moulds which are applicable to the totality of things and which make it possible to think of them.[32]

Durkheim's assertions, as Skaff has observed, are echoed in "Eliot's contention in his later writings that society should by nature embody the religion of its people unconsciously, beyond any deliberate and overt religious profession and observance."[33] Eliot used Durkheim's idea of collective conscience to form his notion of a social, immediate experience that functions largely at an unconscious level. Furthermore, both Durkheim and Eliot shared the belief that logical analysis should aim to achieve the unity of immediate experience. As Durkheim lamented: "logical thought tends to rid itself more and more of the subjective and personal elements which it still retains from its origin."[34]

While Durkheim uncovered the social aspect of the unconscious, Lévy-Bruhl, via a comparative study between primitive thought and modern mentality, revealed its historical dimension. Eliot was so enamoured with Bruhl's work that he based, partly at least, his paper for Royce's seminar on his *Les Fonctions mentales dans les sociétés inférieures*.[35] Here, Bruhl argued that when a primitive mind perceives an object, a process occurs which he called "mystical participation."[36] During this process, the perceiver and the object are felt to be one.[37] Eliot was fascinated by the idea of mystical participation, a state of mind allowing thinking of oneself as two things simultaneously while never losing consciousness of each object. Eliot wrote a review of Clement Webb's *Group Theories of Religion and the Religion of the Individual*, which discussed (among others) Durkheim and Levy-Bruhl. Eliot wrote:

> In practical life, the Bororo never confuses himself with a parrot, nor is he so sophisticated as to think that black is white. But he is capable of a state of mind into which we cannot put ourselves, in which he is a parrot, while being at the same time a man. In other words, the mystical mentality, though at a low level, plays a much greater part in the daily life of the savage than in that of the civilized man. M. Levy-Bruhl goes on to insist quite rightly upon a side of the primitive mind which has been neglected by older anthropologists, such as Frazer, and produces a theory which has much in common with the analyses of mythology recently made by disciples of Freud.[38]

While Eliot greeted positively Levy-Bruhl's theory, he was nevertheless critical of his tendency to differentiate between primitive and modern mentality. In Eliot's words, "Levy-Bruhl draws the line between the crude mentality of primitive [man] and his own [mentality] too sharply." Eliot also gave immediate experience a historical dimension, asserting that it exists at a certain time in "the development of consciousness in biological evolution" (*KE* 17). Looking into the "primitive consciousness," he discovered many similarities between the two: "We do not find feeling without thought, presentation without reflection: we find both feeling and thought, presentation, reintegration and abstraction, all at a lower stage" (*KE* 17). For Eliot, "the mystical mentality, though at a low level, plays a much greater part in the daily life of the savage than in that of the civilised man."[39]

James Frazer's *The Golden Bough* also inspired much of Eliot's belief in the existence of a historical unconscious, in which past and present intermingle.[40] Frazer's impact on the formulation of Eliot's own conception of the unconscious is made evident in several places. For example, Eliot characterized Frazer's work as "a revelation of that vanished mind of which our mind is a continuation."[41] Through Frazer, Eliot discovered a death/rebirth pattern in all religious ceremonies and beliefs which he considered to be innate and to participate in the structure of the unconscious. Frazer's hero-gods underwent violent deaths and resurrections at sacred places, from which they continued to exercise their powers at festivals that recreated their drama. According to Eliot, the rituals associated with Osiris, Attis and Adonis are similar to the ritual during the Eucharist. According to Eliot, Frazer "has extended the consciousness of the human mind into as dark a backward and abysm of time as has yet been explored."[42] The primitive mentality is for Eliot part of our own mind. He, therefore, reads Frazer as an archaeologist of the primitive mind, which lives on as our unconscious and shapes our spiritual feelings and religious systems.

Eliot also identified a similarity between Levy-Bruhl's theory of primitive mentality and the recent interpretation of mythology formulated by Freud's followers.[43] Eliot initially assumed psychoanalysis to be relevant to his own conception of the unconscious. Jung in *Psychology of the Unconscious*, Freud in *Totem and Taboo* and Eliot relied on the same anthropological sources to develop their respective theories of the unconscious.[44] Unlike Eliot and Jung, however, Freud added that rituals are symptoms of a mental disorder caused by an inability to adjust to sexual desire. In this way, Freud reduced religious experience to a psychological disease. Freud's transformation of religion into sexual aberration is an interpretation Eliot could not accept. Instead, Eliot sought an integration of sexual desire with religious experience. Jung's theory proved to be closer to Eliot's own thought. For Jung, myths and rituals do not reveal an individual's maladjustment to their sexual drives, because the psychic impulse is not narrowly sexual but spiritual. Myths embody psychological archetypes derived from a deeper level of the unconscious; they represent our collective inheritance and point the way to spiritual fulfilment. Psychoanalytic theory, for Eliot, represented a limited point of view attempting to subsume all others. In sharp contrast to such an approach, he sought a synthesis of the variety of perspectives formidable to describe the metaphysically imbued religious experience in a way that approximates the absolute. In Eliot's view, psychoanalytic terminology fails to facilitate such an integration of perspectives, and so he was vocal in his critique of its legitimacy: "a word half-understood, torn from its place in some alien or half-formed science, as of psychology, conceals from both writer and reader the meaninglessness of a statement" (*SE* 305). Echoed in this statement is his definition of such ideas as "half-objects," which are "half-understood." Eliot, then, rejected psychoanalytic "half-objects," and saw the unconscious approximating the mind of primitive man. Frazer's depiction of a primitive mind led Eliot to assume that his legacy would be more lasting than either Freud's[45]—who conceived of primitive rituals and myths as evidence of his own theory of sexuality—or Jung's—who categorized myths and rituals according to archetypes.

Eliot would come to be publicly dismissive of Freud's psychoanalytic methods, particularly when it came to psychoanalytic interpretations of literary works, stating that: "I sometimes think that our own time, with its elaborate equipment of science and psychological analysis, is even less fitted than the Victorian age to appreciate poetry as poetry."[46] He viewed the psychoanalytic readings of his work as "attempt[s] to find origins [...] in the darker recesses of my private life."[47] This resentment was partly caused by the various psychobiographical analyses of *The Waste Land* which had even characterized sections of the work written while Eliot was under therapy as "a form of partial self-analytic work."[48] Similarly to Lawrence and Woolf, Eliot reacted to what he saw as psychoanalytic reductionism: "with or without the tools of the psychologist [...] the attempt to explain the poem by tracing it back to its origins will distract attention from the poem."[49]

Eliot was informed about the research on hysteria and the related theory of the unconscious as early as 1910, and saw its relevance to Freudian psychoanalysis.[50] The theoretical point of view of psychoanalysis, which focusses on the sexual and the aberrant, provided for Eliot a distorted view of the unconscious, which is collective and historical. Eliot also located the origins of psychoanalysis in the investigations conducted at the French school for psychological disturbances at Nancy, as well as in those of the French psychiatrists Jean-Martin Charcot, Ribot and Janet. Whereas modern French psychology concentrated "prudently" upon the "care of cases," Eliot admitted in 1920 to having been acquainted with the "more surprising developments" that occurred in Vienna (*SE* 49).[51] Initially, Eliot received approvingly aspects of psychoanalysis, but he came to believe that psychoanalysis was "a dubious and contentious branch of science."[52] He further asserted that Mary Sinclair's psychoanalytic fiction did not offer an opportunity for "tapping the atmosphere of unknown terror and mystery in which our life is passed and which psychoanalysis has not yet realized."[53] Eliot expressed a similar attitude towards the psychoanalytically oriented Dadaism. He characterized it as artistic "chaos,"[54] which becomes the "diagnosis of a disease of the French mind."[55] His sarcastic tone is also evident in his review of *Vingt-cinq poèmes* by Tristan Tzara, one of the founders of Dadaism: Eliot observed that the passage quoted should be taken "very seriously" as a "symptom of 'experiment.'"[56]

Eliot's Literary Theory and the Unconscious

Immediate Experience, the Physiological Unconscious and the Art of Writing

The unconscious for Eliot has a physiological basis and is continuous with the metaphysical unconscious, an aspect in his thought intimately related to Bradley's ideas of immediate experience. It is also collective and historical, as suggested by anthropological studies of Durkheim and Frazer. This conception makes the mind of past cultures part of our own mentality, shaping the way we experience the world. Frazer's work on primitive ritual was mainly continued by C.B. Cook at Oxford and by the Cambridge Classicists Jane Harrison, Gilbert Murray and F.M. Cornford, who applied the anthropological method to Greek

culture.[57] By tracing the origins of Greek religion, art and philosophy
to primitive rituals, these scholars gave further credence to Eliot's idea
that the unconscious mind is a historical continuum. Harrison argued
that primitive rituals evolved into later Greek religion. At the same time,
Murray and Cornford—also following the evolution of Greek primitive experience—revealed a relationship between these rituals and later
Greek art and philosophy. Murray asserted that "Tragedy is in origin a
Ritual Dance"[58] and Cornford, in *The Origin of Attic Comedy*, added
that comedy evolved not only out of primitive ritual, but also out of the
same ritual as tragedy: "Athenian Comedy arose out of a ritual drama
essentially the same type as that from which Gilbert Murray has derived
Athenian Tragedy."[59] The theory of the development of tragedy and
comedy out of a "common form" had a significant appeal to Eliot, given
the idea of a pre-existing unity characteristic of immediate experience.
Although commonly perceived as disparate, Eliot conceived of these two
genres as springing from a common source: rituals. Hence, when we
study Greek we are studying "our own mind."[60] Modern man's "categories of thought" are predominantly the "outcome" of Greek thought,
and our "categories of emotion are largely the outcome of Greek literature."[61] Arguing for the existence of a collective unconscious, Eliot asserted that "what analytic psychology attempts to do for the individual
mind, the study of history—including language and literature—does for
the collective mind."[62] He stressed that the main challenge of historians
is to reconstruct for modern man the mind of the Renaissance and the
pre-Renaissance so vividly that they will no longer be dead. Bringing
into consciousness the archaic modes of thought and feeling, the "unconscious parts of our own mind," we can make better use of them for
our benefit and "future development."[63] In Eliot's preoccupation with
mystical moments, the archaic part of the mind plays a major role; it
is the portion of the mind that Eliot, following Frazer, would try to recover and integrate into his modern sensibility. He held the belief derived
from Frazer that the structure of that unconscious mind is symbolized
through the pattern of death and rebirth.

Eliot believed that the "highest forms" of dance are "the ballet and
the mass,"[64] and that modern ballet could lead to the birth of a "new
drama" if it reintegrated primitive experience.[65] The examples that Eliot
used in order to corroborate his argument come from the Ballets Russes
of Serge Diaghiev,[66] as well as from the folk art of the music hall with
its unique sense of humour.[67] More specifically, he saw, as Skaff has observed, the "music hall comedian to be the modern incarnation of a very
old stock character —the Fool."[68] For Eliot, the fool in *King Lear* is "a
very cunning and very intuitive person; he has more than a suggestion
of the shaman or medicine man."[69] In addition to the Fool's evolutionary origin from the priest of primitive societies, the Fool is not merely
comic, but also has a serious side. He can even become a "master of the

situation." Eliot located the "prototype" of the "true" Fool in *St. George and the Dragon*, the Mummer's play based upon a Perseus myth.[70] The Fool—with his tragicomic status—blends the two into a form of humour moving beyond such dualities. Eliot found, both in Shakespeare and Ben Jonson, a "point of view which can be called neither comic nor tragic," and which approximates the unity of primitive experience and incorporates these mental abstractions (*SE* 141).

In Royce's seminar, Eliot expressed his objection to the attempts of certain anthropologists to discover the meaning behind primitive rituals and dances. He accused W.O.E. Osterly, the author of *The Sacred Dance*, of falling into the trap of offering "intelligible reasons" why primitive people performed these dances. Eliot believed instead that primitive dancers "acted in a certain way and then found reason for it," articulating a theory wherein actions precede reason.[71] Going a step further, Eliot believed that these rituals may have begun even "before 'meaning' meant anything at all."[72] Although Eliot found appealing theories that assumed the evolution of drama from ritual dances, he was nevertheless also critical of them, since he thought they only explain its content rather than its origin. Instead, he defended the instinctual, physical response or desire that urges a man to beat a drum, and the pragmatism inherent in this response which explains its continuity:

> An unoccupied person, finding a drum, may be seized with a desire to beat it; but unless he is an imbecile he will be unable to continue beating it, and thereby satisfying a need (rather than a "desire"), without finding a reason for doing so.[73]

The rituals of drama and religion that migrate from generation to generation have a physiological origin which evolves and has a significant role in shaping one's consciousness, feelings, thoughts, and behaviour.

If ritual practices are rooted in unconscious, instinctual drives, then this should be the starting point of religion and art as well, to which they must always return: "all art emulates the condition of ritual. This is what it comes from and to that it must always return for nourishment."[74] He considered some examples of fine art, like "the Egyptian who first fashioned gold into a likeness of a cowrie-shell, the Cretan who designed an octopus on his pottery, the Indian who hung a necklace of bear's teeth about his neck," concluding that they "were not aiming primarily at decoration, but invoking the assistance of life-giving amulets." The consideration of primitive ritual led him to ask if art can recover its original social function: "At what point [...] does the attempt to design and create an object for the sake of beauty become conscious? At what point in civilization does any conscious distinction between practical or magical utility and aesthetic beauty arise?" Put another way, artistic creation should emerge freely from its unconscious source, and this process serves practical purposes as well. Eliot went on to support the need for art to work towards the wholeness of primitive, immediate experience: "Is it possible and justifiable for art, the creation of beautiful objects and of literature, to persist indefinitely without its primitive purposes: is it possible for the aesthetic object to be a *direct* object of attention?"

Eliot synthesized the relationship between dance and religious ritual in his essay "The Ballet," written for *The Criterion*. Seeking the unconscious origin of our sense of rhythm (which develops from the beating of the drum into ritualistic dancing), Eliot asserted that to understand the "spirit" of dancing we must consider the

> evolution of Christian and other liturgy. (For is not the High Mass—as performed, for instance, at the Madeleine in Paris—one of the highest developments of dancing?) And finally, he should track down the secrets of rhythm in the (still undeveloped) science of neurology.[75]

The source of reasoning is referred to the physiological unconscious and the neurological system. That is the part of our physiology directly related to brain activity and thus to thought and emotion. Hence, the sense of rhythm in our nervous system gives rise to dance, and then to ritual and ceremony, the religious impulse being inherent in our body; it is a mystical moment of unity, similar to immediate experience. For Eliot, the same impulse which springs from the body and which prompts modern man to beat his drum prompts the modern man to go to church. Ritual is able to stir the unconscious mind and to serve as an expression of it, through rhythm, reaching into the unconscious by stimulating us physiologically.

For Eliot, it is the primary duty of artists to stir the unconscious elements of drama by uncovering its ritual foundation and making its purpose akin to a religious service. "The play," he wrote, "like a religious service, should be a stimulant to make life more tolerable and augment our ability to live; it should stimulate partly by the action of vocal rhythms on what, in our ignorance, we call the nervous system."[76] Rhythm becomes a way to stir the physiological unconscious. Eliot hinted at the importance of our physiology by claiming that, "in our ignorance," we call it the nervous system, implying that its impact on our lives tends to be diminished to numb physiology. Primitive people responded bodily to rhythm by participating in a collective ritual. Eliot referred to the decline of art that neglects the primal forms of enchantment and the endurance of those forms of entertainment that cleave to the original rhythms:

> It is the rhythm, so utterly absent from modern drama, either verse or prose, and which interpreters of Shakespeare do their best to

suppress, which makes Massine and Charlie Chaplin the great actors that they are, and which makes the juggling of Rastelli more
cathartic than a performance of "A Doll's House."[77]

Despite the efforts to eliminate rhythm from the modern stage and prose,
its innate power stirs our physiological unconscious and is the cause of
the impact of Massine, Rastelli and Charlie Chaplin.

Eliot attempted to achieve the same effect by including ritualistic elements in his poetry: chants, invocations and supplications. This surrep-
titious method of the modern poet is made only too clear in *The Use of
Poetry and the Use of Criticism*, which says that the

> chief use of the "meaning" of a poem, in the ordinary sense, may
> be [...] to satisfy one habit of the reader, to keep his mind diverted
> and quiet, while the poem does its work upon him: much as the
> imaginary burglar is always provided with a bit of nice meat for the
> house-dog.
>
> (*UP* 151)

That is, the main cognitive process of a poem takes place in the unconscious and its "meaning" is merely a way to preoccupy the conscious
mind. We encounter again the idea of two separate cognitive mechanisms operating simultaneously. Eliot follows the above observation by
concluding that the "ideal medium for poetry" is "the theatre" (*UP* 153).
Drama is just a way of bringing the "pleasures of poetry" to a larger
audience than is otherwise possible in civilized society (*UP* 154). Verse
drama is, after all, only poetry in a disguise that will make it acceptable for ordinary people, the most fundamental of schemes used to keep
"the bloody audience's attention engaged" so that the poet may pull
off "monkey tricks [...] behind the audience's back."[78] Drama provides
the optimum conditions for the poet, mainly because it can "cut across
all the present stratifications of taste," providing meaning or "plot" to
"the simplest auditors" and giving to others, "the more literary" and
"the more musically sensitive," the "words and phrasing" and "rhythm"
(*UP* 153).

Eliot's insistence in his later criticism upon the use of verse in drama
illustrates his intention that, while the artist keeps his listeners occupied
with the "monkey tricks" of plot and meaning, he feeds them the "primitive" bolus, the "feeling for syllable and rhythm" that, he claimed,
constitutes the origin of literary art. The unconscious that emerges as
the source of literary creation is achieved through a combination of the
primitive elements, which appeal to both the historical unconscious
and the physiological unconscious, and these latter are stirred through
rhythm. The dramatist, then, is the Eliotic shaman who keeps the tribe
entertained while working the magic of poetry upon the audience. That

magic—what distinguishes poetry from prose—Eliot associated with the poet's "auditory imagination," a primitive, prelogical instinct:

> the feeling for syllable and rhythm, penetrating far below the conscious levels of thought and feeling, invigorating every word; sinking to the most primitive and forgotten, returning to the origin and bringing something back, seeking the beginning and the end. It works through meanings, certainly, or not without meanings in the ordinary sense, and fuses the old and obliterated and the trite, the current, and the new and surprising, the most ancient and the most civilised mentality.
>
> (*UP* 118–9)

By formulating the sound of verse, by building up "syllable and rhythm," the poet fuses past and present, the "primitive" and the "civilised." That process, inherently mystical or prelogical, involved a return to "primitive" origins, as shown in the conclusion to *The Use of Poetry and the Use of Criticism*: "Poetry begins, I dare say, with a savage beating a drum in a jungle, and it retains that essential of percussion and rhythm; hyperbolically one might say that the poet is older than other human beings" (*UP* 155). That sense of "syllable and rhythm"—which unites poetry and drama and provides the bridge between "primitive" and civilized—also bonds audience to performer.

Eliot incorporated into his literary aesthetics the role of the physiological unconscious, which is awakened through rhythm. Bringing together such diverse literary works as Joyce's stream of consciousness novel, Lewis's satire and Shakespearean tragedy, Eliot drew attention to the fact that physical reaction is characteristic of all literature of whatever genre and period. French literary author and critic Remy de Gourmont inspired Eliot to consider the effect of the physiological unconscious in literature. In his 1928 preface to *The Sacred Wood*, Eliot acknowledged the influence of de Gourmont's work, and two epigraphs to "The Perfect Critic" show familiarity with the Frenchman's sensualist theory of style. Commenting on his first literary essays, Eliot remarked that "at that time I was much stimulated and much helped by the critical writings of Remy de Gourmont."[79] Eliot first encountered de Gourmont's writings probably during his year in France as a visiting student, as de Gourmont is mentioned in his retrospective account of 1910 Paris.

The first direct evidence of de Gourmont's influence is in the early literary essays beginning in 1919.[80] Of de Gourmont's work, we know for certain that Eliot read *Le Problème du style* (1902) and *Lettres à l'Amazone* (1914), as well as his essay on Laforgue's *Promenades littéraires I* (1904) (*SE* 192–3).[81] Eliot's later essays were written "when I was somewhat under the influence of Ezra Pound's enthusiasm for Remy de Gourmont," noting that Pound intensified his interest in de Gourmont (*UP*

10). De Gourmont's ideas on literature derived from the central role he placed on the physiological basis of mental phenomena. Eliot praised de Gourmont as "an amateur, though an excessively able amateur, in physiology."[82] De Gourmont postulated that reality and the self are entirely material, and feeling and thought are strictly physiological processes. Moreover, mental activity is the product of sensations, which are first transformed into images (*mots–images*), then into ideas (*mots–idées*), and then they finally become emotions (*mots–sentiments*). Ideas emerge, therefore, out of sensory impressions. For language to have any meaning, it must remain as close as possible to sensory experience. Our mental life is a constant revitalizing of concepts and words through the continuing imbibing sensations. According to de Gourmont, image transmutation and language formation are entirely physiological. A writer's style is determined by his physiology inasmuch as their writing is determined by the sensations they receive on the day and the corresponding conceptual apparatus that is activated as a result.

Eliot's formulation of the unconscious is an elaborate synthesis of the metaphysical, psychological, historical and physiological unconscious. De Gourmont reinforced Eliot's ideas on the physiological unconscious. Eliot reconstructed de Gourmont's theory through the Bradleyan concept of immediate experience in which object, emotion and thought are united as feeling. In "La Création subconsciente" of *La Culture des idées*, de Gourmont stated that the unconscious mind is physiological, and affects us through physical processes. Eliot corroborated this idea, but he did not restrict himself to a solely materialist conception of the unconscious as de Gourmont did. Moreover, de Gourmont was a historical relativist: as periods of history change, sensations change accordingly, and so does art. For him, the physiological unconscious is differentiated among people, whereas for Eliot it is what remains relatively permanent in human nature like the body does and unchanged throughout history, embedded in the physiology of our unconscious. For Eliot, the unconscious is also continuous with experience; it is a unified state of thought and emotion. Eliot's belief in the physiological unconscious and its role in creativity is vividly depicted in his reference to the poet John Davies: "his appeal is, indeed, to what Hallam calls the heart, though we no longer employ that single organ as the vehicle of all poetic feeling."[83]

The most lasting influence on Eliot was the concept of "dissociation," which for de Gourmont is a method "analogous to what is called analysis in chemistry," *viz.*, the dissociation of material into its various elements "in order to prepare for a new synthesis."[84] In de Gourmont's theory, the term refers to the need for the critic to "dissociate" the commonplaces that pass for deep truths. Eliot, however, adjusted the term to signify the disintegration of a unified tradition, specifying Milton and Dryden for ending a period when feeling and thinking made up a single process. From a technique to refine sensibility, "dissociation" came to signify in Eliot's theory a splitting in communal consciousness. Following de Gourmont's belief that poetry springs from physiology, Eliot saw the physiological unconscious as the source of all poetry "'look into our hearts and write' [...] is not looking deep enough [...] One must look into the cerebral cortex, the nervous system, and the digestive tracts" (*SE* 250). The element revealing the essence of a writer is the rhythm present in a writer's neurological system, which governs the poetic composition. Rhythm is not the verse form or the scansion. It is instead a "highly personal matter" and "very uncommon." It is the "scheme of organization of thought, feeling, and vocabulary, the way in which everything comes together."[85] Nor is the discursive separate from the bodily, for "every vital development in language is a development of feeling as well" (*SE* 185). The physiological unconscious plays a significant role in the creative process, as the poet's sense of rhythm allows him or her to recover the primitive experience inherent in the historical unconscious. Eliot described "auditory imagination" as a feeling for the architectonics of language, a feeling which has the ability both to return the human mind back to its primitive roots and forgotten drives, and to fuse opposites and shape the aesthetics and ideological undercurrents of modern art.

Tradition, the Unconscious and Individual Talent

Eliot's theory of the involvement of the unconscious and tradition in the act of creating literary art is best exemplified in "Tradition and the Individual Talent." A letter describing the original impetus behind the composition of this essay explains his position to Mary Hutchinson:

> I have now got started on a long subject which I have not now either time or energy to carry out—instead of replying simply to a question of civilization and culture. I think two things are wanted—civilisation which is impersonal, traditional (by "tradition" I don't mean stopping in the same place) and which forms people unconsciously [...] and culture—which is a personal interest and curiosity in particular things.[86]

Tradition represents a "simultaneous order," that is, a historical timelessness and, at the same time, a sense of present temporality (*SE* 5). The idea of tradition not as chronology, a succession or a series of events, but as a possession of an unconscious knowledge of tradition as a whole, is also evident in Charles-Louis Philippe's *Bubu de Montparnasse*, the novel which became Eliot's guide to early 20th-century Paris. Philippe introduces his hero: "A man who walks carries all the things of his life and turns them in his mind. One sight arouses them, another excites them."[87] Eliot's conception of tradition, giving a culture its sense of continuity and wholeness, emerges out of the collective and physiological unconscious: "What I mean by tradition," Eliot wrote in *After Strange Gods*, "involves all those habitual actions, habits, and customs [...] which represent the blood kinship of 'the same people living in the same place.'"[88] Blood and territorial kinship encompass the conscious elements of living, such as the love of bocce by rural Italians, as well as those elements lying below consciousness and woven into a community's fabric of existence. Communal solidarity and cohesion offer individuals great strength, by grounding identity in a collectively intuitive life.

Eliot described tradition as a combination of conscious and unconscious elements, the interaction of which shapes societies:

> I hold in summing up that a tradition is rather a way of feeling and acting which characterizes a group throughout generations; and that it must largely be, or that many of the elements in it must be, unconscious; whereas the maintenance of orthodoxy is a matter which calls for the exercise of all our conscious intelligence.[89]

Such unconscious forms of cognition shape the larger part and essence of a tradition and individual human behaviour, whereas conscious intelligence is restricted to the "maintenance of orthodoxy." Hence, "The two will considerably complement each other."[90] Eliot's concept of the unconscious as a cognitive mechanism that shapes and directs the streams of consciousness is integral to his theory of tradition, as is the importance of a "historical sense" for the production of lasting literary works. One should

> write not merely with his own generation in his bones, but with a feeling that the whole of the literature of Europe from Homer and within it the whole of the literature of his own country has a simultaneous existence and composes a simultaneous order.
>
> (*SE* 14)

Eliot located tradition in the body, in the very bones of the author. He can fuse the "timeless" and the "temporal," through a form of writing that returns the reader to the roots from within which the author's creativity sprung: the physiology of the human body and unconscious forms of cognition. In Eliot's thought, successful literary art operates to bring feeling and thought, mind and body, to a unity. Tradition—registered in the physiology of the human body and awakened by the power of literary art—is the means through which such an enriching unity can be achieved:

> Tradition may be conceived as a by-product of right living, not to be aimed at directly. It is of the blood, so to speak, rather than of the brain: it is the means by which the vitality of the past enriches the life of the present. In the co-operation of both is the reconciliation of thought and feeling.[91]

The unconscious, tradition and literary creation are therefore tightly intertwined. They share the same fate; they are subject to the same conditions and alterations, for a change in literary creation will cause a change in our perception of tradition, as well as in our unconscious and consciousness. However, "this change is a development which abandons nothing en route, which does not superannuate either Shakespeare, or Homer, or the rock drawing of the Magdalenian draughtsmen" (*SE* 6). The introduction of a new work alters the cohesion of this existing order, and causes a genuine readjustment of the old for the inclusion of the new work, both altering the way the past is seen and also altering the present:

> The persistence of literary creativeness in any people, accordingly, consists in the maintenance of an unconscious balance between tradition in the larger sense—the collective personality, so to speak, realized in the literature of the past—and the originality of the living generation.[92]

Tradition represents a universal mind that is a "greater, finer, more positive, more comprehensive mind than the mind of any period."[93] For Eliot, "A common inheritance and a common cause unite artists consciously or unconsciously: it must be admitted that the union is mostly unconscious. Between the true artists of any time there is, I believe, an unconscious community" (*SE* 13). Authors must possess a sound knowledge of literary history. This will form an unconscious union between a poet and the literary tradition that precedes him. After recognizing that this process takes place in the artist's unconscious, Eliot argued that it is possible to have these unconscious cognitive processes transferred to consciousness:

> There is accordingly something outside of the artist to which he owes allegiance, a devotion to which he must surrender and sacrifice himself in order to earn and to obtain his unique position [...] And, as our instincts of tidiness imperatively command us not to leave to the haphazard of unconsciousness what we can attempt to do consciously, we are forced to conclude that what happens unconsciously we could bring about, and form into a purpose, if we made a conscious attempt.
>
> (*SE* 24)

Authors are not affiliated with a particular period, but are "related so as to be in light of eternity contemporaneous, from a certain point of view cells in one body."[94] The historical sense of a writer must consist in an awareness of tradition, "a perception not only of the pastness of the past, but of its presence." The writer should have a "feeling" that the "whole" of the literature of the Western world has a "simultaneous existence and composes a simultaneous order" (*SE* 14). Bringing the collective unconscious of literary history into the light of individual consciousness means that "we have borrowed, we have been awakened, and we become bearers of a tradition."[95] This allows us to fuse past and present, giving rise to "a sense of the timeless and of the temporal together" (*SE* 14). In this way, we live in an enlightened present. It is no surprise, then, that Joyce's *Ulysses*—with its employment of styles occurring throughout the English language and the use of words that recall their own history—became the paradigm of modern literature for Eliot. Joyce succeeded in writing with a "consciousness" of tradition, as he put the "whole weight of the history of the language behind his word."[96] In this way, *Ulysses* "realises untried possibilities" and "revivifies the whole of the past."[97]

Moreover, the poet has to engage in a "continual surrender of himself" to the vast order of tradition (*SE* 17). Eliot wrote of the "universal sameness" of people despite the "superficial variations" of the "uniformity of human nature," emphasizing that personality is nothing but a superficial psychological experience.[98] In addition, great poetry involves the stretching of language to accommodate unconscious elements that represent the collective, the impersonal; they express "in perfect language, some permanent human impulse" (*SE* 137). Impersonality in poetry becomes synonymous in Eliot's ontology with the unconscious, with the "struggle" of the great poet "to transmute his personal and private agonies with something rich and strange, something universal" (*SE* 137). This unconscious process involves the transmutation of the personal into a "superior organisation," and that is "impersonal in the sense that personal emotion, personal experience, is extended and completed in something impersonal—not in the sense of something divorced from personal experience and passion. No good poetry is the latter."[99] The creative process thereby involves a loss of selfhood: "The creation of a work of art is like some other forms of creation, a painful and unpleasant business; it is a sacrifice of the man to the work, it is a kind of death."[100] In this process of depersonalization, the mature poet is viewed as a medium through which tradition is channelled and elaborated. When the poet reaches this state, "impressions and experiences combine in peculiar and unexpected ways" (*SE* 20), the poet becoming "a more finely perfected medium in which special, or very varied, feelings are at liberty to enter into new combinations" (*SE* 18). Thus, if writing with a sense of tradition involves the complete annihilation of any sense of individual personhood, then "Impressions and experiences which are important for the man may take no place in the poetry, and those which become important in the poetry may play quite a negligible part in the man, the personality" (*SE* 20). What lend greatness to a work of art are not the feelings and emotions themselves, but the nature of the artistic process by which they are synthesized.

In Eliot's theory of poetic creativity, the poet is compared to a catalyst in a chemical reaction, in which the reactants are feelings and emotions, synthesized to create an artistic image that captures and relays these same feelings and emotions. While the mind of the poet is necessary for artistic production, it emerges unaffected by the process. The artist stores feelings and emotions and unites them into a specific combination, which is the artistic product (*SE* 18–9). This cognitive process involves the ability to combine disparate elements in new patterns to produce lasting literary works: "mind is in fact a receptacle for seizing and storing up numberless feelings, phrases, images which remain until all particles which can unite to form a new compound are present together" (*SE* 19). The creative process entails a continual sacrifice of the self: "The progress of an artist is a continual self-sacrifice, a continual extinction of personality. There remains to define this process of depersonalization and its relation to the sense of tradition" (*SE* 17). It is therefore not "the intensity of the emotions, the components, but the intensity of the artistic process, the pressure, so to speak, under which the fusion takes place, that counts" (*SE* 19). The "intensity" of an author's "imagery" depends upon its "saturation [...] with feelings too obscure for the authors even to know quite what they were" (*UP* 147–8).

Eliot emphasized the transformation of the personal into an impersonal experience impossible to comprehend through conscious reason: "an author's imagery [...] comes from the whole of his sensitive life since early childhood [...] [S]uch memories may have symbolic value, but of what we cannot tell, for they have come to represent the depths of feeling into which we cannot peer" (*UP* 148). Within these depths into which we are unable to peer rests the "poetic sensibility," the "sensitiveness necessary to record and bring to convergence" on a given experience "a multitude of floating but universal feelings" (*SE* 352). The role of perception and the senses in poetic creativity is pivotal: they have cognitive characteristics, and there is also evidence of an emotional consciousness, that blurs the distinction between emotion and intelligence. This constitutes a movement away from personal emotion—since these are "feelings which are not in actual emotions at all"—towards an embracing of a faculty that is universal and impersonal (*SE* 21). Poetry becomes an "escape from emotion," an "escape from personality"; it no longer expresses the conscious world, but "the emotion of art [which] is impersonal" (*SE* 21–2). But there is a real difficulty in reaching this "impersonal" state: "instead of thinking with our feelings (a very different thing) we corrupt our feelings with ideas; we produce the public, the political, the emotional idea, evading sensation and thought."[101] We need to disrupt the binary thinking that conceives of emotion as the diametrical opposite of thought, and realize that our predicament lies in the way idealism has superseded any other form of thinking. The poet's "passive attending upon the event," his waiting for these unpredictable crystallizations, reinforces the idea that creative potential lies mainly in the cognitive unconscious (*SE* 21).

The Objective Correlative and Immediate Experience

Eliot made many attempts in his literary theory to reinvigorate poetry with the cognitive insights located in the unconscious. Poetry should have a vital relation to tradition, and this led to the notion of "poetic impersonality." But poetry must also affect us as a direct sensation. This is achieved through the "objective correlative," a literary technique highlighting the union of thought and emotion: "there is no greater mistake than to think that feeling and thought are exclusive" (*KE* 18). This literary concept is a natural outcome of the philosophical theory expressed in *Knowledge and Experience*: immediate experience is a state where thought and emotion are united. Through the objective correlative, Eliot attempted to bring poetry closer to immediate experience. Since it is "impossible [...] to draw any line between thinking and feeling, [...] 'feeling,' in a work of art, is any less an intellectual product that is 'thought.'"[102]

The "objective correlative" is "a set of objects, a situation, a chain of events which shall be the formula of that *particular* emotion; such that when the external facts, which must terminate in sensory experience, are given, the emotion is immediately evoked" (*SE* 145). Given the idea of the physical unconscious, poetic emotion should arise out of physical sensations or images linked to these sensations, and expressed through "sensory experience." When a work has its own unique patterning, then the whole experience from which the work emerges will be "immediately evoked." The term "immediately" is indicative of the fact that the reader's response to such a patterning is instinctual. The response is automatically activated without the involvement of any conscious mental effort, thereby invoking contemporary physiological theories of emotion. The James-Lange theory of emotion had a special appeal to Eliot. As we have seen, not only did he corroborate the theory; he also added that the physiological process of perceiving an object and the emotional response associated with it are more "inextricably related" than even the James-Lange theory claims. Moreover, there is no "priority of image over emotion, or vice versa" (*KE* 116). Instead, an emotion and the physical object are indeed simultaneous.

Furthermore, Eliot's emphasis on the formation of a unity between the two echoes his insistence, following Bradley, on "the unity and continuity of feeling and objectivity" (*KE* 115). More specifically, it recalls the state of immediate experience characterized by a transcendence of subject/object distinctions. The effect of the "objective correlative" is only achieved through the stimulation of the physiological unconscious. Eliot stressed this aspect in his praise of Dante as a master of the "objective correlative," because he makes his readers both experience the reality of

Hell "by the projection of sensory images," and "apprehend sensuously the various states and stages of blessedness" (*SE* 250, 265). Long before forming his theory of the objective correlative, Eliot asserted that art is not just an expression of emotion, but "in really great imaginative work the connections are felt to be bound by as logical necessity as any connections to be found anywhere" (*KE* 75). The operative term in this passage, "logical," characterizes the latent structure of a poem. After appealing to the cognitive aspects of the unconscious, Eliot asserted that these connections cannot be comprehended by the conscious mind. Instead, they require an affective response, they are "felt." At the same time, through this literary technique, Eliot aimed for a relative objectivity, just as he did when he focussed on a living tradition and the consensus it can provide: specific external stimuli evoke "a *particular* emotion" (*SE* 145). In italicizing the word "*particular*," he wished to achieve a certain level of uniformity and objectivity. In a similar manner, Eliot sought objectivity in aesthetic response, when he urged the perceiver "to apply exact measurement to our own sensations" (*SE* 206). The cognitive unconscious present in every individual leads beyond the subjective and towards the impersonal and the objective. After appealing to the physiological unconscious, Eliot's final test and verification of his theory lie in the readers' collective unconscious: the "objective correlative" has essentially the same effect in every individual. Eliot advances a theory of how works of art convey not just ideas or themes, but the full breadth and texture of experience.

In "The Metaphysical Poets," Eliot wrote that these poets exemplified the highest level of unified sensibility. A "unity of sensibility" is displayed when a poet reaches beyond distinctions of thought and emotion, and into the unconscious where they are fused. The interplay of this poetics to the objective correlative is expressed in the idea that poets of a unified sensibility "feel their thought as immediately as the odour of a rose" (*SE* 287). These poets allow for thoughts to grow naturally out of sensory experience, with which they are inextricably connected. Poetry of a unified sensibility demonstrates the quality of "transmuting ideas or sensations, of transforming an object into a state of mind" (*SE* 290). Realizing the purpose of the "objective correlative," such poets succeeded in fusing object, thought and emotion.

In poets such as Donne, Herbert and Marvell, and in playwrights such as Chapman and Webster, Eliot found a "direct sensuous apprehension of thought, or a recreation of thought into feeling" (*SE* 286). Unlike writers like Tennyson and Browning, the Metaphysical poets were intent on "trying to find the verbal equivalent for states of mind and feeling" (*SE* 289). Without being very specific about the social factors that contributed to this change, Eliot said that the Metaphysical poets were fortunate to live in an age before "a dissociation of sensibility set in, from which we have never recovered" (*SE* 288). For example, Shakespeare's era was a "period when the intellect was immediately at the tips of the senses." In the "period of Milton," however, one deplored the "decay of the senses" and also Massinger's failure to be "guided by direct communications through the nerves" (*SE* 210, 215). The two main reasons for this failure are the lack of "intellectual courage" and the "dissociation of sensibility," characteristic of this age when even morality had turned into an abstraction (*SE* 220). Massinger's age was only the beginning of the "dissociation."

Blake's time is characterized as a "formless age," even further removed from the 17th century.[103] Living in the formless Romantic period, Blake had to shape his own philosophical framework, which distracted him from the "problems of the poet," namely, the expression rather than invention of ideas and emotions.[104] Tennyson, further into the "dissociation," was "almost wholly encrusted with parasitic opinion, almost wholly merged into his environment."[105] Less critical of Blake than of Massinger or Tennyson, Eliot asserted that the fault did not lie with Blake himself, but with a culture that did not provide the right framework to realize a greater poetic vision.[106] In a comparison of Donne and Chapman to Jules Laforgue and Tristan Corbiere, Eliot argued that "Transmuting ideas into sensations," these poets looked "into the cerebral cortex, the nervous system, and the digestive tracts," as well as into the heart (*SE* 290). In his praise of Racine and Baudelaire, Eliot asserted that they are "The greatest two masters of diction [and] also the greatest two psychologists, the most curious explorers of the soul" (*SE* 290). For Eliot, insight into the human nervous system and psychology is indispensable for the composition of lasting literary works.

In Dante's age, philosophy and theology, religion and actual belief, and public and private morality were not dissociated. Hence, Dante benefited from "a mythology and a theology which had undergone a more complete absorption into life."[107] Dante's creative powers were spent in the right direction "to *realize* ideas." This is because the challenge for the poet lies in translating ideas, thoughts and emotions into sensory images: "Poetry can be penetrated by a philosophic idea, it can deal with this idea when it has reached the point of immediate acceptance, when it has become almost a physical modification."[108] Eliot insisted that an idea has to be presented in such a way as to stir the physiological unconscious, which possesses a higher cognitive potential than we realize. For Eliot, "Hell, though a state, is a state which can only be thought of, and perhaps only experienced, by the projection of sensory images; and that the resurrection of the body has perhaps a deeper meaning than we understand" (*SE* 250). Criticizing abstract thinking, he proposed another way of reasoning which leads us to the poetic emotion: "the reasoning takes only its proper place as a means of reaching these states [of feeling]" (*SE* 266). In his essay "Dante," Eliot introduced the possibility for a new mode of thinking in images, even a logic of images, both multi-dimensional and popularly accessible. The unconscious quality—that mark of "genuine poetry"—is manifested in Dante's work, which "can communicate before it is understood" (*SE* 238).

Dante's poetry is not simply characterized by the use of clear visual images; he invests them with meaning. He uses them as a way to recreate meaning through sensual means, and thus achieves the "objective 'poetic emotion'" (*SE* 238). Moreover, such unified sensibility as a mark of genuine poetry arises from privileging immediate experience as an unconscious state, in which division between idea and emotion collapses. Eliot supported the use of sensory means that shape a somatic, unconscious experience as a way of transcending dualism. He also attributed to Dante's "*visual* imagination" another level of meaning, linking his theory of "dissociation" to the need for incorporating unconscious structures in poetry:

> Dante's is a *visual* imagination. It is a visual imagination in a different sense from that of a modern painter of still life: it is visual in the sense that he lived in an age in which men still saw visions. It was a psychological habit, the trick of which we have forgotten, but as good as any of our own. We have nothing but dreams, and we have forgotten that seeing visions—a practice now relegated to the aberrant and uneducated—was once a more significant, interesting, and disciplined kind of dreaming.
>
> (*SE* 243)

In this passage, Eliot embraced visions as another way through which the unconscious is manifested while consciousness is withdrawn. Trying to salvage visions from the negative connotations they have received, Eliot believed they constituted "a more significant, interesting, and disciplined kind of dreaming." Seeing visions is a "psychological habit" more lucid than dreams, and constitutes a valuable access to unconscious forms of cognition. The Freudian model is criticized for the primacy and character it has attributed to dreams: "we take it for granted that our dreams spring from below: possibly the quality of our dreams suffers in consequence" (*SE* 243). The indeterminacy regarding the "type of sexual experience," which the first meeting with Beatrice represented to Dante—as recorded in part two of the *Vita nuova*—provided Eliot with a new opportunity further to criticize the authoritative status of Freudian psychology: "the same experience, described in Freudian terms, would be instantly accepted as fact by the modern public" (*SE* 273). Dante, however, "quite reasonably, drew other conclusions," and led "the experience in a different direction from that which we, with different mental habits and prejudices, are likely to take" (*SE* 273). The *Vita nuova* is "a very sound psychological treatise on something related to what is now called 'sublimation.'" Eliot thereby expressed the embodiment of his poetic ideal of a unified sensibility, along with its need for a different conceptual system of the unconscious (*SE* 275).

In the essay "Andrew Marvell," Eliot introduced another key term, namely, "wit." This term signifies the cognitive processes taking place in a Metaphysical poetry which is the result of a unified sensibility. Marvell's poetry owes its beauty to "a connection with that inexhaustible and terrible nebula of emotion which surrounds all our exact and practical passions and mingles with them" (*SE* 300). These words echo Eliot's account of Bradley's definition of immediate experience, which the poet described as "a sort of confusion, and a nebula which would grow distinct on closer scrutiny" (*KE* 19). The linguistic echoes of the two passages suggest that Marvel connected emotions with their unconscious source. Eliot also applied Coleridge's definition of the "Imagination" to Metaphysical verse: "the balance or reconcilement of opposite or discordant qualities: of sameness with difference; of the general with the concrete; the idea with the image; the individual with the representative" (*SE* 298). It is not surprising that Eliot used this definition as part of his attempt to define "wit," because it aptly renders the artist's unifying point of view, one that fuses objects and events with ideas and emotions. Eliot further demonstrated the quality of unifying discordant elements, in writing that "characteristic of the sort of wit we are trying to identify" is the "alliance of levity and seriousness" (*SE* 296). A key point in the attempt to define this concept is its relation to impersonality. Eliot regarded this as a primary attribute of the unconscious, when he wrote, it has a "certainly impersonal virtue—whether we call it wit or reason" (*SE* 304). This cognitive ability of the unconscious to overcome polar opposites is essential for a poet.

The Unconscious, the Creative Process and the Reader

For Eliot, the formative mystery of poetry was a fusion of feelings and thoughts into a "concentration which does not happen consciously or of deliberation." As such, there can only be "a passive attending upon the event" (*SE* 21). Sarah Kennedy also argues that Eliot's "conception of the creative impulse as a latent but powerful presence in the unconscious appears to draw on depth psychology, which emphasizes the psychodynamics of the unconscious."[109] Since the primary impetus behind a poem lies in the unconscious, a literary writer cannot explain his own work; he or she "does many things upon instinct, for which he can give no better account than anyone else" (*UP* 122). That said, Eliot did not underestimate the involvement of the conscious mind in the creative process. Both cognitive mechanisms play a defining role in the act of creating literary art: "There is a great deal, in the writing of poetry, which must be conscious and deliberate. In fact, the bad poet is usually unconscious where he ought to be conscious, and conscious where he ought to be unconscious" (*SE* 21). The impetus of a poem originates in the unconscious. When it erupts in consciousness, it is in a raw state, "it is not used: the poem has not been written" (*UP* 139). The conscious effort of the poet lies in his attempt to translate this logic in consciousness and shape it in discourse. The collaboration of the conscious and the unconscious in the creative process also involves a re-creation of word and image, since the poet has to "give a new meaning" to words or "extract a latent one" (*UP* 140). As Eliot explained in an account of Shakespeare's creative genius, "the right imagery, saturated while it lay in the depths of Shakespeare's memory, will rise like Anadyomene from the sea. In Shakespeare's poetry this reborn image or word will have its rational use and justification" (*UP* 140).

Eliot's own experience as a poet led him to argue that feelings will be found "inhering for the writer in particular words or phrases or images" (*SE* 18). According to his aesthetic theory, a poet seizes upon the unconscious material that erupts into consciousness. He then fashions a poem which should reflect these subliminal feelings, not only in its structure and stylistic techniques, but also in its content. For Eliot, it is crucial to retain the formative mystery of the poem through a "form" that reflects the unconscious impetus behind it:

> to create a form is not merely to invent a shape, a rhyme or rhythm. It is also the realization of the whole appropriate content of this rhyme or rhythm. A sonnet of Shakespeare is not merely such and such a pattern, but a precise way of thinking and feeling.[110]

Eliot also stressed the selective role of the unconscious, which stores and redeems relevant impressions during the creative process: "the mind of any poet would be magnetised in its own way to select automatically [...] the material—an image, a phrase, a word—which may be of use to him later" (*UP* 69–70). In *The Use of Poetry and the Use of Criticism*, Eliot cited John Livingston Lowes's *The Road to Xanadu: A Study of the Ways of the Imagination* as proof of the role of subliminal memory in the creative act, demonstrating "the importance of instinctive and unconscious, as well as deliberate selection" (*UP* 69). Eliot does not adhere to the Romantic maxim, Be true to "one's self"—which urges the poet to write by following his subjective feelings. Rather, the challenge to the poet lies in bringing the unconscious processes to light; the poet is "responsible to a much more difficult consciousness and honesty," namely, to "expressing his genuine whole of tangled feelings."[111] Such words express the difficulty of translating latent material into consciousness. Eliot's translation of unconscious material in poetry "represents an attempt to extend the confines of human consciousness and to report things unknown, to express the inexpressible."[112] In other words, it is an attempt to confound and transgress the very thought it relies on, but cannot trust. Genuine poetry arises from an unconscious need, and then searches for a linguistic leap, advancing "Into another intensity/ For a further union, a deeper communion."[113] Hence, the locus of poetry lies in a unified immediate experience and it is manifest as an instinct or "obscure impulse."[114]

This unconscious realm involves a "fusion of feelings so numerous, and ultimately so obscure in their origins, that even if there be communication of them, the poet must hardly be aware of what he is communicating" (*UP* 131). For Eliot, this locus lies in "depths of feeling into which we cannot peer." It is impossible to comprehend the unconscious processes by means of the conscious mind not the least because the form of these processes inevitably changes as they emerge in discourse. They are "the deeper, unnamed feelings which form the substratum of our being" and which take on a new verbal form in poetry (*UP* 149). The restless pursuit of truth through necessary but inadequate means constitutes a "raid on the inarticulate/ With shabby equipment always deteriorating," but points through its very inadequacy to a transcendental truth.[115] If reality entails intimations of immediate experience unavailable to reason, then truth must be conceived by an intuitive "wisdom [...] communicated on a deeper level than that of logical propositions."[116] In his play *The Elder Statesman*, the limits of language are discussed: "It's strange that words are so inadequate. / And yet we go on trying to compel them to our service. / Though all words fail us, even falsify our meaning."[117] These linguistic limitations are not, however, an impasse. Rather, they are an incentive encouraging writers to a perennial production of literary art. Poetry should embody the processes of the unconscious; it should reveal the facets of this other level of experience and represent the "logic of the imagination."[118] Unconscious logic is therefore sanctioned by something beyond the figments of consciousness and the illusions of language, since the "path of consciousness reflecting on itself leads us nowhere."[119] In order to gesture towards a mystical truth beyond consciousness, Eliot made extensive use of logical contradictions, because unconscious cognition can only be made visible by revealing the darkness of thought. In *Ash Wednesday*, for instance, we read:

> End of the endless
> Journey to no end
> Conclusion of all that
> Is inconclusible
> Speech without word and
> Word of no speech[120]

The extensive use of paradoxes and oxymorons hints at a truth reaching beyond linguistic limitations, not because it is irrational—it does not resist logic—but because it transcends logic, an aspect in Eliot's thought and art to which we will return in the last section. We can only discover truth through experience rather than linguistic signification. The completion of thought is only possible by overcoming the false rift between word and thing: "Redeem / The unread vision in the higher dream."[121]

Eliot discussed at length how the latent meaning of a poem is communicated to the reader's unconscious. His preface to *Anabase* (by St-Jean Perse) gives an analysis of poetic logic. Regarding the apparent incoherence of the poem, he wrote: "Any obscurity of the poem, on first readings, is due to the suppression of 'links in the chain,' of explanatory and connecting matter, and not to incoherence, or to the love of the cryptogram." A rapid combination of disjunctive images can stir the unconscious as the reader must permit the "images to fall into his memory successively without questioning the reasonableness of each at the moment; so that, at the end, a total effect is produced."[122] A relaxation of conscious censorship allows for an unconscious comprehension. The meaning of the poem can emerge only if readers engage in an imagistic free play, a play reenacting the poet's unconscious formative mystery. Eliot provides a description of the reader's cognitive process that follows a condensed work like *Anabase*:

> Such selection of a sequence of images and ideas has nothing chaotic about it. There is a logic of the imagination as well as a logic of concepts. People who do not appreciate poetry always find it difficult to distinguish between order and chaos in the arrangement of images; and even those who are capable of appreciating poetry cannot depend upon first impressions. I was not convinced of Mr. Perse's imaginative order until I had read the poem five or six times. And if, as I suggest, such an arrangement of imagery requires just as much "fundamental brainwork" as the arrangement of an argument, it is to be expected that the reader of a poem should take at least as much trouble as a barrister reading an important decision on a complicated case [...] But *Anabase* is poetry. Its sequences, its logic of imagery, are those of poetry and not of prose.[123]

Two forms of logic are described in this passage, a non-discursive logic offering "one intense impression" or vision (which triumphs over the apparent disorder that produces it), and a "logic of concepts." The latter involves the conscious process that provides "the arrangement of an argument." The unconscious processes involved in the act of creating and receiving literary art are characterized by a disruption of the logical sequence of meaning. Within discourse, it therefore takes the form of an enthymeme, or a condensed syllogism that has suppressed some of its premises. Literary response depends not only on an intuition of intense impressions, but also on an orderly contemplation: "I was not convinced of Mr. Perse's imaginative order until I had read the poem five or six times." Once he recognized the rationality of the imaginative system, he saw the "reasonableness" of the poem.

The reader's inability to consciously grasp the wholeness of the poetic logic completes the circle of its conception as it was formed in the poet's unconscious mind. The poem's effect lies squarely in the experience of the reader, and the "experience of poetry, like any other experience, is only partially translatable into words" (*UP* 8). In the greatest poetry there is "something which must remain unaccountable," not only because it is so obscure but because, by its very nature, it is ineffable:[124]

> It is commonplace to observe that the meaning of a poem may wholly escape paraphrase. It is not quite so commonplace to observe that the meaning of a poem may be something larger than its author's conscious purpose [...] If, as we are aware, only a part of the meaning can be conveyed by paraphrase, that is because the poet is occupied with frontiers of consciousness beyond which words fail, though meanings still exist [...] the poem means more, not less than ordinary speech can communicate.[125]

The impetus for a poem begins in the poet's unconscious, and the communication of a poem ultimately ends in the reader's unconscious. Eliot's theory of the unconscious shows how the conscious mind's cognitive operations comprise only a fraction of the human subject as a thinking being. His displacement of the conscious mind as the governing principle of cognition has significant consequences for our understanding of Eliot's literary art.

Immediate Experience and the Death of Consciousness in the *Four Quartets*

Eliot's *Four Quartets* is a notoriously difficult poem to understand. G. Douglas Atkins has contended that

> *Four Quartets* is inexhaustible. No one can master it, and no one should try. I sometimes think that Eliot—at pranks, perhaps—sought to frustrate his reader, to embody a poetics of difficulty and adversity, to make his essay poem too strange for misunderstanding.[126]

It is a poem that relies, in Roger Bellin's words, "on paradox, contradiction, tautology, and the performance of self doubt."[127] And yet, Eliot insists that the *Quartets* is straightforward, told in the simplest language possible, "like conversing with your reader [...] Sometimes the thing I am trying to say, the subject matter, may be difficult, but it seems to me that I am saying it in a simpler way."[128] This part of the chapter discusses Eliot's language and its ability to describe spatio-temporality in the light of his philosophical outlook and literary theory. A study of this relation opens, in turn, a new window into our understanding of the role of the unconscious during the process of reading the poem.

Although the function of the unconscious has not received adequate attention, time and language in the *Quartets* have been the subjects of extensive critical scrutiny. However, they are usually studied separately. Nancy K. Gish argues that Eliot's poetic form and content depend largely on philosophical concepts of time and timelessness.[129] R.L. Brett contends that the "main preoccupation for the *Four Quartets* is the Christian doctrine of time and eternity." He maintains that Eliot finds in the Christian position of the intersection of time and eternity a way of transcending the notion that time is an endless process with no direction and the notion that time is an illusion.[130] Vincent Miller also considers how Eliot's Christian views shape his notions of time and concludes that time "exists as an essential and unending purgation."[131] Corey Latta too argues for a theological reading of time in the *Quartets*, but it is one modelled on the Bergsonian idea of duration. Latta continues to assert that Eliot chose to employ a Christian reading of time by incorporating Bergson's influential ideologies, rather than drawing from biblical statements of time or on the theories of past or contemporary prominent theologians. *The Four Quartets*, on Latta's account, is a poem that promotes, through its reliance on Bergsonian ideas, a theological understanding of time. *Four Quartets* demonstrates an absorption of 20th-century philosophy for the purpose of constructing theology.[132] Kenneth Paul Kramer has argued that the poem contemplates "how timeless moments—of redeeming reciprocity, of graced consciousness— shine through physical landscapes and release the poet from temporal enchainments."[133] Kramer continues to assert that this release is accomplished by what he refers to as "acts of spiritual resistance" that liberate the reader from an imprisoning relation to time.[134]

According to Eliot's critics, one of the main issues of *Four Quartets*, along with time, is language and the poet's struggle to express his meanings and experiences through words.[135] Indeed, on many occasions Eliot wonders if he can successfully interpret and communicate his thoughts via the medium of language. According to David Moody,

> When the poet's double declares "our concern was speech, and speech impelled to us / To purify the dialect of the tribe," the subtext implies that the poem's language should itself be passed through the refining fire. Its diction is in fact remarkably purified. That is to say, the words carry only the sense intended, neither more nor less.[136]

The central question that arises here concerns the intended sense of this purified diction and syntax that, to use Eliot's words, "you would have to put off/ Sense and notion" (*FQ* 192).

This section seeks to complement these studies by showing how Eliot's (and the reader's) liberation from time and language is accomplished through a language that consumes itself, the end product of which is a conceptually incomprehensible notion of spatio-temporality that can nevertheless be communicated to and make sense at an unconscious level. It is within this alien to consciousness spatio-temporality that the intended sense of Eliot's purified language is communicated. In *Four Quartets*, as Alireza Farahbakhsh has observed, "sometimes it seems that Eliot is deliberately testing the limits of language to prove the inadequacy of the available vocabulary and syntax for what he aspires to express."[137] But more than a testimony to the inadequacy of language, Eliot pushes language to the point of breakdown in such a way as to deconstruct the reader's consciousness into an unconscious mode of thinking and perceiving as a means to intuit what eludes the symbolic order of signification and understanding. Reading Eliot's *Quartets* becomes a form of a prayer that gives rise to a mystical and inarticulate immediate experience that liberates us from the finiteness of logocentric thinking and experiencing, of consciousness itself.

The first few lines of the first quartet may seem to serve as an introduction to the tetralogy, but we should bear in mind that time (and by extension chronological sequence) in this poem is constructed only to deconstruct it, to let it crumble under the weight of a reality in which everything is congregated at a point where traditional concepts of linear time and logic collapse. This is the main import of "Burnt Norton's" opening lines:

> Time present and time past
> Are both perhaps present in time future,
> And time future contained in time past.
> If all time is eternally present
> All time is unredeemable.
>
> (*FQ* 171)

These lines have enjoyed extended discussion. Readings range from "a treatment of Bergsonian duree" to that of "Roycean and Bradleyan metaphysical idealism," that is, as "absolute time (or, better, 'timelessness')" as well as a "concurrence of Bradleyan and Bergsonian Temporal conceptions."[138] For Doris T. Wight, in these lines Eliot "sets forth the metaphysical paradoxes of time" appropriately in the beginning, "setting forth the task of explaining through poetic logic the precise workings of these suprarational truths."[139] Here, Wight continues to assert, "Eliot mystically resolves all problems and questions concerning time and place—the material of this world—by stepping outside time and outside place and into the Unnamed." Yet, this enterprise entails a fundamental difficulty: "Of course, the poet does not do this rationally, explicitly, openly; to do so would defeat his entire project." Rather, according to Wight,

> "Eliot must create insights within the reader through poetry's emotional, hypnotic manipulations, must force the reader to suffer through the intellectual contradictions and paradoxes of life in time until he, with Eliot, is completely ready to abandon himself to the idea of the timeless.[140]

Indeed, one of the main purposes of these lines, and of the poem more generally, is to deconstruct temporal categories and by extension our habitual, intuitive sense of time. However, the central question that arises from this reading concerns the ways in which Eliot accomplished this deconstruction of time and how he is able to communicate it via emotional and hypnotic manipulations. If the present and the past are contained in the future and the future is contained in the past, we have a cyclical dialectic whereby the one is contained in the other. On the one hand, the notion of "containment" signifies a finite temporal dimension, but on the other, the fact that that which contains is also contained by that which it contains deconstructs these boundaries and thrusts the reader into a temporal dimension that knows no limits, linearity or logical-sequential construction. This is a pervasive aspect in Eliot's poem. A few lines later, we are invited to enter a door that leads into a rose garden, and so "Through the first gate, / Into our first world" we enter (*FQ* 171). Once we are in, we get the sense that we have entered the garden in autumn, where we get to witness "the dead leaves / In the autumn heat" (*FQ* 171–2). However, what Eliot gives in one breath he takes in the other, as autumn is injected with images that signal other seasons. For example, we soon confront the image of a pool "filled with water out of sunlight, / And the lotos rose" (*FQ* 172). The image of the sun beaming out waves that fill up a pool is a reference to contemporary advances in physics where the fundamental particles' dual nature as both corpuscles and waves became central to discussions of objectivity and reality. At the same time, the surreal image of a light-wave filled pool, seasoned with blooming lotos, steers the reader's mind away from autumn and into the summer, a reverse trajectory that continues through the next lines where vegetation rises from the mud in order to ascend to summer (*FQ* 172). Just like Eliot's botanic entities, which instead of progressing from autumn to winter as one would expect following the traditional linear edifice of time, we move from autumn to summer. This is a kind of reality that "human kind / Cannot bear" because it undermines the logical structures of language itself, the means by which we construct reality and acquire our knowledge of its nature (*FQ* 172). What are we to make of Eliot's "Time past and time future / What might have been and what has been / Point to one end, which is always present"? (*FQ* 172) It might seem that what Eliot is telling us here is that the past and the future converge at a single point, the present, which encompasses both the past and the future, in a dialectics where the present has an objective reality as a point in time, one that reproduces the Christian feeling that St Augustine describes about the immediacy of time, "the all-at-onceness of the past, the present, the future, fused in the ongoing living of human experience as it is happening."[141] However, we have already been warned that the present, along with time past, is "present in time future/ And time future contained in time past" (*FQ* 171). Here, indeed,

> Words strain,
> Crack and sometimes break, under the burden,
> Under the tension, slip, slide, perish,
> Decay with imprecision, will not stay in place,
> Will not stay still.
>
> (*FQ* 175)

All our understanding of the world around us and within us is built upon language, the tool that does not merely describe what we experience but participates in the emergence of what we experience and how we experience it. To attain knowledge of the new reality that Eliot proposes we must resist the signifying import of language itself, but since language is linked to our consciousness, we must cease being conscious of language's referentiality. Thus, Eliot's understanding of time requires the loss of consciousness as a means of liberating ourselves from ingrained modes of logocentric thinking:

> Time past and time future
> Allow but a little consciousness.
> To be conscious is not to be in time
> But only in time can the moment in the rose-garden,
> The moment in the arbour where the rain beat,
> The moment in the draughty church at smokefall
> Be remembered; involved with past and future.
> Only through time time is conquered.
>
> (*FQ* 173)

The third line of this passage may seem to introduce a logical contradiction, as is so often the case in Eliot's *Quartets*, because as long as one is conscious, they are so at a certain point in time. But the consciousness of which Eliot is speaking corresponds to a new type of consciousness, one which rises above the traditional form of consciousness as it is defined by and structured around language. It is only through a linear understanding of time that we can say that we actually remember something. However, Eliot tells us, the content of this remembrance does not belong to a point in the past, but it is also involved in the future, presumably the future of that past, which is our present, and which is itself contained, as we were told, in the past and the future. The key idea here is that "Only through time time is conquered," just like it is only through consciousness that consciousness is conquered and only through language that language is conquered. It is a type of conquer that is predicated on erecting before us a concept (i.e. present, past, future, autumn) and allowing it to collapse via the very means through which it was originally constructed (language-consciousness). This dialectic creates a space between consciousness and unconsciousness where our notion of time and its implicational relations (i.e. sense of temporal linearity, progression towards an end, beginning, sequence of events) are confused. In Eliot's words,

> Here is a place of disaffection
> Time before and time after
> In a dim light: neither daylight
> Investing form with lucid stillness
> Turning shadow into transient beauty
> With slow rotation suggesting permanence
> Nor darkness to purify the soul
> Emptying the sensual with deprivation
> Cleansing affection from the temporal.
>
> (*FQ* 173–4)

As we read the poem and journey through a garden wherein traditional notions of time and space collapse, we become "disaffected" from ordinary consciousness in order to witness the "transient beauty" of a cognitive experience that hovers between light and darkness, consciousness and unconsciousness, temporality and timelessness, "Between un-being and being" (*FQ* 175). The temporality of Eliot's garden allows, indeed, "but a little consciousness" (*FQ* 173). To lift the confusion that the "shadow" casts upon human cognitive psychology is to approach death, it is to "Descend lower, descend only/ Into the world of perpetual solitude, / World not world, but that which is not world" (*FQ* 174). Here we are deprived of sense, imagination ("fancy") and consciousness ("spirit"), the trinity that not only gives meaning to our reality but which participates in its construction (*FQ* 174). It is thus no surprise that in order to escape the circular dialectics embedded within the symbolism of the shadow, one has to withdraw from consciousness, which is rooted in the aforementioned trinity. The rose garden is the world of the shadow, where both temporal and spatial linearity lose their meaning. It is a world where not only seasons and time itself more generally are warped and stretched to the point of ripping apart, but also where "the light is still" (*FQ* 175). Light, we know, is nothing if not photons in motion. Spatial progression, just like temporal linearity, are evacuated of their traditional signification in a philosophical system where space and time are interlinked and inter-dependent, where they indeed form a single dimension as per Einstein's theory:[142] "Words move, music moves / Only in time; but that which is only living / Can only die. Words, after speech, reach / Into the silence" (*FQ* 175). If words and speech, like everything else, can move only in time, then they are muted by the meaninglessness of the semantic import of the utterance that something actually moves in time. Moving and stay-ing still can be defined only in the context of a time map where there is a well-defined beginning and a well-defined end, where, that is, we can describe a trajectory. In the absence of a time map and trajectories, the binary concepts of movement and stillness lose their meaning. Within this context, it is incomprehensible to assert that something moves in time and space because spacetime has been ripped apart, but it does make sense to say that something "Moves perpetually in its stillness" because a travel-ling object in a crumbled spacetime cannot be said to move towards any direction (*FQ* 175). It is a world wherein motion and stillness describe the same phenomenon and become cognates. Eliot parades before his readers an army of objective correlatives, a series of images tasked to evoke an immediate sensory experience that transcends conceptual specificity.

We may observe the same pattern in the second quartet, which seems to mark a seasonal shift from the autumn of the opening of the previous quartet to the summer. This shift is signalled as early as in the quartet's second stanza, where we read of dahlias sleeping "in the empty silence," flowers that bloom in mid and late summer. The third stanza thus finds the reader "On a summer midnight" listening to music around a bonfire (*FQ* 177). Once again Eliot is warping the linearity of time, for as we enter through the gate of this quartet we have progressed from autumn to summer, thereby reversing seasonal sequence. It is as if we are moving backwards into space and time instead of moving forwards, but as we have been warned in "Burnt Norton," linear spacetime has no place in Eliot's garden. "East Coker" mirrors this conceptual framework as the first two stanzas open with the injunction "In my beginning is my end," serving as a constant reminder that this is a world wherein our intuitive notions of time and space must collapse (*FQ* 177). This process of sea-sonal confusion is completed as soon as we proceed to the opening of the second canto, where all seasons have fused:

> What is the late November doing
> With the disturbance of the spring
> And creatures of the summer heat,
> And snowdrops writhing under feet
> And hollyhocks that aim too high
> Red into grey and tumble down
> Late roses filled with early snow?

(*FQ* 178)

The four epochs have joined together to orchestrate a spatio-temporal phenomenon that defies logic. Eliot complains that this way of expressing what he has intuited is unsatisfactory. It is coated "in a worn-out poetical fashion, / Leaving one still with the intolerable wrestle / With words and meanings" (*FQ* 179). Words fail to convey successfully Eliot's meaning, driving a wedge between signified and signifier. Conceptually, Eliot's remote place and time make no sense. Logos, the tool of thought that is inextricably connected to the process of making sense, seems to be an unfit agent in any attempt to describe the phenomenon that Eliot has intuited and struggles to convey. Intuition remains in an embryonic state that cannot deliver conceptual and logocentric understanding. Words thus provide only "a periphrastic study," and so the reader is urged to "Wait without thought, for you are not ready for thought: / So the darkness shall be the light, and the stillness the dancing" (*FQ* 180). Consciousness is intimately connected to thought and language, as per the Cartesian adage "cogito ergo sum." Eliot is describing a cognitive phenomenon here wherein we should no longer struggle to deliver what has been intuited to conceptual understanding and attempt to arrest its signifying drift, not because it is difficult but because it is impossible. It is a cognitive state where "the mind is conscious but conscious of / nothing," where we intellectually and physically stand still in a state of unconsciousness divested of any logocentric channels towards conceptual understanding (*FQ* 180). And so "We must be still and still moving / Into another intensity / For a further union, a deeper communion / Through the dark cold and the empty desolation" (*FQ* 183). Once we withdraw from sentient perception and lay down our thinking tools (language), we leave the surreal, dreamy world of the garden and take a turn towards the depths of a state that resembles death. Two lines later, the quartet ends with the following line: "In my end is my beginning" (*FQ* 183). This line enjoys a multi-layered signification.[143] Among these, it suggests a metaphysical argument, referring to the human state after physical passing, the soul migrating to another realm that signals a new beginning. It is also suggestive of a human condition whereby the conscious self, what defines us as thinking agents, ceases to operate and comes to an end in order to elevate human understanding to a higher, more intuitive level in this life. Eliot's literary ploy also suggests that there is an analogy between our progressive mode of reading and the spatio-temporality it describes: the beginning of the poem is its end and its end is its beginning. In the first instance, we might be tempted to go back to "Burnt Norton" and read it as the last quartet, but by the time we come to the end of the second quartet, which is spatio-temporally in the middle of the four quartets, we realize that if we do so we will have implicated ourselves in a process where going back is the same as going forward, and so there is no sense in trying to adopt and follow a linear spatio-temporal reading order. Whether we choose to read the line as referring to physical passing, to an unconscious state of being, to the reader's own reading strategy or to a combination of all three if we are tolerant of semantic polyphony, the central idea is that logocentrism, the centre of thought and consciousness, has to give way to another mode of consciousness, to an unconscious type of consciousness wherein everything that have been constructed upon the foundations of language and discursive understanding and perception collapse.

The next quartet, "The Dry Salvages," finds the reader "Here between the hither and the farther shore," where it is possible, "While time is withdrawn, [to] consider the future / And the past with an equal mind" (*FQ* 188). This poem, like the preceding ones, insists on constructing and situating the reader in logically remote places where time is deconstructed. However, the only means by which time can be withdrawn is time itself, so that we must first conceive of a future and a past as separate chronological categories within a temporal continuum and then fuse them together. The mere poetic injunction "consider the future / And the past" presupposes the automatic evocation of separate periods of time in a fixed sequential order. Even the term "timeless" evokes the presence of that which its semantic import is supposed to have signified as absent (*FQ* 189). The problem, then, is rooted in language itself and by extension in consciousness, and so the temporal withdrawal of which the poet sings can be realized by surrendering one's self:

> But to apprehend
> The point of intersection of the timeless
> With time, is an occupation for the saint—
> No occupation either, but something given
> And taken, in a lifetime's death in love,
> Ardour and selflessness and self-surrender.
>
> (*FQ* 189–90)

In this state of being, there are only "hints and guesses," not fully fledged conceptual understanding, as "The hint" is only "half-guessed, the gift half understood." We may recall here that, for Eliot, immediate experience remains in its pristine state only in the unconscious, while conscious thinking can only process its faint echoes, which emerge in consciousness as fragmented residues. Any attempt to reconstitute these fragments into their wholeness is futile. Poetry figures as the vehicle that can trigger in readers this type of immediate experience, which implicates consciousness in an attempt to hear its echoes as clearly and loudly as possible. This is what the poet refers to as "Incarnation" with a capital "I," an "I" that migrates in order to occupy a place where consciousness is withdrawn and, along with it, time: "Here the impossible union / Of spheres of existence is actual, / Here the past and future / Are conquered and reconciled" (*FQ* 190). The fourth quartet, "Little Gidding," continues along similar lines of thought:

> If you came this way,
> Taking any route, starting from anywhere,
> At any time or at any season,
> It would always be the same; you would have to put off
> Sense and notion.
>
> (*FQ* 192)

Regardless of whether the reader-wanderer has arrived here via any time or season, that is, via any of the other quartets or started off in "Little Gidding's" everlasting "Midwinter spring," they would have to suspend their aesthetic and conceptual means of perceiving and understanding (*FQ* 191). Reading the poem becomes a kind of a prayer, a surrendering of one's self to something higher, a sort of incarnation or ecstasy outside the self where what is intuited remains in an embryonic state that cannot be delivered to conceptual articulation and discursive processes: "You are not here to verify, / Instruct yourself, or inform curiosity / Or carry report. You are here to kneel / Where prayer has been valid" (*FQ* 192). Our book of prayers, the words we whisper to ourselves, are the words that synthesize Eliot's book of poetry. But we should be reminded that this kind of "prayer is more / Than an order of words, the conscious occupation / Of the praying mind, or the sound of the voice praying" (*FQ* 192). To remain faithful to the semantic and aesthetic import of words and language becomes a form of a sacrilege, a violation of the piety that the process of this particular prayer requires. To lose faith in the word is tantamount to withdrawing from consciousness, to allowing the praying self to "put off / Sense and notion" (*FQ* 192) and so come to witness a realm where the spatio-temporality that underpins the way we think about and feel the world around and within us gives way to a "Here" where "the intersection of the timeless moment / Is England and nowhere. Never and always" (*FQ* 192). Recalling "East Coker," Eliot describes this religious experience as a kind of a death in life, which establishes a form of communication to which the living and fully conscious people are unable to attune themselves: "And what the dead had no speech for, when living, / They can tell you, being dead: the communication / Of the dead is tongued with fire beyond the language of the living" (*FQ* 192). The Barthian death of the author assumes a different signification in Eliot's poem, for there has to be communion between the dead author and the dead reader, a process that ministers the death of consciousness as the only means by which true communication between poet and reader can be established via a purified language. The text necessitates the death of the author's consciousness, the death of the referent and the death of the reader's consciousness. To recall Eliot's words, the formative mystery of poetry, on both the reader's and the writer's part, is a fusion of feelings, emotions and thoughts into a "concentration which does not happen consciously or of deliberation" (*SE* 298) in an attempt to "extend the confines of human consciousness and to report things unknown, to express the inexpressible."[144] Immediate experience does not survive in its pure form in the conscious subject. Rather, we must

> turn to inspect a lower stage of mind [...] when it is least active, we do not find one or another of these elements into which we analyse the developed consciousness, but we find them all at a lower stage. We do not find feeling without thought, or presentation without reflection: we find both feeling and thought, presentation, redintegration and abstraction, all at a lower stage.
>
> (*KE* 17)

Notes

1 T.S. Eliot, "Commentary," *Criterion*, 13: 52 (1934): 452.
2 Manju Jain, "Appendix: List of Courses Taken by Eliot while at Harvard," Harvard University, A.B., June 1909; A.M., February 1911. Reproduced by permission of the Harvard University Archives in *T.S. Eliot and American Philosophy: The Harvard Years* (Cambridge: Cambridge University Press, 1992), 255.
3 T.S. Eliot, *The Varieties of Metaphysical Poetry*, ed. and introduced by Ronald Schuchard (London: Faber and Faber, 1993), 81.
4 Jain, "Appendix," 256.
5 Harry Todd Costello, *Josiah Royce's Seminar: 1913–1914*, ed. by Grover Smith (New Brunswick: Rutgers University Press, 1963).
6 Charles Blakewell, "Novum Itinerarium Mentu in Deum," *Philosophical Review*, 24: 3 (1816). Reprinted in E. Auxier, *Papers in Honor of Josiah Royce on His Sixtieth Birthday* (New York: Longmans, Green, 1916), 32.
7 Arthur O. Lovejoy, *The Revolt Against Dualism: An Inquiry Concerning the Existence of Ideas* (La Salle, IL: W. W. Norton and the Open Court Publishing Company, 1930), 1–4.
8 See, for instance, Thomas S. Kuhn, *The Structure of Scientific Revolutions* (Chicago, IL: University of Chicago Press, 1962) and Gerald Holton, *Thematic Origins of Scientific Thought* (Cambridge, MA: Harvard University Press, 1973).
9 Richard Wollheim, "Eliot and F. H. Bradley: An Account," in *Eliot in Perspective: A Symposium*, ed. by Martin Graham (London: Macmillan, 1970), 173.
10 For Eliot's treatment of Bradley's philosophy see also William Skaff, *The Philosophy of T. S. Eliot: From Skepticism to a Surrealist Poetic* (Philadelphia: University of Pennsylvania Press, 1986).
11 Jewel Spears Brooker, *Mastery and Escape: T.S. Eliot and the Dialectic of Modernism* (Amherst: University of Massachusetts Press, 1994), 197.
12 F.H. Bradley, *Essays on Truth and Reality* (New York: Cambridge University Press, 2011), 159.
13 F. H. Bradley, *Appearance and Reality* (London: Routledge, 2002), 462.

14 Eliot, *Varieties*, 55, 51.
15 Ibid., 247.
16 Ibid., 54–5.
17 Eliot, "Commentary," 452.
18 Lyndall Gordon, *Eliot's Early Years* (Oxford: Oxford University Press, 1977), 141.
19 Jain, *T.S. Eliot and American Philosophy*, 167.
20 See also Costello, *Royce's Seminar*, 173–4.
21 See Eliot's review of Wundt's *Elements of Folk Psychology: Outlines of a Psychological History of the Development of Mankind*, *International Journal of Ethics*, 27: 2 (1917): 252–4 which reveals knowledge of Wundt's earlier work that treats the mind-body problem.
22 T.S. Eliot, *After Strange Gods: A Primer of Modern Heresy* (London: Faber and Faber 1934), 60.
23 On this point, see also, Skaff, *The Philosophy of T. S. Eliot*, 48.
24 See also, Ibid., 49.
25 T.S. Eliot, Review of *Theism and Humanism*, by A. J. Balfour, *International Journal of Ethics*, 26: 2 (1916): 288.
26 Ibid.
27 Ibid., 49.
28 Costello, *Royce's Seminar*, 74.
29 T.S. Eliot, Review of *Group Theories of Religion and the Religion of the Individual, by Clement J. Webb*, *International Journal of Ethics*, 27: 1 (1916): 117.
30 Emile Durkheim, *The Elementary Forms of the Religious Life: A Study in Religious Sociology*, trans. Joseph Ward Swain (London: G. Allen & Unwin, 1915), 439.
31 Ibid., 441.
32 Ibid., 444.
33 Skaff, *The Philosophy of T. S. Eliot*, 61.
34 Durkheim, *The Elementary Forms of the Religious Life*, 445.
35 Costello, *Royce's Seminar*, 74.
36 Lucien Lévy-Brühl, *How Natives Think*, trans. Lilian A. Clare (New York: Washington Square, 1926), 31.
37 On this point, see also Skaff, *The Philosophy of T. S. Eliot*, 63.
38 T.S. Eliot, Review of *Group Theories of Religion and the Religion of the Individual, by Clement C. J. Webb*, *International Journal of Ethics* (1916): 116.
39 Ibid.
40 Costello, *Royce's Seminar*, 76, 78.
41 T.S. Eliot, "London Letter," *Dial*, 71: 4 (1921): 453.
42 T.S. Eliot, "A Prediction in Regard to Three English Authors, Writers Who, though Masters of Thought, Are likewise Masters of Art," *Vanity Fair*, 21: 6 (1924): 29.
43 Eliot, Review of *Group Theories*, 116.
44 See Stephen Spender, *T.S. Eliot* (New York: Penguin Books, 1976), 101–2.
45 Eliot, "Commentary," 342.
46 T.S. Eliot, "Introductory *Essay to London: A Poem and the Vanity of Human Wishes* by Samuel Johnson" (1930), in *The Complete Prose of T. S. Eliot: The Critical Edition, vol. IV: English Lion, 1930–1933*, ed. by Jason Harding, and Ronald Schuchard (Baltimore, MD: Johns Hopkins University Press, 2015), 173.
47 T. S. Eliot, *On Poetry and Poets* (London: Faber & Faber, 1957), 113.

48 Harry Trosman, "T. S. Eliot and The Waste Land: Psychopathological Antecedents and Transformations," *Archives of General Psychiatry*, 30: 5 (1974): 717.
49 Eliot, *Poetry and Poets*, 98–9.
50 Eliot, "Commentary," 452 and Gordon, *Eliot's Early Years*, 141.
51 See also T.S. Eliot, "The Search for Moral Sanction," *Listener*, 7 (1932): 445.
52 T.S. Eliot, "London Letter," *Dial*, 73 (1922): 330.
53 Ibid.
54 T.S. Eliot, "Ulysses, Order, and Myth," *Selected Prose of T.S. Eliot* (London: Faber and Faber, 1975), 175.
55 T.S. Eliot, "Notes on Current Letters: The Lesson of Baudelaire," *Tyro*, 1 (1921): 4.
56 T.S. Eliot, "Reflections on Contemporary Poetry," *The Egoist*, 6: 3 (1919): 39.
57 T.S. Eliot, "War-Paint and Feathers," in *Primitivism and Twentieth-Century Art: A Documentary History*, ed. by Jack Flam and Miriam Deutsch (Berkeley: California University Press, 2003), 121–2; Eliot mentions Harrison, Cornford, Murray and Cooke in *SE*, 49; and in "A Prediction in Regard to Three English Authors," Harrison, Cornford, and Cooke.
58 Gilbert Murray, "Excursus on the Ritual Forms Preserved in Greek Tragedy," in Jane Harrison's *Themis: A Study of the Social Origins of Greek Religion* (1912), 2nd ed. (Cambridge: Cambridge University Press, 1927), 341.
59 Francis Macdonald Cornford, *The Origin of Attic Comedy* (London: Edward Arnold, 1914), 165.
60 T.S. Eliot, "The Importance of Greek," *The Criterion*, 3: 2 (1925): 341.
61 Ibid.
62 Ibid., 342.
63 T.S. Eliot, "Hooker, Hobbes, and Others," *Times Literary Supplement*, 1293 (1926): 789.
64 T.S. Eliot, "The Ballet," *Criterion*, 3 (1925): 441.
65 Eliot, "London Letter," 214.
66 Eliot viewed their performances in London in 1919, 1921, and 1924. See "London Letter," (August 1921) and (October 1921) and "A Commentary," *Criterion*, 3 (October 1924) and (January 1925).
67 T.S. Eliot, "The Possibility of a Poetic Drama," *The Dial*, (1920): 447.
68 Skaff, *The Philosophy of T. S. Eliot*, 94.
69 T.S. Eliot, "The Beating of a Drum," *The Nation and Athenaeum*, (1923): 11.
70 Ibid., 11.
71 Ibid., 12.
72 T.S. Eliot, "Introduction," in Charlotte Eliot's *Savonarola: A Dramatic Poem* (London: R. Cobden-Sanderson, 1926), viii.
73 Eliot, "Beating," 12.
74 T.S. Eliot, "Marianne Moore," *Dial*, 75 (1923): 567.
75 Eliot, "Ballet," 441–2.
76 Eliot, "Introduction," *Savonarola*, xi–xii.
77 Eliot, "Beating," 12.
78 T.S. Eliot, "Five Points on Dramatic Writing," *Townsman* 1 (1938): 10.
79 T.S. Eliot, *The Sacred Wood: Essays on Poetry and Criticism* (London: Methuen, 1928), viii.
80 Glenn Stephen Burne, "T S. Eliot and Remy de Gourmont," *Bucknell Review*, 13 (1959): 113–26, and *Rémy de Gourmont: His Ideas and Influence in England and America* (Carbondale: Southern Illinois University Press, 1963).
81 See also Eliot, *Sacred Wood*, 1, 8.

82 Ibid., 13–4.
83 Eliot, *Poetry and Poets*, 153.
84 Remy de Gourmont, "La Création subconsciente," *La Culture des idées* (Paris: Mercure de France, 1964), 68–9.
85 Eliot, "Marianne Moore," 595.
86 T.S. Eliot, *The Letters of T.S. Eliot*, vol. I, ed. by Valerie Eliot (London: Faber & Faber, 1948), 317–8.
87 Charles-Louis Philippe, *Bubu de Montparnasse* (Paris: Garner-Flammarion, 1978), 53.
88 Eliot, *After Strange Gods*, 18.
89 Ibid., 29.
90 Ibid.
91 Ibid., 32.
92 Eliot, *Poetry and Poets*, 58.
93 T. S. Eliot, "Was There a Scottish Literature?," *Athenaeum* 4657 (1919): 680.
94 Ibid., 680.
95 T.S. Eliot, "Reflections on Contemporary Poetry," *Egoist*, 6 (1919): 39.
96 T.S. Eliot, "The Three Provincialities," *Tyro*, 2 (1922): 13.
97 T.S. Eliot "A Preface to Modern Literature," *Vanity Fair*, 21 (1923): 118.
98 T.S. Eliot, "Turgenev," *Egoist*, 4: 11 (1917): 167.
99 T.S. Eliot, "A Brief Introduction to the Method of Paul Valéry," in *Le Serpent par Paul Valéry* (London: R. Cobden-Sanderson, 1924), 7–15.
100 Eliot, *Letters*, vol. I, 387.
101 T.S. Eliot, "In Memory of Henry James," *Egoist*, 5 (1918): 2.
102 T.S. Eliot, "Prose and Verse," *Chapbook*, 22 (1921): 9.
103 Eliot, *Sacred Wood*, 64.
104 Ibid., 158.
105 Ibid., 154.
106 Ibid., 158.
107 Ibid., 163.
108 Ibid., 162–3.
109 Sarah Kennedy, *T. S. Eliot and the Dynamic Imagination* (Cambridge: Cambridge University Press, 2018), 166.
110 Eliot, *Sacred Wood*, 63.
111 T.S. Eliot, "John Donne," *The Nation and Atheneum*, 33 (1923): 332.
112 Eliot, *Poetry and Poets*, 193.
113 T.S. Eliot, *Collected Poems, 1909–1962* (London: Faber & Faber, 1963), 204.
114 Eliot, *Poetry and Poets*, 107.
115 Eliot, *Collected Poems*, 203.
116 Eliot, *Poetry and Poets*, 264.
117 From a typescript of the play. Eliot retained only the first of these lines. Quoted from Anne Barton, "Shakespeare and the Limits of Language," in *Shakespeare Survey 24: Shakespeare: Theatre Poet*, ed. by Kenneth Muir (Cambridge: Cambridge University Press, 1971), 19.
118 T.S. Eliot, "Preface," in *Anabasis* (London: Faber and Faber, 1931), 10.
119 Altieri, Charles, "Steps of the Mind in T.S. Eliot's Poetry," *Twentieth Century Poetry, Fiction, Theory, Bucknell Review*, 22 (1976): 201.
120 Eliot, *Collected Poems*, 98.
121 Ibid., 100.
122 Eliot, "Preface," 9–10.
123 Ibid., 8–9.

124 Eliot, *Poetry and Poets*, 124.
125 T.S. Eliot, *Selected Prose of T.S. Eliot*, ed. by Frank Kermode (London: Faber and Faber 1975), 110–1.
126 G. Douglas Atkins, *Reading T.S. Eliot: Four Quartets and the Journey towards Understanding* (New York: Palgrave Macmillan, 2012), 2.
127 Roger Bellin, "The Seduction of Argument and the Danger of Parody in the 'Four Quartets'," *Twentieth Century Literature*, 53: 4 (2007): 422.
128 T.S. Eliot, "The Art of Poetry I," *Paris Review*, 21 (1959): 63.
129 Nancy K. Gish, *Time in the Poetry of T. S. Eliot: A Study in Structure and Theme* (Totowa, NJ: Barnes & Noble, 1981).
130 R. L. Brett, *Reason and Imagination: A Study of Form and Meaning in Four Poems* (London: Oxford University Press for the University of Hull, 1960), 120.
131 Vincent Miller, "Eliot's Submission to Time," *The Sewanee Review*, 84: 3 (1976): 458.
132 Corey Latta, "T. S. Eliot's Bergsonism 'Always Present': Incarnation and Duration in Four Quartets," in *When the Eternal Can Be Met: The Bergsonian Theology of Time in the Works of C.S. Lewis, T.S. Eliot and W.H. Auden* (Cambridge: Lutterworth Press, 2014), 115–66.
133 Kenneth Paul Kramer, *Redeeming Time: T.S. Eliot's Four Quartets* (Lanham: Cowly Publications, 2007), xiii.
134 Ibid., xvii.
135 H. Reid MacCallum, "Time Lost and Regained," in *Imitation and Design and Other Essays*, ed. by William Blisset (Toronto: University of Toronto Press, 1963), 137.
136 David Moody, "Four Quartets: Music, Word, Meaning and Value," in *The Cambridge Companion to T.S. Eliot* (Cambridge: Cambridge University Press, 2006), 150.
137 Alireza Farahbakhsh, "Postmodern Word in Eliot's Four Quartets," *Journal of the Australasian Universities Language and Literature Association*, 107 (2007): 63.
138 Ronald Moore, *Metaphysical Symbolism in T.S. Eliot's Four Quartets* (Stanford, CA: Stanford University Press, 1965), 25.
139 Doris T. Wight, "Metaphysics through Paradox in Eliot's 'Four Quartets'," *Philosophy & Rhetoric*, 23: 1 (1990): 63.
140 Ibid., 64.
141 Elliott Jaques, "The Enigma of Time," in *The Sociology of Time*, ed. by John Hassard (New York: Palgrave Macmillan, 1990), 24. On this point, see also Kevin Hart, *Poetry and Revelation: For a Phenomenology of Religious Poetry* (London: Bloomsbury, 2017), 54.
142 Ole Bay-Petersen, "T. S. Eliot and Einstein: The Fourth Dimension in the Four Quartets," *English Studies*, 66: 2 (1985): 143–55.
143 See, for instance, Barry J. Faulk, "Eliot and the Music-Hall Comedian," in *The Edinburgh Companion to T. S. Eliot and the Arts*, ed. by Frances Dickey, and John D. Morgenstern (Edinburgh: Edinburgh University Press, 2016), 192, and Paul Murray, *T.S. Eliot and Mysticism* (Basingstoke: Macmillan, 1994), 137–8.
144 Eliot, *Poetry and Poets*, 193.

6   Conclusion

From Modernism to
21st-century Cognitive Science

The notion of the intelligent unconscious is not idiosyncratic to the authors discussed in this book. They are representative of a wider tendency in modernist literary culture to adopt a theory of the unconscious hitherto unexplored, a theory that shifts emphasis from Freudian psychoanalysis to intelligent forms of cognition performed unconsciously. For example, H.D. openly declared her admiration for Freud's theories, but often portrayed the unconscious in ways that are more congenial to Carpenter's, James's and Lawrence's outlooks. Out of the sessions she conducted with Freud emerged the classic memoir *Tribute to Freud* of 1944. This account is full of insights into the intimate aspects of Freud's practice and into the way in which psychoanalysis was perceived by H.D. As she noted, Freud would "sit there quietly, like an owl in a tree,"[1] or pound the head-piece of the horsehair sofa with his hand and complain: "The trouble is—I am an old man—*you do not think it worth your while to love me.*"[2] At the heart of this account is a series of visions she experienced on a wall in Greece while on a trip with Bryher—a face, a chalice, a tripod, a Nike. As H.D. has it, these are things which "had happened in my life [...] actual psychic or occult experiences."[3] The text constitutes an interesting account of how H.D., while seeking Freud's opinion of these experiences, also resisted it. Freud insisted that they are a narcissistic desire for wonder and religious renewal. H.D., however, sees them as being outside the purview of psychoanalysis and wishes to move "outside the province of established psychoanalysis."[4] In her resistance to Freud's "caustic implied criticism," she promoted a different approach to psychic life, "another region of cause and effect, another region of question and answer."[5]

H.D.'s essays on cinema grouped together as "Cinema and the Classics" (1919) provide significant insights into this non-Freudian psychological region. Here, H.D. laments the contemporary "dissociation" of body and soul, which gave rise to a Cartesian experience that provides a limited "point of view."[6] H.D.'s preoccupation with unconscious cognitive processes is further exemplified in her personal manifesto, *Notes on Thought and Vision*, where she expands on the notion of the "over-mind." The "over-mind" suggests a sphere beyond the control of the conscious mind, where unconscious processes are at work, bringing about a higher, transcendental cognitive experience. This mechanism promotes two kinds of "sight" or "knowing," that of the womb and that of the brain, both of which are located "*in* the body" and are "equally important."[7] H.D. asserts the cognitive capacity of these centres of "knowing," which she defines as "over-mind intelligence," while noting that "both [are] capable of thought."[8] "Jelly-fish consciousness" is H.D.'s term for this unconscious experience, in which the "over-mind" was first revealed to her. As she describes it, she felt a "cap of consciousness" over her head.[9] From this cap or "super-mind," "super-feelers" reach down through the body and outwards like the tentacles of a jelly-fish.[10] The "jelly-fish consciousness" has a controlling function as it "seemed to come definitely into the field or realm of the intellect or brain," directing and shaping the thinking process.[11] In *Advent*, H.D. relates the jelly-fish directly to the unconscious state, which she calls the "'jelly-fish' experience of double ego."[12] As a transparent and elusive entity, the jelly-fish became an ideal metaphor to represent the hidden processes that belong to the unconscious mind. The wave-like movements of this almost unformed presence represent a resistance to a specific structure. The absence of any internal or external structure by the lack of skeleton or shell in the jelly-fish aptly reflects the ability of the unconscious to move beyond a well-ordered form and conceptual clarity and escape the boundaries of discursive consciousness.

H.D. related her personal experience of the overmind: "a cap is over my head, a cap of consciousness over my head, my forehead, affecting a little my eyes. Sometimes when I am in that state of consciousness, things about me appear slightly blurred as if seen under water."[13] H.D. visualizes it as a new form of consciousness that takes her into a semi-hypnotic state. In a passage from an earlier draft of the *Notes*, H.D. used the terms "overmind" and "subconscious" as near cognates:

> the jelly-fish—or to use the terminology of the modern psychologists— the sub-conscious mind. The realisation of this sub-conscious world is the concern of the artist. Nevertheless, the sub-conscious world is there for everyone. The minds of men differ but the over-minds or sub-conscious minds are alike.[14]

She later substituted "sub-conscious" for "over-conscious," and deleted the phrase "the terminology of the modern psychologists." This earlier draft is suggestive of not only the affinities between the two terms, but also her tortuous struggle to find her own approach to the mapping of the mind. Lisa Rado argued that the language of transcendence used to describe this experience attempts to "authorize itself by 'over' combining the paralyzing power of literary fathers such as Pound, Freud, Aldington, and Lawrence by incorporating power within herself, creating an 'over' mind and joining it to her womb."[15]

This unconscious mechanism, portrayed as a kind of superconsciousness, emerges as the source of imagination and creativity. As H.D. noted, the highest cultural achievements, such as Leonardo's "Madonna on the Rocks," the sculpture of the charioteer at Delphi and Euripides's choruses, are windows into the world of the pure overmind.[16] The origins of these works of art are thus placed in a transcendent realm accessible only to the overmind. As H.D. wrote, one needs "an over-mind or a slight glimmering of over-mind intelligence to understand over-mind intelligence."[17] The overmind becomes for H.D. a mark of true creative genius: "I believe there are artists coming in the next generation, some of whom will have the secret of using their over-minds."[18] It is this universal and trans-historical attribute that makes great artists "never old, never dead."[19] The ideas treated by the Attic dramatists, for instance, "were eternal, changeless ideas that he had grown aware of by means of his over-mind consciousness."[20] The body constitutes the origin, location and means to approach this ecstatic state: "the human body may be used as an approach to over-mind or universal mind."[21]

H.D.'s concept of the overmind, moreover, forms a link between androgyny and creative or artistic empowerment, as it involves a collapse of gender and mind-body dichotomies alike. As Albert Gelpi pointed out, "the impulse behind 'Notes' is to account for those mysterious moments in which the polarities seemed to fall away."[22] The cognitive potential of the overmind, H.D. argues, can be world-changing: it "could turn the whole tide of human thought, [it] could [...] slash across and destroy the world of dead, murky thought."[23] The overmind becomes for H.D. a way to undermine the mind-body polarity since it provides access into the sources of creativity and a way to move beyond gender differences. H.D. asserted that the overmind is subject to impersonality, echoing the impersonal and universal nature of the unconscious in Lawrence, Woolf and Eliot.[24] Like Woolf, she describes this unconscious experience with water metaphors, and links it with androgyny and creativity. Moreover, H.D., like Lawrence, uses the metaphor of "coal" to showcase the role of the body in achieving this unconscious state. Just "like a lump of coal" can be transmuted to a more ethereal form, the overmind emerges from the physical to achieve a transcendental state. Thus, echoing Lawrence, she stressed the fact that even though the overmind is manifested "in a different form" the substance remains the same.[25] These connections, both thematic and linguistic, warrant further investigation in order to study the undertones of these themes and the ways they form the basis of her conception of the unconscious.

Aldous Huxley, too, repeatedly expressed his opposition to the Freudian system. When Humphry Osmond took him to a conference of the American Psychiatric Association, Huxley crossed himself devoutly every time Freud's name was mentioned, drawing attention to his long-life disrespect.[26] One of Huxley's favourite anecdotes was that of a thoroughly conditioned Freudian, who, having taken LSD, noticed nothing extraordinary, except that "his excreta smelled stronger and sweeter."[27] "Sig Freud's body lies a-mouldering in the grave," Huxley noted sarcastically, "but his soul, or his anus, goes marching along."[28] The pun on "Sig" and the implication that Freudians cannot distinguish the soul from the anus pervades Huxley's interviews, lectures and letters. It also underlies the extensive anti-Freudian satire in *Brave New World*. The major difficulty with Freudian psychology, Huxley told the *Paris Review*, "is that it is based exclusively on a study of the sick. Freud never met a healthy human being."[29] Huxley asserted that Freudianism had a detrimental effect on the intellectual life in the modern period; in *Jesting Pilate* he lamented that moderns "have only a collection of scientific, or sham-scientific, words and phrases to serve as the framework of their philosophy of life."[30] Freud had provided a surplus of such words like "complex" and "wish-fulfilment" that became part of everyone's vocabulary.

Huxley saw Freudian psychoanalysis as a backward-looking science, "only concerned with the past," whereas his own intellectual development can be described as a gradual awakening to what he called man's "future potentialities."[31] "Freud's greatest error," Huxley noted, was "not to have paid sufficient attention" to the "higher Not-Self within and beyond the self."[32] Huxley preferred the theory of the unconscious put forward by F.W.H. Myers to Freud's explanation of human behaviour in terms of libido and repression. Preoccupied with states of mind that lead to disaster, Freud, unlike Myers, "paid very little attention to what may be called the positive side of the unconscious."[33] Huxley juxtaposed Freud's view of the unconscious to Myers's: "Freud is talking all the time about the basement downstairs with the rats and black beetles, whereas Myers is largely concerned with the floors above the ground floor" which, having no roof, remain "open to the sky."[34] The rats and beetles are definitely in the basement, but Huxley believed that one could exterminate them by strengthening the positive elements Freud minimized in his interpretation of human personality. As Huxley noted, by consigning the unconscious to the cellars, Freud was led to consider only "the destructive activities of Até" but blindly to ignore "the influxes of Menos, the visitations of the Muses."[35] Comparing psychologists to sea divers, Huxley decided that Freud and Jung come up too muddy. Myers's *Human Personality* (1903), by contrast, "set forth a theory of the unconscious far more comprehensive than Freud's narrow and one-sided hypothesis." Unlike Freudians, Myers possessed a strong sense of "that impersonal spiritual world which transcends and interpenetrates our bodies."[36]

In *Brave New World*, society conforms to Freudian designs, but Helmholtz Watson—an embryonic mystic and poet-philosopher—matures intellectually, contrary to Freudian and Pavlovian theories, and gradually embraces the theories of F.W.H. Myers and Gerald Heard. Huxley creates a world wherein it was Freud's mechanistic conception of personality that paved the way for the inhuman mistakes of Pavlov and John Watson, as well as for the domination of behaviourist controllers in the brave new world. Dr. MacPhail—Scottish physician and co-founder of the utopian fictional *Island* of Pala—links Freudism and Behaviourism as the West's "two highly touted systems of psychology," both of which are "hopelessly inadequate."[37] The healthy Palanese of *Island* follow "neither Paul nor Freud."[38] Freud dominates *Brave New World*, but the Palanese have banished him from their *Island*. *Brave New World* highlights the inherently positive side of human nature via Helmholtz Watson's rebellion against the Freudian system later in his life. The novel is structured by the principle that man's inspirations and intuitions are as real as the compulsions and aggressions assigned to them by Freud. As Huxley noted, "I think (Freud) omitted too much from his purview of human beings."[39] By ignoring the cognitive potential of the unconscious and playing down the visitation of the Muses, Freud convinced people of their inherent negativity. "I was never intoxicated by Freud as some people were," Huxley told an interviewer, "and I get less intoxicated as I go on."[40] In the opening pages of *Brave New World*, Mustapha Mond lists the accomplishments that have enshrined Freud among the founding fathers of this future society: "Our Ford—or Our Freud, as, for some inscrutable reason, he chose to call himself whenever he spoke of psychological matters."[41] The equation of "Our Freud" with "Our Ford" is premeditated, since both have contributed to and have done their share to make the future perilous for humanity. Rather than an unlikely pairing, the American Industrialist and the Viennese psychologist contributed equally to the reductive behaviourist conspiracy of *Brave New World*.

Often dismissed as "surprising,"[42] this correlation underlines the particularities of Huxley's anti-Freudian critique. Huxley discloses the potential danger of this correlation and attempts to expose how heavily conditioned the society is by a Freudian mechanistic-oriented approach. Ford's utopia is a world that runs like one of his factories. Huxley also accused Freud of conditioning his definition of man entirely on a study of the sick. The goal of the society of the brave new world is to make the populace sick in predictable, socially profitable ways. Mond's society is a Freudian society that reproduces the industrial principle and constitutes a perversion of tendencies latent in Freud's thinking. Mond and his colleagues have learnt from Freud that the causes of human behaviour can often be traced to the repression of childhood experience. This is the stage of development where the germ of behaviourism lies, which attempts to regulate behaviour by implanting the necessary structuring experiences. By controlling childhood experiences, behaviourism could dictate what the individual will repress and consequently manage the way one behaves. The brave new world constitutes a response to the

Pavlovian possibilities inherent in Freudian thought. Inspired by Freud, the behaviourists in the brave new world devise mechanical traumas, socially engineered taboos and contrived primal scenes to produce an easily manipulated collective unconscious. They make the populace sick in foreseeable and socially "useful" ways.

The neo-Pavlovian Conditioning Rooms are based on Watson's actual experiments, but they are ultimately Freudian in being formative, traumatic and concentrated on childhood.[43] Humanity is treated as a complicated machine that can be manipulated by planting certain ideas: neurotics are thus conscientiously created. By instilling artificially stimulated phobias through association, the citizenry is prevented from seeking truth and beauty. The behaviourists of the brave new world apply Pavlovian methodology to Freudian insights about the human personality. This is also a Fordian utopia. The goal of life as defined by the District Hatchery Commissioner is "to increase consumption"; "the consumption of consumption" has been introduced to compel "every man, woman and child [...] to consume so much a year."[44] Freudian and behaviourist psychology combine to support the Fordian preoccupation with production quotas by creating conditioned personalities. The brave new world society, blindly committed to the pleasure principle, makes immediate gratification the purpose of life. *The Brave New World* is populated by spoilt brats of any age, slaves to their ids. The concept of arrested development is another of Freud's discoveries implemented in *The Brave New World*. Everyone's development is arrested scientifically with the help of Freud's discoveries on the reasons and the ways through which such arrests can take place. Shorter hours, improved working conditions, better benefits, all these demands that Ford had to deal with are beyond the imagination of the new working class. For Huxley, if 20th-century science is cutting man down to a size it can handle, a "Procrustes in modern dress," then Ford, Freud and Watson are also in Procrustean uniforms.[45] Freud, along with Ford and Watson, is satirized for his essentially mechanistic conception of human behaviour. Our Ford is our Freud because Huxley saw both as glorified mechanics. Both provided behaviourists with the information needed to construct the brave new world. A combination of Freudian theory and Pavlovian methodology has the potential to produce the ideal Fordian worker: a model citizen who is a perfectly stable behaviouristic phenomenon with socially useful neuroses. Borrowing from Freud and Pavlov, the brave new world knows how to manufacture the kind of worker Ford wanted while Freud becomes emblematic of a reductive conception of the human mind.

Huxley emerges as an outspoken critic of Freud, explicitly stating his admiration for Myers's psychology. The mark of genius depended, for Huxley, on a "particularly active and good positive unconscious."[46] The "uprush of helpful material from the deep levels of the unconscious, which is then worked up by the conscious self into an appropriate form" is too brilliant, Huxley believed, to have come by the conscious self alone.[47] He also believed that the unconscious is teleological in nature, possessing the ability to direct the mind in order to achieve certain aims: "The mind, it seems to me, is a roulette board which is very frequently tampered with by a purposeful being."[48] Huxley was also interested in the scientific and experiential study of the use of psychedelic substances as catalysts for psychological transformation. He was experimenting with substances as a means of reaching an expanding consciousness and ultimately a visionary state. His interest in unconscious states was profoundly influenced by his close relationship with D.H. Lawrence. It was also under Lawrence's guidance that Huxley embraced a stance grounded in personal experience and corporeal knowledge.[49] Huxley described Lawrence after their first meeting in 1915 as "a good man more than most" as well as "a novelist and poet and genius."[50] After Lawrence's death, Huxley portrayed him as "the most extraordinary and impressive human being I have ever known."[51]

The influence of psychoanalysis on the movement of Surrealism is well known. However, it often tends to be exaggerated, thereby obscuring the ways surrealists understood the unconscious.[52] André Breton was expecting a thrilling encounter with Freud when he began his trip to Vienna in 1921. What was confirmed instead was a lack of common ground.[53] Freud's letter to Breton validated the impossibility of a fruitful dialogue between them: "I am not in the position to explain what surrealism is and what it is after. It could be that I am not in any way made to understand it."[54] In 1933, Breton asserted that the attempt to undermine rationalism as the only reality was not solely indebted to psychoanalysis: "I think we owe more than is generally conceded to what William James justly called the *gothic psychology* of F.W.H. Myers."[55] He embraced Myers's approach to the unconscious and committed Surrealism to "the Myers problem (strictly psychological): the determination of the precise nature of the subliminal."[56] The conception of the unconscious in Surrealism as an intelligent mechanism was also reflected in the approach to dreams. Dreams depict an unconscious reality, a reality of wider potential that the one experienced through our waking self. Rather than distorted instinctual traces, dreams for Breton have a revelatory aspect. Breton emphasized the temporality of the present in relation to the future (not the past) and dismissed Freud's approach to dreams: "Freud is again quite surely mistaken in concluding that the prophetic dream does not exist."[57] Breton conceived of dreams, like James and Myers, as looking into the future, resolving issues with an eye towards achieving certain aims. For Breton, to believe that the dream is "exclusively revelatory of the past is to deny the value of motion."[58] Surrealists also experimented extensively with automatic writing. "The First Manifesto of Surrealism" defined it as "pure psychic automatism," and the Surrealists as "modest recording devices" for "thought dictated in the absence of all control exercised by reason."[59] Automatic writing, as a means of revealing the thinking processes of the unconscious, was also practised by many writers like Rainer Maria Rilke, Gertrude Stein and H.D. Automatic writing, practised by researchers, Surrealists and literary writers alike offered a way of reaching the intelligent unconscious. As Sonu Shamdasani noted, "automatic writing and 'its' unconscious was an 'other' unconscious" explored at the time.[60]

We can also find this alternative view of the unconscious in Henri Bergson's philosophy, which influenced immensely literary writers, especially in the first half of the 20th century. As Suzanne Guerlac noted, "After Deleuze and Guattari's critique of psychoanalysis we can appreciate in Bergson another way to think unconsciousness."[61] Bergson's first publication in 1886, "On Unconscious Simulation in States of Hypnosis," concerns the results of his observations at experiments on hypnosis.[62] This foreshadowed Bergson's interest in the role of unconscious memories—an interest that culminates in his election as president of the London-based Society for Psychical Research in 1913.[63] Bergson was immensely influenced by the work of his friend, William James, whom he met in 1908.[64] He wrote the Preface, "Truth and Reality," to the French translation of James's *Pragmatism*. James was also immensely impressed by Bergson's philosophy; he called it a second Copernican revolution, and wrote that "in philosophy the present epoch will be a sort of turning point in the history of philosophy."[65] Bergson distinguished between two kinds of memory: habit-memory, which facilitates automatic behaviour, and true or "pure" memory,[66] which consists of the accumulation of personal memories, an accumulation that, for Bergson, "is latent and unconscious."[67] Bergson singled out memory as "a privileged problem" precisely because an adequate conception of it would enable us to gain a better insight into the nature of unconscious psychical states.[68] In *Bergsonism*, Deleuze suggests that Bergson introduces an ontological unconscious over and above the psychological one, and it is this which enables us to speak of the being of the past and to grant the past a genuine existence. The past is not simply reducible to the status of a former present, and neither can it be reduced to mere recollections.[69]

Bergson's understanding of the unconscious is far removed from the psychoanalytic paradigm; it did not depend on repression or the Oedipal complex. Instead, the unconscious facilitates consciousness so that the distinction between the two systems becomes subtle and fluid; action and memory inform each other interactively. Bergson based his system of philosophical psychology on a form of unconsciousness that he called *intuition*.[70] Seeing in the mind a dynamic system of constant flux, he analysed the mystical *élan*, an element which draws his theories closer to psychical researchers and their conception of the intelligent unconscious.[71] His belief that "pure intellect is a contraction, by condensation, of a more extensive power," a power of "duration" beneath the mechanistic divisions of discursive logic, shared many similarities with James's and Myers's unconscious consciousness.[72] His attribution of intelligence to the unconscious is further exemplified in his understanding and adoption of Aristotle's concept of νοῦς, that is, the direct and immediate apprehension of basic truths:

> in the philosophy of Aristotle, by the active intellect, the νοῦς that has been called ποιητικός that is, by what is essential and yet unconscious in human intelligence. The νοῦς ποιητικός is Science entire, posited all at once, which the conscious, discursive intellect is condemned to reconstruct with difficulty, bit by bit.[73]

Dissatisfied with the rationalistic method, Bergson also turned to the concept of the "fringe," "vague nebulosity," or "halo," which, however "delicate and indistinct, it should have more importance for philosophy than the bright nucleus it surrounds."[74] For Bergson, the fringe constitutes the origin of "conceptual thought." However, the intellect that constitutes the solid nucleus "has detached itself from a vastly wider reality" to which the fringe provides access.[75] Bergson noted that speculating and focussing solely on the intellect will never allow you to "succeed in going beyond it. You may get something more complex, but not something higher nor even something different."[76] The "fringe"—through its affinity with intuition—has the ability to move beyond the nucleus of rational perception and envelop the object under consideration by an act of sympathetic identification. Intuition establishes an "expansion of consciousness," which allows a realization of "psychological osmosis." This enables one mind to understand and penetrate another mind as well as the coinciding of subject and object that gives access to absolute knowledge.[77]

The coinage of the term "involuntary memory" by Marcel Proust has led literary critics to see a possible influence in Proust's cousin by marriage, Henri Bergson. Other possible influences include Théodule Ribot, Pierre Janet and Edouard Brissaud.[78] Proust's pairing of "my intelligence and my unconscious" suggests that he conceived of the unconscious as a cognitive agent.[79] This understanding of the unconscious is further reflected in his conception of art as the movement of unconscious contents into consciousness.[80] In addition, he characterized *In Search of Lost Time* as "an attempt at a sequence of novels of the unconscious."[81] As Joshua Landy has explained, "he is taking the term [unconscious] in its pre-Freudian, more inclusive sense. Proust did not read Freud."[82] Involuntary memory, which recurs in Proust's *In Search of Lost Time*, is typically activated by sensory stimuli and emerges as more "genuine" than recollections deliberately evoked by conscious memory. The past in this context figures as an unseen dimension of perception, which generates multiple layers of perception. Authentic memory is shaped for Proust by unconscious processes because "reality is formed only in the memory," only when an object is charged with associations of memory can it be "in direct communication with my heart."[83]

In his discussion of the implications of technologies for memory, Walter Benjamin took up the Proustian notion of "involuntary memory" which he privileged as richer and more "authentic" than voluntary memory. Benjamin understood involuntary memories as unconscious processes inspired by taste and smell and emerging from "the realm of the unwilled, unmediated [...] recollection" without the control of the conscious mind.[84] These moments provide insight and a feeling of joy; this positive impact led Proust to cite them as "moments bienheureux" (fortunate moments). This sense of joy overcomes the individual immediately, well before the memory reaches consciousness. Stirred from bodily sensations and perceived by the unconscious mind which processes them, involuntary memories are activated independently of the conscious mind. The occurrence of an involuntary memory in the novel brings about an immediate intellectual satisfaction or expansion, linking the intelligent unconscious with memory: "What I could have remembered would have been given to me only via unconscious memory, the memory of intelligence."[85] It is through these insights about life gained through involuntary memory that the protagonist comes to understand time lost and regained through the intellectual crystallization of memory. It is only through reflection stimulated by involuntary memory that the protagonist realizes by the end of the novel the proper role of time, art and memory. Involuntary memory with the insight it provides becomes the most crucial intellectual process upon which the meaning and convergence of the most important themes of the novel depend. The conception of involuntary memory as an unconscious intellectual process as well as an aesthetic device, in its ability to recapture time, provided the unity and design of *In Search of Lost Time*. Involuntary memory becomes the organizing principle of the novel for Proust. It allows the protagonist to realize his mission as a writer and comprehend his psychological life. Treating the heightened intellectual nature of involuntary memory in conjunction with theories of the intelligent unconscious may yield further insight into the workings of involuntary memory and the unconscious as they were being examined at the time Proust was utilizing and recounting in fiction the intricacies of this psychological process.

Over the last five decades or so, advances in the field of the cognitive sciences have breathed new life into the nature of the unconscious, which is seen as capable of executing complex, rational and productive cognitive processes. This is what cognitive scientists often refer to as the "new unconscious." The roots of this new, non-Freudian unconscious are often argued to begin in 1987, when John F. Kihlstrom published the seminal essay, "The Cognitive Unconscious."[86] Kihlstrom has defined this concept as "mental structures and processes that, operating outside phenomenal awareness, nevertheless influence conscious experience, thought, and action."[87] Kihlstrom's theory has since been adopted and elaborated by many scientists. James S. Uleman, for instance, has argued that "Unconscious processes seem to be capable of doing many things that were, not so long ago, thought of as requiring mental resources and conscious processes."[88] In this way, Thomas Mies has noted, the cognitive unconscious has evolved from a "marginal theme" to a "legitimate and important object of research."[89] Kihlstrom, Barnhard and Tataryn explain that "much contemporary research on unconscious mental life is dismissed on the grounds that Freud had said it all before and that our carefully designed and painstakingly executed experimental work is either trivial or merely a gloss on the clinical insights of the Master."[90] As Kihlstrom, Barnhard and Tataryn note here, the cognitive unconscious is based on entirely different premises than Freud's theories. And as Kihlstrom has noted more assertively, "this is not your psychoanalyst's unconscious."[91] This new interpretation of the unconscious entails the assumption that mental processes are not driven by "primitive sexual and aggressive ideas and impulses" nor are the "mental processes necessarily irrational, imagistic, or in any other way qualitatively different from conscious ones."[92] Cognitive psychologists emphasize that it "evolved independently of psychodynamic theory."[93]

In "Unconscious Processes," Kihlstrom reviews extant research in the field with the aim of establishing the categories that drive the concept of the cognitive unconscious, "implicit" being the established term he uses in order to denominate unconscious mental processes and contents in cognitive research: automaticity, implicit perception, implicit memory, implicit thought, implicit learning, implicit emotion and implicit motivation.[94] These contents of the cognitive unconscious are suggestive of complex and rational thinking processes. Cognitive psychologists argue that "implicit thought" affects conscious thought, behaviour and decision making in fundamental ways. Kihlstrom defines it as "a mental representation [...] that influences ongoing experience, thought, and action in the absence of conscious awareness of that thought."[95] Accordingly, the unconscious does not merely store and process contents, such as memories and percepts, but it can autonomously produce new contents and "mental representation[s]," which "may consist of ideas, beliefs, or images."[96] In other words, we are not only unaware of the ways in which our brains process information, but "we do not always know *what* we think and know."[97] It is often the case that we become aware of such unconscious contents as they reach consciousness, which is popularly known as "intuition." Within this framework, intuition is not to be seen as a random process, but as the consequence of unconscious information processing. It is in this light that Kenneth Bowers defines "intuition" as "sensitivity and responsiveness to information that is not consciously represented, but which nevertheless guides inquiry toward productive and sometimes profound insights."[98] Kihlstrom has provided a more detailed account of the various stages of this process. He argues that implicit thought "may underlie the phenomena of intuition, incubation, and insight in problem solving."[99] In this context, intuition defines the moment "when the thought is unconscious" and a gut feeling, as it were, hints at the existence of said thought.[100] Incubation, in turn, which is largely defined as a process of unconscious recombination of thought elements that were stimulated through conscious work at one point in time, resulting in novel ideas at some later point in time, "may be thought of as the process by which the transformation from unconscious influence to conscious access takes place."[101] The essential elements in the process of incubation are "cues contained in the original statement of the problem, inferences generated by the subject's initial work on the problem, and new contextual cues processed during the ostensibly dormant period."[102] The last stage, insight, "occurs when the unconscious thought emerges into consciousness," which often happens in unexpected situations and specifically when one is not pondering the problem underlying the insight.[103] Intuition, a cognitive phenomenon that everybody has probably experienced at some point, is not a random spark of inspiration. Rather, in Ap Dijksterhuis and Loran F. Nordgren's words, they "may well be the result of extensive unconscious thought."[104] Intuition, incubation and insight describe the various stages via which an unconscious mental representation becomes a conscious one, often culminating in the well-known eureka effect. Even if there is no intuitive awareness of unconscious mental contents and no insight emerges from implicit thought, the latter still exerts considerable influence.

Moreover, Dijksterhuis and Nordgren argue that "decision making, impression formation, attitude formation and change, problem solving, and creativity" heavily rely on unconscious thought.[105] Their unconscious thought theory (UTT) entails the notion that when it comes to simple decisions, these are better made consciously, but when the issue is more complex, then the outcome is better if decisions are the result of unconscious cognitive processes. The implication is that compared to conscious thought, unconscious thinking is characterized by a larger capacity. Scott Barry Kaufman has similarly proposed that "complex decisions will benefit from tacit processing,"[106] and Pawel Lewicki, Thomas Hill and Maria Czyzewska have maintained that "our nonconscious information-processing system appears to be incomparably more able to process formally complex knowledge structures, faster and 'smarter' overall than our ability to think and identify meanings of stimuli in a consciously controlled manner."[107] In this view, implicit thought is not simply the unconscious counterpart of conscious thought, but differs in respect to its capacity and the modes of information processing. Cognitive psychologists argue that conscious thinking can only process a limited amount of data and it is slower due to the sequential procedures of logic. In Kaufman's terms, the "*rational system* is analytic, logical, abstract, experienced actively and consciously, is slower to process information, and requires justification via logic and evidence."[108] As Dijksterhuis and Nordgren continue to assert, implicit thought has more capacity, it works "aschematically," "naturally weights the relative importance of various attributes" and is "better under very complex circumstances."[109] The question that cognitive psychologists now explicitly try to answer "is whether we can sensibly ask whether the percepts, memories, and thoughts that would be represented by the output layer, normally in consciousness, can be inaccessible to phenomenal awareness yet nonetheless influence the person's ongoing experience, thought, and action."[110] This brings us back to the question of whether the cognitive unconscious is "routinized and inflexible—in a word, stupid," or "sophisticated, flexible, and adaptive—in a word, intelligent."[111]

The historical scope of this book hopes to have shown that today's notion of an intelligent unconscious is not a crackpot theory. Rather, it is to be found at least as early as in the 19th and early 20th centuries, spiralling its way forward to our own era. Its implicational relations for modernist literary art and thought were fundamental, as it did not only shape the style and technique of such canonical and influential writers as Lawrence, Woolf and Eliot, but it also informed their philosophical and theoretical takes on various pressing dilemmas that characterize their cultural milieu, including notions about reader response, gender and sexuality, language, perception and subjectivity. From Carpenter's, Myers's, James's and Janet's thesis on an unconscious consciousness (to mention but a few indicative names) to Lawrence's Woof's and Eliot's adaptations of this overarching ontological outlook, modernist theorists, experimentalists and literary writers often drew upon and complicated the notion of the intelligent unconscious in their scientific, philosophical, aesthetic and artistic projects. The writers and the particular works examined in this study are by no means the only ones who showed an intense interest in the intelligent unconscious and its implicational relations. They represent a carefully selected sample of case studies that demonstrate the potential this strand of thought offered to scientists, psychologists and literary writers in an age when psychoanalytic pressures made even more pertinent the reconsideration of the process that remain hidden from consciousness. As with any study that situates a particular ontological theory within the longer context of intellectual history, more could be said both to extend and to limit the claims that are made here. But the significance of this book's contribution lies in part in the way it makes these extensions and limitations interesting, productive and urgent. At the same time, the insurgence of the ontological phenomenon of the intelligent unconscious in the work of authors that have been only broadbrushed here, such as Aldous Huxley, Mina Loy, H.D., the Surrealists and Bergson, is indicative of the diversity of the analytical work needed to capture its importance and consequences for the period's literary writing and intellectual output.

Notes

1 Hilda Doolittle, *Tribute to Freud: Writing on the Wall and Advent* (Manchester: Carcanet, 1985), 22.
2 Ibid., 62.
3 Ibid., 39.
4 Ibid.
5 Ibid., 99.
6 James Donald, Anne Friedberg and Laura Marcus, *Close up, 1927–1933: Cinema and Modernism* (London: Cassell, 1998), 105. For the emergence in the late 19th century of new theories of vision that challenged the prevailing Cartesian model of perception, see Jonathan Crary, *Techniques of the Observer: On Vision and Modernity in the Nineteenth Century* (Cambridge, MA: MIT Press, 1990) and *Suspension of Perception: Attention, Spectacle, and Modern Culture* (Cambridge, MA: MIT Press, 1999) and Andrea Goulet, *Optiques: The Science of the Eye and the Birth of Modern French Fiction* (Philadelphia: University of Pennsylvania Press, 2006).
7 Hilda Doolittle, *Notes on Thought and Vision; and, The Wise Sappho* (London: Peter Owen, 1988), 20, 21.
8 Ibid., 22.
9 Ibid., 18.
10 Ibid., 19.
11 Ibid., 20.
12 Doolittle, *Tribute to Freud*, 116.
13 Doolittle, *Notes*, 18
14 Hilda Doolittle, *Notes on Thought and Vision: Second Draft, Typescript, Corrected by H.D.*, Yale Collection of American Literature, Beinecke Rare Book and Manuscript Library, 17.
15 Lisa Rado, *The Modern Androgyne Imagination: A Failed Sublime* (Charlottesville: University Press of Virginia, 2000), 66.
16 Doolittle, *Notes*, 24, 26.
17 Ibid., 24.
18 Ibid., 21.
19 Ibid., 24.
20 Ibid., 23.
21 Ibid., 47.
22 Albert Gelpi, "Introduction" to *Notes on Thought and Vision*, 12.
23 Doolittle, *Notes*, 27.
24 Ibid., 47.
25 Ibid., 47–8.
26 Sybille Bedford, *Aldous Huxley: A Biography* (London: Papermac, 1993), 525.
27 Aldous Huxley, *Letters of Aldous Huxley*, ed. by Grover Smith (London: Chatto and Windus, 1969), 813.
28 Ibid.
29 George Wickes and Frazer Ray, "Aldous Huxley," in *Writers at Work: The Paris Review Interviews*, ed. by George Plimpton (New York: Viking Compass, 1965), 202.
30 Aldous Huxley, *Jesting Place* (London: Chatto and Windus, 1962), 34.
31 Huxley, *Letters*, 647.

32 Ibid.
33 Bedford, *Aldous Huxley*, 261.
34 Ibid.
35 Ibid.
36 Aldous Huxley, *Collected Essays* (New York: Bantman, 1960), 83.
37 Aldous Huxley, *Island* (London: Chatto & Windus, 1962), 119.
38 Ibid., 243.
39 Bedford, *Aldous Huxley*, 259.
40 Ibid.
41 Aldous Huxley, *Brave New World* (London: Chatto & Windus, 1932), 43.
42 Peter E. Firchow, "Science and Conscience in Huxley's *Brave New World*," *Contemporary Literature*, 6 (1975): 312–4.
43 See, for instance, John B. Watson, *Psychology from the Standpoint of a Behaviorist* (Philadelphia: Lippincott, 1919), 278–81.
44 Huxley, *Brave*, 34, 49.
45 Aldous Huxley, "Foreword," in *Brave New World* (London: Chatto & Windus, 1950), xii.
46 Aldous Huxley, MIT Lecture *What a Piece of Work Is Man* (Audiocassette, Dolphin Tapes, 1961).
47 Aldous Huxley, *The Human Situation* (London: Chatto & Windus, 1978), 160.
48 Aldous Huxley, *Selected Letters*, ed. by James Sexton (Chicago: Ivan R. Dee, 2007), 308.
49 Dana Sawyer, *Aldous Huxley: A Biography* (New York: Crossroad Publishing Co., 2002), 57–8.
50 Huxley, *Letters*, 88.
51 Ibid., 332.
52 See, for instance, David Lomas, *The Haunted Self: Surrealism, Psychoanalysis, Subjectivity* (New Haven, CT: Yale University Press, 2002); Hal Foster, *Compulsive Beauty* (Cambridge, MA: MIT Press, 1993) and Natalya Lusty, *Surrealism, Feminism, Psychoanalysis* (Aldershot: Ashgate, 2007).
53 André Breton, "Interview du Professeur Freud," in *Les Pas Perdus* (Paris: Gallimard, 1969), 94–5.
54 André Breton, *Communicating Vessels*, trans. by Mary Ann Caws and Geoffrey T. Harris (Lincoln, NE: University of Nebraska Press, 1997), 152.
55 André Breton, "The Automatic Message," in *What Is Surrealism?: Selected Writings*, ed. by Franklin Rosemont (London: Pluto Press, 1978), 100.
56 Ibid.
57 Ibid., 13.
58 Ibid.
59 André Breton, "Manifesto of Surrealism" (1924), in *Manifestos of Surrealism*, ed. by Richard Seaver and Helen R. Lane (Ann Arbor: University of Michigan Press, 1997), 26.
60 Sonu Shamdasani, "Automatic Writing and the Discovery of the Unconscious," *Spring*, 54 (1993): 121.
61 Suzanne Guerlac, "Forward," in *Understanding Bergson, Understanding Modernism*, ed. by S.E. Gontarski, Paul Ardoin, and Laci Mattison (London: Bloomsbury Academic, 2013), 1.
62 Henri Bergson, "On Unconscious Simulation in States of Hypnosis," *Revue Philosophique*, 22 (1886): 525–31.
63 For Bergson's Presidential Address, see *Proceedings of the Society for Psychical Research*, XXVI (London: Society for Psychical Research, 1912–13), 462–79.

64 Francesca Bordogna, *William James at the Boundaries: Philosophy, Science, and the Geography of Knowledge* (Chicago, IL: University of Chicago Press, 2008), 106.

65 John Alexander Gunn, *Bergson and his Philosophy* (London: Methuen & co., 1920), 6.

66 Henri Bergson, "The Two Forms of Memory," in *Matter and Memory* (London: Swan Sonnenschein, 1911), 86–105.

67 Ibid., 181.

68 Ibid., 83.

69 Gilles Deleuze, *Bergsonism*, trans. Hugh Tomlinson and Barbera Habberjam (New York: ZoneBooks, 1988).

70 Henri Bergson, *Creative Evolution* (Mineola, NY: Dover, 1998), 70–84.

71 Ibid., 87–102.

72 Ibid., 46.

73 Ibid., 340.

74 Ibid., 49.

75 Ibid., 203.

76 Ibid., 204.

77 Henri Bergson, *The Creative Mind*, trans. by Mabelle L. Andison (New York: The Citadel Press, 1992 [1946]), 159–62.

78 Douglas W. Alden, "Origins of the Unconscious and Subconscious in Proust," *Modern Language Quarterly*, 4 (1943): 343–57.

79 Marcel Proust, *In Search of Lost Time*, trans. by C.K. Scott Moncrieff, Terence Kilmartin, and D.J. Enright (London: Chatto & Windus, 1992), 709.

80 Ibid., 274 and Marcel Proust, *Essais et Articles* (Paris: Gallimard, 1994), 288.

81 Marcel Proust, *Letters of Marcel Proust*, ed. and trans. by Mina Curtis (New York: Random House, 1949), 226.

82 Joshua Landy, *Philosophy as Fiction: Self, Deception, and Knowledge in Proust* (Oxford: Oxford University Press, 2004), 165.

83 Proust, *In Search*, 170, 182.

84 Walter Benjamin, *Illuminations*, trans. by Harry Zohn (London: Pimlico, 1999 [1968]), 158.

85 Proust, *In Search*, 68.

86 John F. Kihlstrom, "The Cognitive Unconscious," *Science*, 237 (1987): 1445–52.

87 Ibid., 1445.

88 James S. Uleman, "Introduction," in *The New Unconscious*, ed. by Ran R. Hassin, James S. Uleman, and John A. Bargh (New York: Oxford University Press, 2007), 3.

89 Thomas Mies, "The Cognitive Unconscious," in *Activity and Sign*, ed. by Michael H. G. Hoffmann, Johannes Lenhard, and Falk Seeger (New York: Springer, 2005), 204.

90 John F. Kihlstrom, Terrence M. Barnhardt, and Douglas J. Tataryn, "The Psychological Unconscious: Found, Lost, and Regained," *American Psychologist*, 47: 6 (1992): 789.

91 John F. Kihlstrom, "The Psychological Unconscious," in *Handbook of Personality: Theory and Research*, ed. by Oliver John, Richard W. Robins, and Lawrence A. Pervin, 3rd ed. (New York: Guilford Press, 2010), 595.

92 Ibid., 585.

93 Kihlstrom, et al., "The Psychological Unconscious," 789.

94 John F. Kihlstrom, "Unconscious Processes," in *Oxford Handbook of Cognitive Psychology*, ed. by Daniel Reisberg (New York: Oxford University Press, 2013), 176–86.

95 Kihlstrom, et al., "The Psychological Unconscious," 589.
96 John F. Kihlstrom, Shelagh Mulvaney, Betsy A. Tobias, and Irene Tobis, "The Emotional Unconscious," in *Cognition and Emotion*, ed. by Eric Eich et al. (Oxford: Oxford University Press, 2000), 34.
97 Jennifer Dorfman, Victor A. Shames, and John F. Kihlstrom, "Intuition, Incubation, and Insight: Implicit Cognition in Problem Solving," in *Implicit Cognition*, ed. by Geoffrey Underwood (Oxford: Oxford University Press, 1996), 286.
98 Kenneth S. Bowers, "On Being Unconsciously Influenced and Informed," in *The Unconscious Reconsidered*, ed. by Kenneth S. Bowers and Donald H. Meichenbaum (New York: Wiley, 1984), 256.
99 Kihlstrom, et al. "The Psychological Unconscious," 589.
100 Ibid.
101 Ibid.
102 Dorfman, et al., "Intuition, Incubation, and Insight," 271.
103 Kihlstrom, et al. "The Psychological Unconscious," 589.
104 Ap Dijksterhuis and Loran F. Nordgren, "A Theory of Unconscious Thought," *Perspectives on Psychological Science*, 1: 2 (2006): 106.
105 Ibid., 95.
106 Scott Barry Kaufman, "Intelligence and the Cognitive Unconscious," in *The Cambridge Handbook of Intelligence*, ed. by Robert J. Sternberg and Scott Barry Kaufman (Cambridge: Cambridge University Press, 2011), 454.
107 Pawel Lewicki, Thomas Hill, and Maria Czyzewska, "Nonconscious Acquisition of Information," *American Psychologist*, 47: 6 (1992): 801.
108 Kaufman, "Intelligence," 454.
109 Dijksterhuis and Nordgren, "A Theory," 97, 99, 104.
110 Kihlstrom et al., "Unconscious Processes," 178.
111 Rhianon Allen and Arthur S. Reber, "Unconscious Intelligence," in *A Companion to Cognitive Science*, ed. by William Bechtel and George Graham (Oxford: Blackwell, 2017), 314.

Index

Note: Page numbers followed by "n" denote endnotes.

Alcott, William A. 69, 70
Allbutt, Clifford 86
Arnold, Matthew 110
automatic writing 12, 19, 25–29, 126, 198, 199; *see also* planchette writing

Bain, Alexander 108, 112
Beard, Miller George 85, 86
Beecher, Catharine 72
Benjamin, Walter 201
Bergson, Henri 38, 147, 178–179, 199–200, 204
Binet, Alfred 2, 6, 12, 24, 25, 26–27, 32, 36, 37–38, 39, 41, 44, 71, 90
Bird, William Francis 72
Bradley, F.H. 13, 148, 150, 152, 169
Braid, James 38
Breton, André 198

Caldwell, Charles 69
Carpenter, William 2, 6, 7, 8, 9, 22, 23, 39, 40, 43, 192
Charcot, Jean-Martin 32, 36, 86, 157
coconsciousness 2, 35
cognitive science 6, 14, 201–204
collective unconscious 158, 167, 170, 197
consciousness of consciousness 2, 154
Cornford, F.M. 157–158

Dante, Alighieri 169, 171, 172
De Gourmont, Remy 162–163
De Quincey, Thomas 6, 122, 142n56
Descartes, René 8, 24, 30, 45, 68, 69, 77, 79, 88, 147, 148, 184, 192
Deschamps, Albert 86
Despine, Prosper 26
Doolittle, Hilda 192–4, 199

Dostoevsky, Fyodor 120, 121
Durkheim, Émile 147, 153–155, 157

Eliot, T.S.: amended behaviourism 146, 151–153; *Ash Wednesday* 175; auditory imagination 162, 164; dance 158–160; dissociation 163, 170, 171–172; *The Four Quartets* 177–186; impersonality 167, 169, 173; myth 153–156, 171; objective correlative 169–173; ritual 155–161; "Tradition and the Individual Talent" 164–169; *visual* imagination 172; and *The Waste Land* 157
Ellenberger, Henri 5
eureka moment 23, 203

Fechner, Gustav Theodor 108, 110, 112, 113
Féré, Charles 36, 37, 38, 86
fields of consciousness 20
Fliess, Wilhelm 85
Frazer, James 155–156, 157, 158
Freud, Sigmund 1–5, 18–20, 33; Aldous Huxley 194–198; cognitive science 201–202; D.H. Lawrence 67–68, 72, 80–88, 91; Hilda Doolittle 192–193; intelligent unconscious 59–62; T.S. Eliot 155–157, 172; and Virginia Woolf 110, 116–117, 130, 133
fringe of consciousness 22, 34

Graham, Sylvester 70
Gurney, Edmund 6, 28, 30, 31, 41, 42

Hall, Marshall 7
Harrison, Jane 157–158
Henry, Charles 71

Herbart, Johann Friedrich 108, 109, 110–111
hidden soul 2, 39
historical unconscious 155, 161, 164
Hooker, Worthington 69
Huxley, Aldous 4, 117, 194–198
hypnosis 8, 12, 30–33, 36, 38, 42, 199

immediate experience 13; amended behaviourism 151–157; *The Four Quartets* 177–187; literary writing 157–164; objective correlative 169–173; and unconscious 146–150
instinctive mind 9
intellectual experience 148

James, William 2, 3, 6, 7, 10, 11, 12; AndréBreton 198; automatic writing, 28–30; D.H. Lawrence 79–84, 90; emotions 53–59; Henri Bergson 199; Hilda Doolittle 192; hypnosis 31–32, 38–39; intelligent unconscious 18–24; May Sinclair 111; neural system 43–45; percept 45–49; Sigmund Freud 59–62; stream of thought 49–52, 108–116; T.S. Eliot 147, 151–152, 169; Virginia Woolf 108–109, 116–118, 120–123, 125–129; and unconscious cerebration 41–42
Janet, Pierre 2, 3, 6, 10, 12, 19, 20, 24, 26, 28–31, 32, 33, 41, 42, 44, 59, 60, 90, 111, 147, 151, 157, 200, 204
Joyce, James 3, 127–128, 162, 167
Jung, Carl 3, 72, 130, 131, 156, 195

Kekulé, August 22

Labriffe, Charles 71
Lahy, Jean-Marie 71
Lambert, Thomas 69
Landmann, Samson 41
latent consciousness 2, 39
latent thought 2, 39
Lawrence, D. H.: allotropy 67, 89–92, 100; blood consciousness 78, 84, 89; human motor 69–73; industrialism 70, 73, 80, 92–97; instinct of community 92, 93, 98; as monist or dualist 67–68; psychoanalysis 80–89; *Psychoanalysis and the Unconscious*

and *Fantasia of the Unconscious* 68, 72–80, 81–87; societal instinct 92, 94; *Sons and Lovers* 88–89, 117; *Women in Love* 67, 83, 89, 96–102
Laycock, Thomas 7, 8, 22
Lévy-Bruhl, Lucien 147, 153, 154, 155, 156
Lewes, George Henry 2, 8–10, 108–109
Lewis, Wyndham 3, 112
Liegeois, Jules M. 32
Lipps, Theodor 151
Lovejoy, A.O. 147–148
Loy, Mina 4, 204

Mann, Thomas 3, 4
Marey, Etienne-Jules 71
Marvell, Andrew 170, 173
mesmerism 5, 7
metaphysical unconscious 157
Morel, Augustin 85
Murphy, Joseph John 9–10
Murray, Gilbert 157–158
Myers, F.W.H. 2, 3, 4, 6, 7, 10, 12, 20, 24, 28, 32, 40–41, 43, 44, 60, 90–92, 195, 197, 198, 200, 204

neurasthenia 85–86
neurosis 82, 85–87; *see also* neurasthenia
Nordau, Max 85

obscure perception 2, 39
organic memory 43–44

Peirce, C.S. 9, 41, 48
Pierce, Arthur H. 41
planchette writing 25, 28
Poe, Edgar Allan 83
Poincaré, Henri 22
Pound, Ezra 3, 162, 193
Prince, Morton 2, 3, 6, 7, 10, 12, 32–36, 60
Proust, Marcel 122, 200, 201
psychoanalysis 1, 3–5, 33, 59–62, 80–88, 116, 129–130, 156–157, 192, 195–199
psychological automatism 25–26

reflex action 2, 39, 40
reflex arc 39
reflex thought 2, 39; *see also* latent thought

Ribot, Théodule 6, 19, 151, 157, 200
Richardson, Dorothy 108,
    110–112, 114
Rilke, Rainer Maria 3, 4, 199
Royce, Josiah 147, 151–154, 159, 179

secondary consciousness 2, 12, 24,
    26–28, 30, 33–34, 36, 41, 59;
    see also secondary personalities;
    secondary selves; subconscious
    personalities; and subliminal
    consciousness
secondary intelligence 31
secondary personalities 24, 26, 90, 91
secondary selves 6, 24
sensational consciousness 9
Shakespeare, William 159, 160,
    166, 174
Sidis, William James 2, 42–43
Sinclair, May 108, 110–112, 114, 157
Society for Psychical Research (SPR)
    4, 7, 19, 90, 111, 199
somnambulism 7, 29, 30, 37
Stein, Gertrude 28, 199
Stout, G.F. 110, 151
stream of consciousness 9, 10, 18,
    50–52, 81–83, 108–115, 118, 120,
    136, 162; chain of thought 40, 50,
    120–121; stream of unconsciousness
    112; substantive parts 49–51, 55,
    111, 115; train of thought 10, 40,
    50, 120–121; and transitive parts
    49–52, 115, 118, 123
stream of thought *see* stream of
    consciousness
subconscious incubation 34, 36
subconscious intelligence 2, 35–36;
    see also secondary intelligence;
    andunconscious intelligence
subconscious personalities 24, 59
subliminal consciousness 2, 10, 25,
    41; *see also* hidden soul; latent
    consciousness; obscure perception;

subwakingconsciousness;
    supraliminal consciousness;
    unconscious psychical activity;
    unconscious psychical processes;
    and unconscious sensual and
    volitional processes
subwaking consciousness 2, 25, 48
supraliminal consciousness 41
Svevo, Italo 4

Taylor, Winslow Frederick 70, 71
Thayer, Scofield 4
Titchener, E.B. 151
tip-of-the-tongue phenomenon 12,
    21–23; *see also* eureka moment
Toulouse, Édouard 71
transcendent experience 148, 150

unconscious cerebration 2, 6, 8, 22,
    23, 39–41, 43
unconscious intelligence,
    definition of 2
unconscious judgements 9
unconscious logical processes 9
unconscious memory 2, 37, 201; *see
    also* organic memory
unconscious psychical activity 3, 39
unconscious psychical processes 3, 39
unconscious reasoning 2, 9, 37,
    49, 84; *see also* unconscious
    judgements; and unconscious
    logical processes
unconscious sensual and volitional
    processes 3, 39

Ward, James 151
Woolf, Virginia: androgyny 129–134,
    137–138; *To the Lighthouse* 129;
    Orlando 136–140; theory of the
    unconscious 117–121; unconscious
    and writing 122–128; and *The
    Waves* 134–136
Wundt, Wilhelm 9, 60, 151

For Product Safety Concerns and Information please contact our EU
representative GPSR@taylorandfrancis.com
Taylor & Francis Verlag GmbH, Kaufingerstraße 24, 80331 München, Germany